195

W9-BYF-056

SEPARATED BRETHREN

Separated Brethren

A SURVEY OF NON-CATHOLIC CHRISTIAN DENOMINATIONS IN THE UNITED STATES

(REVISED EDITION)

WILLIAM J. WHALEN

ILLUSTRATED WITH PHOTOGRAPHS

THE BRUCE PUBLISHING COMPANY
MILWAUKEE

NIHIL OBSTAT:

JOHN A. HARDON, S.J.
Censor Deputatus

IMPRIMATUR:

✝ JOHN J. CARBERRY
Bishop of Lafayette in Indiana
September 8, 1960

First printing — January, 1958

Second printing — December, 1958

Third printing (Revised edition) — January, 1961

Fourth printing — September, 1963

Library of Congress Catalog Card Number: 61–8014

© 1961 THE BRUCE PUBLISHING COMPANY

MADE IN THE UNITED STATES OF AMERICA

PRAYER FOR THE REUNION OF CHRISTENDOM

O LORD JESUS CHRIST, who when Thou wast about to suffer didst pray for Thy disciples to the end of time that they might all be one, as Thou art in the Father and the Father in Thee, look down in pity on the manifold division among those who profess Thy faith and heal the many wounds which the pride of man and the craft of Satan have inflicted on Thy people.

Break down the walls of separation which divide one party and denomination of Christians from another. Look with compassion on the souls who have been born in one or other of these communions which not Thou, but man, has made.

Teach all men that the See of Peter, the Holy Church of Rome, is the foundation, center, and instrument of unity. Open their hearts to the long-forgotten truth that the Holy Father, the Pope, is Thy Vicar and Representative; and that in obeying him in matters of religion, they are obeying Thee, so that as there is but one company in heaven above, so likewise there may be one communion, confessing and glorifying Thy Holy Name, here below. Amen.

— CARDINAL NEWMAN

PREFACE

T HIS volume is intended to offer American Catholic readers a survey of Protestant, Eastern Orthodox, Old Catholic, and Polish National Catholic churches and sects in the United States. In addition I have included examinations of a number of religious cults which are sometimes mistaken for Christian groups and which themselves sometimes appropriate the Christian name.

The two introductory chapters present an overview of American Protestantism and the basic theological differences between Catholicism and Protestantism. This was done in order to avoid the necessity for continually restating fundamental Protestant principles such as the sole sufficiency of the Bible or the priesthood of all believers in the subsequent chapters on particular denominations. Only the exceptions to the general Reformation positions are pointed out in these chapters. Those who wish to use this book as a handbook for reference will want to keep this in mind when turning to any particular chapter. The chapters on the major denominations outline the history, doctrine, ritual, organization, and traditions of each group.

In the past half century only three book-length studies of non-Catholic denominations for Catholic readers have appeared in this country. They are Krull's *Christian Denominations* which was first published in 1911, Algermissen's book by the same title which was translated from the German, and the thoroughly documented appraisal by Fr. John A. Hardon, S.J., entitled *The Protestant Churches in America*. The other published works in this rather neglected area are more often than not pamphlets or magazine articles, sometimes uncharitable, frequently inaccurate, and perhaps nothing more than expositions of classical Lutheranism or Geneva Calvinism.

This book does not encompass Catholic apologetics as such nor does it attempt a point by point refutation of non-Catholic theology. The aim has been to explain these theologies in terms the average educated Catholic will understand. Many excellent apologetics works are available for those who wish to re-examine their Catholic faith and review the reasons for their acceptance of Catholic truths.

Footnotes have been kept to a minimum. SEPARATED BRETHREN was written for the parish priest, religious, and intelligent Catholic layman rather than for the professional theologian or student of comparative religion who would naturally be more concerned with details and extensive documentation.

In completing the research for this book over a period of years I relied heavily on personal interviews, official church publications, correspondence, published studies, and observation. If space permitted and I were not afraid of inadvertently omitting someone's name, I would like to acknowledge my indebtedness to the scores of church officials, ministers, and laymen who generously gave of their time to enable me to get a current picture of the life of their denominations. My first interest in writing a book of this type developed while I was specializing in religious journalism in graduate study at Northwestern University in 1949–50.

I would like to thank my wife who read the manuscript chapter by chapter, offered innumerable suggestions, and maintained those conditions of domestic tranquillity conducive to writing.

Several people were kind enough to review sections of the book and offered valued comments. In particular I would like to thank Abbot Ambrose Ondrak, O.S.B., and Prof. Eric L. Clitheroe. Of course, they must not be held accountable for my errors nor must the reader presume that they share my views in all instances. I would also like to express my appreciation to the National Council of Churches of Christ and to Editor Benson Y. Landis for permission to use statistics compiled for the *Yearbook of American Churches*.

Thanks are due to the following copyright holders for permission to use quotations: Association Press, B. Herder Book Co., *Life* magazine, Newman Press, W. W. Norton & Co., Inc., Review and Herald Publishing Association, Sheed and Ward, *Time* magazine, and the Watchtower Bible and Tract Society, Inc.

W. J. W.

CONTENTS

CONTENTS

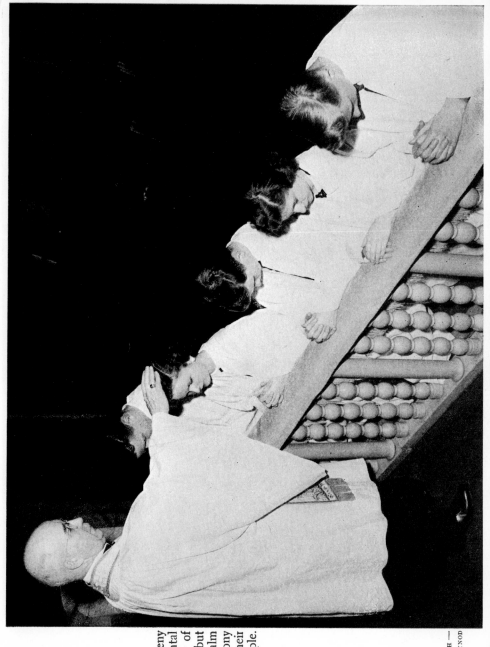

Lutherans deny the sacramental character of confirmation but emphasize the Palm Sunday ceremony in the lives of their young people.

LUTHERAN CHURCH —
MISSOURI SYNOD

Baptism of adults by immersion is a
characteristic practice of the Baptists,
largest U. S. Protestant denomination,
the Disciples of Christ, Churches of Christ,
and Seventh-Day Adventists.

— *Baptist Leader*, PHILADELPHIA

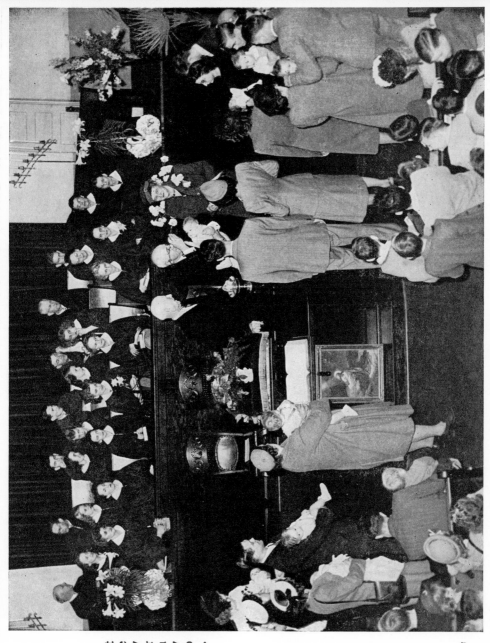

Other Protestant churches baptize infants by sprinkling or pouring at a regular Sunday morning worship service.

— Julian Jacobson

Baptists and Methodists won their
large followings on the American
frontier through the efforts of such men
as Bishop Francis Asbury.

— METHODIST PRINTS

American Methodism meets every four years in a general conference to vote on matters of doctrine and discipline.

— METHODIST PRINTS

Liturgical Episcopalian and Lutheran churches
often resemble Catholic churches
in ecclesiastical appointments.

— WERNER C. BRUCHLIS

A liturgical movement in American Protestantism substitutes an altar-centered sanctuary for one which used to feature the pulpit, choir, or organ, such as this example.

— JULIAN JACOBSON

All denominations observe the Lord's Supper,
although conflicting interpretations of
the sacrament have divided Protestantism
since its earliest days.

— NATIONAL COUNCIL, PROTESTANT EPISCOPAL CHURCH

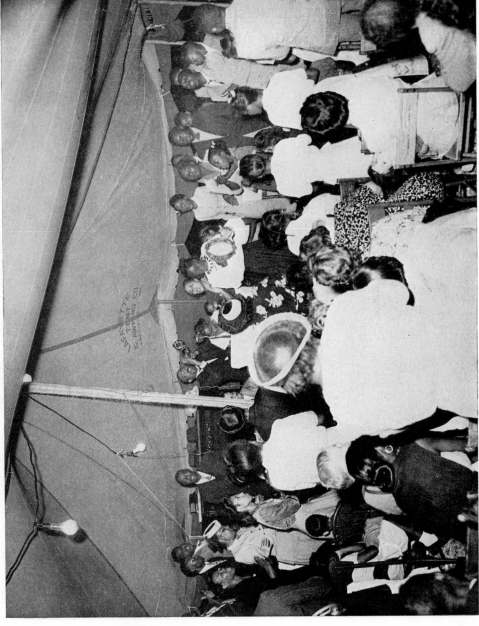

Most Negro Christians in this country belong to separate Baptist and Methodist denominations.

— JULIAN JACOBSON

Faith healers such as Oral Roberts of the Pentecostal church sponsor revivals in tents, auditoriums, armories.

— ORAL ROBERTS

Seventh-Day Adventists support an ambitious
missionary program which includes
the use of medical launches on
the Amazon River.

— GENERAL CONFERENCE OF SEVENTH-DAY ADVENTISTS

Street meetings and social welfare programs carry the message of the Salvation Army to the masses and underprivileged.

— T. KAITILA

This new $6 million Mormon Temple in Los Angeles brings the number of such temples to ten.

—LaMar S. Williams

Dedicated Jehovah's Witnesses operate this modern printing plant in Brooklyn which turns out millions of pieces of literature every year.

— MARLEY COLE

Archbishop Michael, head of the Greek Orthodox Church in North and South America, presides at dedication of the new St. Sophia Orthodox Cathedral in Los Angeles

— RELIGIOUS NEWS SERVICE

Representatives of 179 Protestant and Eastern Orthodox churches gathered in Evanston for the 1954 meeting of the World Council of Churches.

— JOHN AHLHAUSER

SEPARATED BRETHREN

Chapter I

AMERICAN PROTESTANTISM

Protestantism Claims Allegiance of 64,000,000 Americans

SHORTLY after the discovery of America, the unity of Western Christendom was shattered by the Protestant Reformation. That bond of common faith which had cemented the brotherhood of European Christians for a millennium was broken and altar was set against altar. Christians remained brothers in the grace of baptism and in loyalty to the person of Jesus Christ but they became separated brethren.

After the dust of the Reformation and the Counter-Reformation had settled, Protestantism consolidated its position in northern Germany, the Scandinavian countries, Holland, and England. Colonists and missionaries from these areas would carry the new religion to other continents. Meanwhile the Spaniards, Poles, Italians, French, Portuguese, Austrians, Hungarians, southern Germans, Irish, and other nationalities held fast to the ancient faith.

The apologetic exigencies of the times prompted controversialists in both Christian camps to emphasize the separation more than the brotherhood. They segregated and stressed points of doctrine on which Protestant and Catholic disagreed. For the Catholic the possibility of converting the Moslem was remote; the obstinate Jew clung to his religious beliefs in the shelter of the ghetto; the Protestant was the obvious target for theological debate and polemics.

Earlier the Great Eastern Schism had split Eastern and Western

Christians. Most of the Greeks and Slavs were in schism. Efforts at the Council of Lyons in 1274 and the Council of Florence in 1439 failed to effect a permanent reconciliation. Theological differences between East and West, however, were slight compared with those engendered by the wholesale innovations of the Protestant reformers. Moreover, the Eastern Orthodox retained a valid episcopacy, priesthood, Mass, and seven sacraments which Protestantism lacks.

Catholics consider Protestantism a heresy and Eastern Orthodoxy a schism. Technically, a heresy consists in the propagation of a denial of any revealed truth of the faith by a baptized person who retains the name Christian. Practically all Protestants today are heretics only in the sense of being material heretics. They never professed the truths of the Catholic faith themselves and have therefore not participated in the act of rejecting them. These Methodists and Lutherans and Baptists do not incur the guilt of formal heresy providing they do not doubt the validity of their own positions. We can hardly deny that most Protestants today are men of good will but invincibly ignorant regarding the Catholic Church.

A schism, on the other hand, consists in the refusal to acknowledge the authority of the pope or to hold communion with Christians subject to the Holy See. Again, a person born and brought up as an Orthodox Christian can be called a schismatic only in a popular way of speaking since he has probably never deliberately rejected the authority of the Vicar of Christ. The Church has never pronounced a blanket excommunication on the Orthodox bishops, clergy, or laity. Schism usually leads to heresy as in the Anglican and Polish National Catholic schisms, but the Church still considers Orthodoxy to be in a state of simple schism. Individual Eastern theologians have advanced heretical doctrines but Orthodoxy itself has not and cannot establish these ideas as dogma and, therefore, the Holy See continues to view the break as a schism, a disciplinary more than a doctrinal question.

Protestantism soon split into four main branches which persist to this day. The followers of Martin Luther disagreed with the Zwinglians and Calvinists on the Real Presence and other doctrinal issues. England produced its own brand of Protestantism, a blend of Calvinism, Lutheranism, and Catholicism, which moved from schism to heresy and has since lost valid orders. Finally, the left wing of the Reformation, the sects, developed into the Baptist, Methodist, Congregational, Mennonite, Disciples of Christ, Churches of Christ, Holiness and Adventist bodies. The four branches, then, are Luther-

WORLD PROTESTANTISM BY DENOMINATIONS

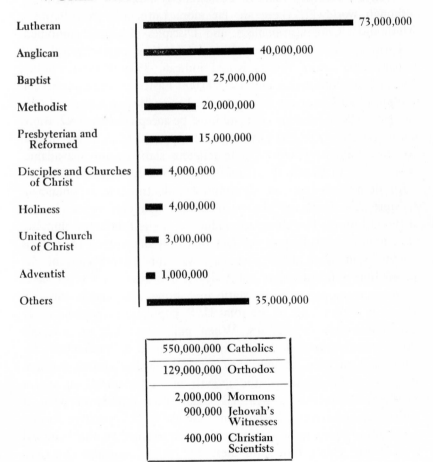

Lutheran	73,000,000
Anglican	40,000,000
Baptist	25,000,000
Methodist	20,000,000
Presbyterian and Reformed	15,000,000
Disciples and Churches of Christ	4,000,000
Holiness	4,000,000
United Church of Christ	3,000,000
Adventist	1,000,000
Others	35,000,000

550,000,000	Catholics
129,000,000	Orthodox
2,000,000	Mormons
900,000	Jehovah's Witnesses
400,000	Christian Scientists

GRAPH A

anism, Calvinism (Presbyterian and Reformed), Anglicanism, and Independent or Radical.

Through historical and geographical circumstances the fourth branch, variously known as Independent, Radical, Nonconformist, and Free church, gained ascendancy in the United States. The despised sects won the battle of the American frontier. World Protestantism has been dominated by the other three wings, but the success of the radical wing in this country exerts a growing influence. Every second American Protestant is a Baptist or Methodist although worldwide there are far more Lutherans than Baptists, Methodists, Congregationalists, and Disciples of Christ combined.

Estimates vary on the number of Christians in the world, but a reasonable set of figures would indicate 550,000,000 Catholics, 220,000,000 Protestants, and 129,000,000 Eastern Orthodox. Several million other Christians belong to the Lesser Eastern Churches long in heresy. The Orthodox estimate must be accepted with reservations since at least 50,000,000 Orthodox are supposed to be living behind the Iron Curtain where accurate religious statistics are unavailable. The extent to which the Russian Orthodox have preserved their faith despite 40 years of Communist indoctrination is unknown.

More Americans are church members than ever before in our national history. The theocratic influence of the Protestant churches in colonial times obscures the fact that only one person in ten was a church member. This percentage was only 16 per cent of the population a century ago but today it has risen to 63 per cent. Protestantism, more or less static in Europe, now claims the allegiance of 35 per cent of the total U. S. population compared to 27 per cent in the late 1920's. When poll takers ask for religious "preference" they find that many more register a "preference" for Protestantism even though they are not on the church register.

What is significant in the growth of Protestantism in recent decades is that this growth has taken place outside of what is called "co-operative Protestantism." Generally "co-operative Protestantism" includes those denominations represented in the National and World Council of Churches: Methodists, northern Baptists, most Lutherans, Protestant Episcopalians, Presbyterians, Disciples,

U. S. MEMBERSHIP OF NON-CATHOLIC
DENOMINATIONS

Baptists	21,400,000
Methodists	12,600,000
Lutherans	8,400,000
Presbyterians	4,300,000
Episcopalians	3,270,000
Eastern Orthodox	2,800,000
United Church of Christ	2,260,000
Churches of Christ	2,250,000
Holiness	1,900,000
Latter-day Saints	1,800,000
Disciples of Christ	1,800,000
Reformed	500,000
Old and Polish National Catholics	445,000
Christian Scientists	350,000
Seventh-day Adventists	330,000
Jehovah's Witnesses	275,000
Brethren	250,000
Mennonites	162,000
Unitarians-Universalists	150,000
Quakers	127,000
Others	2,000,000

Most Protestant denominations count only adults in membership tabulations.
The Protestant Episcopal, Lutheran, and Eastern Orthodox churches count
baptized children and adults. Christian Scientists do not furnish statistics on
membership, therefore, the 350,000 figure is an estimate.

GRAPH B

Negro Baptists, etc. Between 1940 and 1954 while the population was increasing 24 per cent the nonco-operative Southern Baptists increased almost 65 per cent, the co-operative American Baptist Convention decreased 2.4 per cent; the nonco-operative Missouri Synod Lutherans increased 49 per cent, the co-operative Disciples of Christ increased only 10½ per cent; the nonco-operative Christian Reformed Church grew by 61.6 per cent and the co-operative Methodists barely kept up with the national increase with 24.7 per cent. The really amazing membership gains have been made by the Southern Baptists, Jehovah's Witnesses, Missouri Synod Lutherans, Mormons, Nazarenes, Christian Reformed, Seventh-day Adventists, and Holiness sects which are lumped together as "Protestant" using the term in its generic sense.

Since we will not limit our subsequent discussion to Protestantism, we should at the outset make a careful distinction between the Protestant and other non-Catholic Christian bodies. Certainly the Eastern Orthodox, Old Catholics, and Polish National Catholics cannot be classified as Protestants. The Quakers, Unitarians, and Anglo-Catholics do not logically belong in the Protestant category for reasons which will be pointed out in later chapters. We have included a number of cults in this book to which we cannot extend the term Christian, much less Protestant, without emptying these terms of any meaning. These cults include among others, Jehovah's Witnesses, Christian Science, Mormonism, and Spiritualism. Many of these cultists do not consider themselves Protestants, are not classified as Protestants by other Protestants, do not uphold the principles of the Reformation, but are nevertheless included in census tabulations of Protestant churches and sects.

While the sects emerged from the suppressed left wing of the Reformation, the Protestant churches emerged from the right wing. The two terms, church and sect, are not precise. In general, however, the church refuses to cut the ties with the past, tends to seek state support and protection, considers all members of the nation in its constituency, baptizes infants, demands subscription to creeds and confessions, and adopts an episcopal or presbyterian form of government. Our use of the term "church" in referring to a Protestant communion is sociological rather than theological.

The sect denies what the church affirms. It usually latches on to one doctrine such as adventism or perfectionism, rejects infant baptism and often insists on immersion, advocates complete separation of Church and State, prefers a congregational polity, appeals mainly to the poor and uneducated, establishes personal conversion as the chief condition of church membership, enforces a Puritan morality, urges tithing as the divine method of fund raising, and dispenses with art and fixed ritual in worship.

A sect may become a church. As its members rise in social status the sect often modifies its original stand. Methodism, for example, began as a sect within Anglicanism even though it never rejected infant baptism and retained an episcopacy in America. Today Methodism reveals all the characteristics of a church. Disaffected Methodists who preferred the milieu of the sect tended to drift into Holiness and Pentecostal sects. The Evangelical United Brethren Church resulted from a merger of two sects which developed in the Pietist revival within German Lutheranism. We can observe the evolution of some sects into churches in our own day: the Church of the Nazarene has almost completed the transformation and the Pilgrim Holiness Church is about midway. Many sects peter out after the death of the leader or else remain numerically insignificant.

No other nation has witnessed the proliferation of Christian churches and sects which we find in the United States. European nations are likely to have one dominant Christian religion — Lutheranism, for instance, in Sweden or Catholicism in Spain — or two major denominations as in Germany and Holland. Estimates place the number of churches and sects in the United States at 265.

Every European heresy and schism has been transplanted to American soil. Yankee inventiveness sometimes extended into ecclesiastical realms and added further divisions and varieties. Historical circumstances in the young nation combined with the Protestant principles of private interpretation of the scriptures and the denial of religious authority furthered the fragmentation.

When Lutheran immigrants came to the New World they brought

GENEALOGY OF MAJOR CHRISTIAN CHURCHES, SECTS, AND CULTS IN THE U. S.

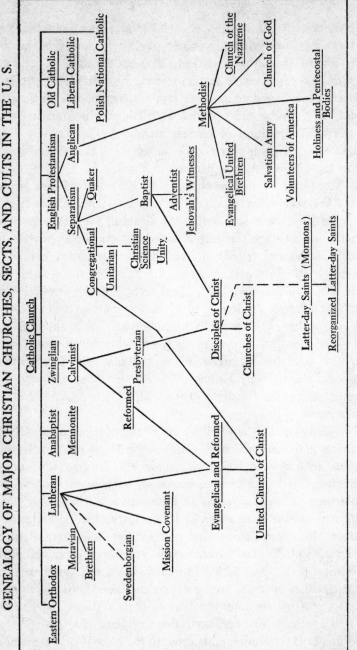

CHART I

their own pastors, languages, and church traditions. As a result the Germans, Swedes, Norwegians, Danes, Finns, and Slovaks organized separate and independent synods. Immigrants from Eastern Europe — the Albanians, Greeks, Russians, Assyrians, Bulgarians, Romanians, Serbs, Syrians, and Ukrainians — set up their own Orthodox denominations with close ties with the autocephalous mother churches in Europe and Asia. Catholicism embraced all nationalities in one Church despite the schism of some Poles in the first part of the present century.

The Civil War and the issue of slavery further split many Protestant denominations into northern and southern branches. The Methodists reunited in 1939 but other such schisms persist: the American (northern) Baptists and the Southern Baptists, the northern United Presbyterian Church in the U. S. A. and the southern Presbyterian Church in the U. S.

Language differences contributed to schisms within the Mennonite denomination and forced German-speaking Methodists to form a separate church, the Evangelical United Brethren.

The conservative Churches of Christ broke away from the Disciples of Christ on a question of worship — they could not find scriptural justification for the use of a pipe organ in church. A serious schism was precipitated among the Mennonites by the problem of whether one man should wash and wipe the believer's feet in the foot washing ceremony or whether one man should wash and another wipe. Mennonites also separated over the use of new fangled buttons instead of hooks-and-eyes.

Nine out of ten Protestant Negroes worship in segregated denominations such as the African Methodist Episcopal Church, the African Methodist Episcopal Church Zion, the Christian Methodist Episcopal Church, and the two National Baptist Conventions. Many smaller denominations are composed entirely of Negro Christians and the number of store front chapels is unknown.

Theological controversies produced Unitarianism, the Christian Reformed Church, and the fundamentalist Evangelical and Orthodox Presbyterian Churches. Dozens of fundamentalist and holiness sects have arisen as a protest against the modernism of the older denomina-

tions or as the personal vehicle of a popular preacher such as Aimee
Semple McPherson.

A number of sects are home grown, including the Seventh-day
Adventist, Christian Science, Church of the Nazarene, Disciples of
Christ, Jehovah's Witnesses, Mormon, Polish National Catholic,
Spiritualist, and Unity School of Christianity. The Adventists and
Witnesses now find the bulk of their membership outside continental
United States and the Mormons also conduct an aggressive foreign
missionary program.

This amazing array of churches, sects, and cults should not mislead the student of the American religious scene. After all the
denominations have been tallied the fact remains that nine out of
ten American Protestants belong to one of the six great denominational families: Baptist and Disciples, Methodist, Lutheran, Episcopalian, Presbyterian and Reformed, and the United Church of
Christ. Even counting separate denominations we find that 90
per cent of the Protestants in this country belong to the 20 largest
denominations.

On the local level the average Protestant can attend a Methodist
church one Sunday, a Baptist the next, a Presbyterian church after
that and find himself more or less at home. So long as he stays
within the predominant Puritan-Independent tradition he can switch
denominational affiliation with a minimum of accommodation and
inconvenience. On the other hand, a monthly cycle of Christian
Science, Anglo-Catholic, Southern Baptist, and Quaker worship would
be conducive to acute schizophrenia. For the Protestant the choice
of church affiliation may be based on family background, the personality and preaching ability of the minister, adequacy of the
physical plant, proximity to home, social advantages, Sunday School
or youth programs, or preference for one type of church polity over
another.

Three types of church government predominate: congregational,
presbyterial, and episcopal. We might mention that in practice
the episcopal form is never so autocratic nor the congregational so
independent as the labels suggest. Some of the most highly organized
denominations in the country, such as the Seventh-day Adventist

and Missouri Synod Lutheran, operate under a congregational or consistorial system. In at least a third of the Protestant denominations the congregation is theoretically supreme and recognizes no authority beyond itself. Besides the two churches just mentioned the Baptists, Disciples of Christ, Churches of Christ, Quakers, Unitarians, Congregational Christians, and many Holiness groups are congregational in polity. The congregational-type church hires and fires the minister whose position then depends on maintaining the good will of his parishioners. The congregation likewise holds title to all property, manages church finances, elects its own officers, and perhaps formulates its creedal statement.

The Episcopalians, Eastern Orthodox, Methodists, and Evangelical United Brethren maintain an episcopal form of church government. In most cases the bishops are elected rather than appointed as in the Catholic Church. The term of office may be limited as in the E.U.B. Church and the church may establish a compulsory retirement age. Methodist and E.U.B. bishops hold a purely administrative office.

The presbyterial system dispenses with bishops but exercises a measure of control over the local congregations by means of representative presbyteries. Clerical and lay delegates cast equal votes and no individual holds an ecclesiastical office superior to another. Besides the Presbyterians themselves other Protestants who are governed by this polity are those in the Reformed and Christian Reformed Churches, the Assemblies of God, and the former Evangelical and Reformed Church (now part of the United Church of Christ). Smaller groups such as the Salvation Army and the Volunteers of America follow a military organization adapted to religious life.

The average Protestant congregation is small with fewer than 350 members (compared to more than 1800 in the average Catholic parish). These parishioners may reside in any part of the city since they are not assigned to a specific church as in the Catholic parochial arrangement. Members usually make an annual pledge to support the church and its benevolences.

Architecturally the familiar Protestant church is a semicircular auditorium. A pulpit, organ, or altar may occupy the chief focal

point in the chancel. Most churches also display an American flag
and a hymn board. A recent liturgical revival in Protestantism is
introducing the cross, central altar, vestments for minister and choir,
stained glass, sculpture, and ecclesiastical furniture common in Catholic churches. Episcopalian and Lutheran churches have always employed art and music to greater advantage than churches in the
Puritan heritage.

The 10:30 or 11 o'clock service is usually the main Sunday worship service although larger churches may offer duplicate services
at other hours. An usher escorts the worshipers to the pews. The
typical nonliturgical Protestant worship service lasts about an hour
and consists of the invocation, Lord's Prayer, hymn, responsive reading, anthem, scripture lesson, anthem, pastoral prayer, offering,
hymns, sermon, closing prayer, and benediction. The sequence of
these elements may vary according to the denomination or the
wishes of the minister or congregation. The vernacular is used
and the music is provided by both the trained choir and the congregation as a whole. Liturgical churches follow the Christian year
and a fixed ritual resembling the Catholic Mass without the canon.

Communion is observed monthly or quarterly except by the Episcopalians and Disciples of Christ who celebrate the Lord's Supper
every week. Communion is distributed under both kinds; all denominations use bread but some use wine, some grape juice, and one
(Mormon) water.

At an earlier hour the children will be listening to Bible stories,
singing hymns, drawing or playing games in the Sunday School.
More than 44,000,000 children are enrolled in these part-time religious schools since fewer than 360,000 attend Lutheran, Christian
Reformed, and Seventh-day Adventist full-time parochial grade and
high schools. Volunteer lay people conduct the 286,000 Sunday
Schools which attempt to provide at least a minimum of religious
instruction. The larger city churches may employ a trained director
of education to supervise the educational program for the various
age groups.

The old-fashioned midweek prayer meeting has fallen into disuse
except in the South and certain rural areas. Many of the sects

sponsor annual revival services either in the church building or in a tent or rented hall. Church facilities may be used during the week for meetings, choir rehearsals, suppers, Boy Scout activities, dances, dramatics, study clubs and the like. During the summer months union services are sometimes scheduled to accommodate depleted congregations and allow pastors to take a vacation. Similar union programs among various churches have been arranged for the Lenten season, Reformation Sunday, Thanksgiving, and other special events.

An increasing number of Protestant ministers are entering their profession with the benefit of college and seminary training. Many Baptist, Methodist, Holiness, and Negro ministers are ordained with little or no education beyond high school or with no regular seminary training. On the other hand, the Lutherans, Episcopalians, Presbyterians, and Congregationalists have always insisted on high educational standards for their clergy.

About 4 per cent of the Protestant ministry in this country are ordained women ministers. Two thirds of these 6000 women serve in The Methodist Church, the Church of God, International Church of the Foursquare Gospel, and the Volunteers of America. Other denominations which now ordain women include the Presbyterian, United Church of Christ, Disciples of Christ, Evangelical United Brethren, Quaker, and Church of the Nazarene. Relatively few women have become pastors of city churches; they generally serve rural parishes or assist as associate pastors.

Few comprehensive studies have been undertaken on the social classes in American Protestantism. Those which have been published indicate that there are more lower class Episcopalians and more upper class Baptists than popularly thought. Nevertheless, many denominations are more or less classbound. The Episcopalian, Presbyterian, Congregational, and Unitarian Churches appeal to the wealthy and privileged; the Baptist, Assemblies of God, and fundamentalist churches find their chief support among the common people in the South and in rural America. The value of many studies attempting to compare social status of American Catholics and Protestants is lessened since the studies are likely to list the relatively wealthy Christian Scientists as Protestants while neglecting the millions of Holiness and Pentecostal Protestants in the lower income brackets. Inadequate data on Negro groups which comprise almost 15 per cent of the Protestants in the country have also distorted the conclusions.

Booker T. Washington once remarked that if you find a Negro who is not a Methodist or Baptist someone has been tampering with his religion. Practically all Negro Christians are Methodists and Baptists and most of them are members of independent Negro denominations. Most of the Negroes in the United States are Christians and of these about 10,000,000 are Protestants and 620,000 are Catholics. Perhaps half a million Protestant Negroes belong to mixed denominations rather than all-Negro bodies and 340,000 of these accept semi-segregated status in The Methodist Church.

The Episcopal, Lutheran, United Church of Christ, and northern Presbyterian denominations have no parallel Negro bodies but their nonwhite adherents are likely to worship in segregated congregations. In fact, it has been estimated that only one tenth of 1 per cent of Negro Protestants worship in local mixed churches. "Sunday morning at 11 o'clock is the most segregated hour in American life" is a Protestant-coined aphorism which emphasizes that Protestantism has so far reinforced rather than circumvented racial segregation in this democracy.

Protestants support home missions to Negroes, Indians, Orientals, Puerto Ricans, and Mexican-Americans, but most of their missionary efforts are directed to foreign lands. For centuries after the Reformation the Catholic Church carried the burden of Christian missions alone. This Catholic head start in the mission fields is illustrated by the fact that today 130,000,000 Catholics reside in mission territories compared to 25,000,000 Protestants. American Protestantism maintains 6000 mission centers in 100 nations and provides two thirds of the support and half the personnel of world Protestantism's missionary program. Since the Chinese missions have been abandoned, Protestant missionaries have turned their attention to Latin America where one fourth of their missioners are now stationed.

In supplying personnel and funds for mission work the smaller sects put the larger Protestant denominations to shame. For example, the Seventh-day Adventists claim 2000 of the 25,000 American Protestant missionaries in the field. The tiny Christian and Missionary Alliance with a membership of 60,000 sponsors more overseas missionaries than the 3,269,000-member Protestant Episcopal Church.

Women missionaries outnumber the men three to two. India gets the largest contingent of U. S. and Canadian missionaries assigned to one country, approximately 1900, with Japan second with 1600.

In the next chapter we shall consider the theological basis of Protestantism and the basic differences between it and Catholicism. So far we have attempted to sketch a capsule picture of Protestantism in mid-century America. Protestantism appears to be less fragmented than many Catholics charge, less united than some ecumenical enthusiasts suggest. Some sections of Protestantism, particularly those which stress solid doctrine and have resisted the corrosive influence of modernism, have registered spectacular gains in the past two decades. In any event the proportion of Protestant church members in our population is many times what it was during colonial times. Protestant Christianity is firmly entrenched in the South and in rural America whose birth rates greatly surpass urban rates. In studying Protestantism in the United States we are not dissecting a corpse but examining an energetic and sprightly youngster, separated it is true from his Mother.

Chapter II

BASIC DIFFERENCES BETWEEN CATHOLICISM AND PROTESTANTISM

Theological Disagreements Divide Western Christians

Compared to the chasm between atheist and theist, between Christian and non-Christian, the differences which separate Catholic and Protestant Christians may seem relatively slight. A Christian world which saw Christendom divided into two neat camps in Western Europe developed rival apologetics which emphasized the theological points of disagreement. Today in what some have labeled the post-Christian era we find Western man offering his allegiance to dozens of religions and ersatz religions: Communism, nationalism, scientism, secularism, hedonism, sentimentalism, cultism. The Weltanschauung of these devotees contrasted with the Christian philosophy of life puts the twentieth-century picture into sharper focus and reveals the Christian camp as a besieged outpost in an aggressively hostile world.

To minimize the real differences between the Catholic and the Protestant interpretations of the gospel would be dishonest. But to fail to recognize the bonds of unity between separated brethren is also dishonest and shortsighted. Of course, we are speaking of those Protestants who believe in a personal God, the divinity of Christ, and other central Christian dogmas. Despite the profound differences between them, the Catholic and the Protestant Christian in the modern world are more often allies than antagonists.

16

Catholic and Protestant share a spiritual outlook which looks beyond material things to spiritual values, which reminds man to live for eternity as well as for time. They share a belief in God and a loyalty to the person of Jesus Christ. They accept the same Ten Commandments as a rule of conduct, acknowledge that fallen man unaided cannot attain his own salvation but needs a Saviour, honor and read essentially the same Bible, recite the same Apostles' and Nicene creeds, pray the same Lord's Prayer. According to Catholic teaching both are admitted to the life of grace through the sacrament of baptism which may be administered by priest, minister, layman, or even Jew or Moslem. Bride and groom, whether baptized Catholics or Protestants, bestow the sacrament of matrimony on each other which brings the necessary graces to their Christian homes and makes their marriage a truly sacramental union. The feasts of Christmas and Easter, the writings of the Fathers of the Church, devotional literature and hymns form a common heritage for Catholic and Protestant Christians.

While insisting that membership in the Catholic Church is the ordinary channel of God's grace, Catholic theologians acknowledge that God is free to bestow His grace on whom He will. The Jansenist proposition that "outside the Church there is no grace" was long ago condemned by Rome even though the grace which non-Catholics receive comes to them somehow in virtue of the Catholic Church.

Certainly the sincere Protestant Christian can receive the graces of baptism and matrimony, sacraments which need not be administered by a priest. True, the Protestant church in which he normally receives these sacraments is a man-made institution. As such it cannot be the vehicle of these graces, but de facto it is the occasion for the bestowal of these graces. Certainly, too, the Protestant can obtain forgiveness of his sins by an act of perfect contrition just as can his Catholic neighbor. Through the sacrament of penance the Catholic may also receive forgiveness with imperfect contrition, a contrition motivated by the fear of the loss of heaven and the pains of hell rather than the pure love of God. Certainly the Protestant is the recipient of actual graces throughout his life and especially at times of temptation and certainly his meritorious good works, his sacrifices, his charity, his prayers are known to God.

As a matter of fact the Church considers all who are baptized according to the proper formula to be Catholics unless and until they affiliate with an heretical or schismatic sect. Just as technically there are no "born Catholics" so there are no "born Protestants" and in Catholic eyes there is no such thing as a Protestant below the age of reason. A child baptized in a Protestant communion ceases membership in the Mystical Body of Christ only when he begins to attend a sectarian Sunday School or worship service at the age of seven or eight. Even then he and all baptized Christians continue to be related to the Church of Christ in some way.

A nonuniversal Catholic Church is a contradiction in terms and the Church cannot recognize rival Christian communions as her equal. Christ founded one Church and one only. The scores of non-Catholic churches and sects have not only distorted the truths of the ancient faith but they have also inherited and preserved a large body of Catholic truths together with certain means of grace such as baptism. Such bodies as the Eastern Orthodox churches have preserved much more: a valid priesthood, divine sacrifice, sacraments.

As we examine the basic differences between Catholicism and Protestantism we should keep in mind the distinction between fundamental and accidental differences. The latter are products of church discipline, historical development, and cultural adaptations which may be amended and changed as the Church sees fit. Fundamental differences touch the core of the Christian faith, dogmas which God has revealed to mankind through His Son.

Immediately we see that most of the differences which seem obvious to the man in the pew do not fall in the area of doctrine at all. He may notice that the Protestant minister is usually married, the Catholic priest celibate. Ignorant of the millions of Eastern Rite Catholics he would not realize that thousands of Catholic priests in these rites follow an ancient tradition in marrying and raising families. Nor is he likely to know that celibacy in the predominant Latin Rite is disciplinary in character, and that, while it was practiced to some extent from the beginning, was not made a matter of general law until the eleventh century. For more than half her history the Church was served, in part at least, by a married parish clergy; celibacy has never been enforced among Eastern Christians although monks and bishops were celibate. Even today papal dispensations have been granted to former Evangelical ministers in Germany who wished to be ordained Catholic priests while remaining married.

Again our average observer may report that Protestant worship services are conducted in English while the Mass is recited in Latin. We can point out that the use of Latin is neither fundamental nor universal in the Church. At least a dozen languages, some of them vernaculars, are employed in the liturgies of the various rites of the Catholic Church. Many liturgists believe that Latin would have given way gracefully to vernaculars about the time of the Reformation had not the Reformers made an issue of the matter. The Church reacted against novelty in religion by "freezing" the language of the Latin Rite. The Holy See has recently authorized a wider use of English in administration of the sacraments and may permit the use of the mother tongue in the Mass in the near future.

Not only did the sixteenth century Reformers promise to give the laity a worship service in a language they understood but they promised to give the layman the cup in communion. While the Catholic faithful usually receive the body and blood of Christ under the species of bread alone, Protestants receive bread and wine (or grape juice) in their communion service. Of course, any Latin Rite Catholic is free to attend an Eastern Rite Catholic church and receive holy communion under both species. In fact, he is encouraged to become acquainted with other rites that he may broaden his understanding of the Church and realize that catholicity does not imply uniformity in liturgies and customs.

Here are three apparent differences between Catholicism and Protestantism — clerical celibacy, a Latin liturgy, communion under one species — which are nothing but disciplinary measures of the Latin Rite, by far the largest rite in the United States. We know that the early church was served by married priests, said Mass in Greek rather than Latin, and distributed communion under both kinds. For good and sufficient reason the Church has changed these practices in the Latin Rite. They continue in other sections of the Catholic Church and are subject to amendment in the Latin Rite. Obviously, nothing contrary to divine truth would be tolerated in any rite of the Church. We cannot doubt that had the fathers of the Council of Trent ever imagined that the new Protestant heresy would be with us 400 years later they would not have altered some of these disciplinary measures in order to blunt the Reformers' weapons and prevent the defection of entire nations from the Church.

By stripping Catholic truth to its essentials we can best see the basic differences which divide some 220,000,000 Protestant Christians from their Catholic (and Eastern Orthodox) brothers.

We can logically classify mankind into two groups: those who believe that man was once better than he is today and those who believe that he was once worse. Christians believe that man was once better but forfeited his favored position through disobedience to God in the Fall. Social evolutionists deny the Fall and maintain that despite occasional temporary setbacks man is getting better and better.

Although Catholics and Protestants attach great importance to the Fall, they disagree on the consequences of that Fall. We discover the first basic difference between the two Christian theologies in the view of man's nature after the Fall. Catholics believe that through the Fall man's natural and religious endowments were weakened. The first transgression by man's first parents lost for them and for their descendants those supernatural and preternatural gifts which were theirs in the Garden of Eden. These gifts included supernatural grace, potential bodily immortality, integrity, impassability. Were it not for the promise of a Redeemer and the sacrifice of the Son of God on the cross man would have been utterly unable to attain his supernatural end, the vision of God. But Catholics hold that these gifts were not due man but were free gifts of God which God withdrew; man, stripped of these gifts, remained man and his nature, though his will was weakened and his intellect darkened, remained intact.

To use a necessarily inadequate example, the Fall was as though someone took back the million dollars which he had given to another person who had previously only fifty cents in his pocket. Without the million dollars the second person realized he had suffered a great loss but he was still solvent. His situation has not changed to bankruptcy, his nature remained intact.

Luther, however, concluded that man's nature was totally corrupted by the Fall. This cardinal principle of Protestantism led logically to most of the other theological innovations. Man's nature is totally depraved and inclined only to evil, declared the German friar. Man is a sinner in whatever he does and all his actions are disgusting to God.

How can such a worthless creature be justified, be made pleasing to God? In an age when religion had become for all too many the mechanical performance of external devotions and Nominalism had undercut the orthodox positions of Thomism, Luther proclaimed his discovery of the truth that justification was by faith alone. Salvation is a free gift of God which man cannot merit. All is grace, pure grace.

Soon justification by faith became associated with three other principles not inherent in the original doctrine nor acceptable to the Church. These were the denial of free will, the doctrine of extrinsic justification, and the denunciation of all good works. Luther denied that man could co-operate with the actual graces God bestowed before justification. The Church, on the other hand, traditionally taught that man could reject God's graces through the exercise of his free will. By extrinsic justification the German Reformer taught that the act of justification is something entirely outside of man. Man remains a sinner, totally depraved, but God, so to speak, looks the other way. God covers man's sins with a cloak but the sins remain. Justification never touches the inherently sinful nature of man. The Catholic view is radically different and is well stated by Algermissen:

This sanctifying grace alters the nature of the soul, blots out what is sinful, permits it to partake in the divine nature, makes it a dwelling place of the Holy Trinity, incorporates man in the mystical body of Christ, makes him a child of God and an heir of heaven, and places him in a position to perform supernaturally good, meritorious works, that is, works that have the power to earn the beatific vision, the participation in God's own unending blessedness.[1]

Catholicism has always denied that good works without justification would avail to man's salvation. After justification, however, the good works which a man performs, ethical or ceremonial, earn merit. Luther flatly denied the idea of merit and urged his followers to perform good works only as fruits or evidence of their justification. But no matter what they do, even in their loving God, they sin. The Church upheld the value of good works after justification in the firm belief that faith without works is dead.

It is one thing to deny Luther's positions on free will, extrinsic justification, and good works, but it is something else to suggest that man can merit his own justification by good works. He must cooperate with the actual graces he receives, do penance, seek the truth, but he cannot thereby earn his justification. The eighth chapter of the Council of Trent states plainly:

> When the Apostle says that man is justified by faith and freely, his words are to be understood in the sense ever held and expressed by the consensus of the Catholic Church; which is, that we are said to be justified by faith, because faith is the beginning of human salvation, the foundation and root of all justification, and without it it is impossible to please God (Heb. XI, 6) and attain to the communion of his sons; yet we are said to be justified freely, because nothing that precedes justification, whether faith or works, merits the grace of justification.

Canon 18 states: "Whatever good works we do are deserving of reward, not through any merit anterior to grace; their performance, rather, is due to a prior gift of grace to which we have no claim."

Most Catholics know or have heard of sincere people who have studied the Catholic faith, accept its teachings, lead upright lives, and pray for light but have not received the "gift of faith." God

---

[1] Konrad Algermissen, *Christian Denominations* (St. Louis: B. Herder Co., 1953), p. 469.

grants this gift to those whom He chooses; their efforts cannot win this gift even though they must co-operate with actual grace and predispose themselves by acts of penance. In its usual context justification by faith alone includes the objectionable Lutheran corollaries we have discussed and as such it has become accepted as a basic principle of the Reformation. The later Pietist and Methodist revivals attempted to disentangle these negative principles from the positive and authentically Christian principle of justification by faith. They stressed personal conversion, holiness, and the performance of good works by "born again" Christians.

A serious complication has clouded theological argumentation since the Reformation. When the Reformers spoke of faith, they did not mean what the Church has always meant by the term. The Church defines faith as an intellectual assent given on the authority of another. For example, if a railroad conductor informs you that the next stop is Chicago and you accept his word, you have faith in him. If the Son of God declares that marriage is indissoluble or that baptism is necessary to salvation, you accept these statements because you have faith in Him. He has not proved these statements by mathematics or laboratory experiments but, because He is who He is, you accept them. Faith, then, is an assent to God's revelation. But to the founders of Protestantism faith became a supreme act of confidence that God had spared you from hell and covered up your sins. Faith became an act of the will and the emotions for the Protestant but remains primarily an act of the intellect for the Catholic.

Early in his revolutionary career Luther saw that the Church would never accept his novel theological views. On the other hand, he soon witnessed Protestant extremists, the Anabaptists, denying any authority in religion or appealing to weird visions and revelations. Unable to appeal to the Roman Church for authority and unwilling to allow the fanatics to overthrow all religious authority, Luther claimed the supreme religious authority to be found not in a man or institution but a book, the Bible. Protestantism dethroned the Church and set up the Bible as the sole rule of faith. Only what the Apostles had committed to writing would be binding on Christians; that oral tradition handed down through the Church from apostolic times was denied. Eventually Protestantism became the religion of the book par excellence.

Catholic controversialists could point out that Christ was a preacher not a writer, that the first Christians never saw a complete Bible, that the Church herself compiled the New Testament and fixed the canon, that the rejection of oral tradition was purely arbitrary, that the Bible itself claimed no supreme authority, and that prior to the invention of printing most of mankind had no access to the Bible even if they could read. But the new religion erected the Bible as the sole rule of faith while vilifying the Church which had compiled, translated, and preserved the Bible through the ages.

Not only was the Bible the sole rule of faith, the source of all that was needed for salvation, but the individual Christian now had the right, the duty, to interpret the Bible for himself. The spectacle of some 210 churches and sects in this country alone gives testimony to the fruits of this disastrous principle of private interpretation. Of course, the masses of the Protestant faithful never exercised this right and duty in the face of a state-supported orthodoxy. Someone has estimated that there are at least 300 distinct interpretations of four words in the New Testament: "This is my body."

Catholics believe that the Church under the ever present guidance of the Holy Spirit is the proper interpreter of scripture. No matter how flattering to the man in the street, the invitation to become his own Bible scholar has always been illusory. Anyone with the slightest acquaintance with the Bible soon admits that a knowledge of languages, theology, history, and archaeology is a prerequisite to mastery of scripture. Apparently Luther believed that once the layman was encouraged to read the Bible, fortified by the principles of the Reformation, he would come to the same interpretations as his fellow Christians. Religious history since the Reformation disproves this theory. Protestant communions sooner or later imposed on their constituencies official interpretations of the Bible which only the most intrepid would dispute.

Searching their Bibles, Protestants came across numerous references to the Church. They knew that the Church of Rome had not adopted Luther's views. Evidently, then, the church must be an invisible rather than a visible body. The members of this invisible church would be known only to God; the head of this invisible church was not the pope, whom Luther branded the anti-Christ, but Christ Himself. Violent opposition to the See of Peter has animated Protestantism for four centuries. Catholics believe in One, Holy, Catholic, and Apostolic Church, founded by Christ, whose visible head is the Vicar of Christ, the successor to St. Peter, the Holy Father, the Bishop of Rome. This visible Church composed of saints and sinners has been the Mother of an estimated 5 billion souls since its founding in Jerusalem.

The traditional Christian sacraments were included in the Reformer's denunciation of good works. Luther reasoned, however, that two sacraments, baptism and the Lord's Supper, were specifically enjoined by Christ and would be observed out of obedience to His will. Penance, confirmation, holy orders, matrimony, and extreme unction were denied any sacramental meaning but were retained as ceremonies of the church.

A simplified worship service patterned after the Catholic Mass but eliminating the idea of sacrifice was introduced. Not sacrifice but the preaching of the Word of God became the central feature of Protestant worship. Without a visible church, a Mass, and five of the seven sacraments, there was little need for a priesthood. Rather, all Christians were declared priests whose only ordination was baptism. Nevertheless some men (and eventually some women) were specially trained for the ministry, ordained in a rite of the church, and given a measure of authority over the congregation. To a great degree this doctrine of the priesthood of all believers suffered the same fate as private interpretation of the scriptures and was compromised by organizational necessities. Catholics believe that all men participate in some way in the royal priesthood of Christ as members of His Mystical Body but that some men are set apart and ordained for sacrifice.

Predestination preoccupied the Reformed branch of Protestantism for several centuries. Catholics flatly deny that absolute or double predestination which teaches that God has elected some to salvation and damned others to hell. This doctrine, so stated, leaves no room for man's free will and has been all but disowned by modern Protestants, even those who fall in the Calvinist tradition.

Protestants deny the doctrine of transubstantiation but differ among themselves on belief in the Real Presence. Lutherans, for example, claim to believe in the Real Presence but propose that the bread and wine and the body and blood of Christ co-exist in the elements; they disclaim the term "consubstantiation" to describe this theory. Calvinists speak of receiving Christ in a spiritual and heavenly manner. Even after the prayer of consecration the bread and wine remain bread and wine. The Methodists, Baptists, Mennonites, and Evangelical United Brethren consider the Lord's Supper a simple memorial service. Anglicans encompass a variety of views from transubstantiation to memorial service, and the Quakers and Salvationists do not observe a communion service.

Other Protestant positions were derived from the basic principles of total depravity, justification by faith alone, the Bible as the sole rule of faith, private interpretation of the scriptures, and the priesthood of all believers. The existence of purgatory was denied; after death the soul was assigned to either heaven or hell. Prayers for the dead were useless and unscriptural. Devotion to Mary as the Mother of God and intercession of the saints were abandoned although Luther kept alive a tender devotion to the Blessed Virgin until his death. The Reformer continued the practice of private confession all during his lifetime but this too died out in the non-Anglican branches of Protestantism although it has been revived in German Lutheranism in recent years.

Catholic controversialists sometimes seek to explain the Reformation in purely political and economic terms or as the result of simple disobedience and pride. That the Reformers incur the guilt of objective disobedience is true, but we cannot deny any genuine, authentically religious impulses of the Reformation. What we must try to do is to separate the positive Christian elements in the theology of Luther and Calvin from the negative elements. Furthermore, we must not judge the principles of the Reformation by certain degenerate types of Protestantism we observe around us. The Protestantism which declared the just man lives by faith is not that of the popular preacher who proposes a salvation by character. The Protestant reverence for the Bible as the Word of God is not that of the Modernist denial of Christianity which treats the scriptures as Hebrew mythology.

A former Lutheran minister now a Catholic priest, Fr. Louis Bouyer, writes in his challenging book, *The Spirit and Forms of Protestantism:*

> It should be quite evident that the principles of Protestantism, in their positive sense — that most consonant with the spirit of the Reformation — are not only valid and acceptable, but must be held to be true and necessary *in virtue of Catholic tradition itself*, in virtue of what makes up the authority of the Church both of today and of all time. Salvation as the pure gift of God in Christ, communicated by faith alone, in the sense that no other way can be thought of apart from faith or even along with faith; justification by faith in its subjective aspect, which means that there is no real religion where it is not living and personal; the absolute sovereignty of God, more particularly of his Word as contained in the inspired writings — all these principles are the heart of Protestantism as a reforming movement. Yet, if we go to the root of them all, to what the Reformers considered most essential, to what is retained by living Protestantism, today and always, we are bound to say that they are all corroborated by Catholic tradition, and maintained absolutely by what is authoritative, in the present, for all Catholics.[2]

While insisting on an understanding of the basic principles of the Reformation and suggesting the harmony between these positive religious insights and Catholic truth, we must bear in mind that we cannot base current judgments of American Protestantism on classical statements. Many classical positions receive lip service at best and concern Protestant seminarians and theologians far more than the man in the pew. The laymen may choose not to dwell on the doctrine of total depravity, abdicate his right to private interpretation of the scriptures by subscribing to detailed creeds and confessions, submit to a clerical system which practically negates

---

[2] Louis Bouyer, *The Spirit and Forms of Protestantism* (Westminster, Md.: Newman Press, 1956), p. 137,

the priesthood of all believers concept, and still consider himself
a genuine Protestant.

Perhaps the majority of Protestants in the United States can be
classified as activist evangelicals, neither theological liberals nor
fundamentalists. They probably hold most of the traditional Protestant principles which we have discussed without hesitating to modify
any particular position. A thorough theological examination would
doubtless also reveal considerable unorthodoxy among lay Catholics
who also consider themselves in good standing.

In the succeeding chapters we shall see how these basic Protestant
principles, especially private interpretation of the scriptures in the
American context, have led to the proliferation of Christian churches
and sects claiming a worldwide allegiance of 220,000,000 souls.

Chapter III

THE LUTHERANS

"The Just Man Lives by Faith"

A GERMAN Augustinian friar touched off the explosion which shattered the unity of Western Christendom in the sixteenth century. Except for the Eastern schism of 1054 and the minor defections of the Waldensians and Moravians, this unity had remained intact for almost 1500 years after the death of Christ.

Soon after the initial revolt and the spread of its doctrinal innovations, the Protestant movement split into two camps which remain divided to this day. The followers of the ex-priest Martin Luther consolidated their position in northern Germany and Scandinavia while the Reformed or Calvinists captured Scotland and Holland, parts of Switzerland, and for a while threatened to win France and England.

American Catholics may be especially sensitive to the tragedy of the Reformation since nowhere are the fruits of the revolt more apparent than in the more than 200 Protestant churches and sects in this country. They cannot help comparing the salvation-by-character and modernism of many heirs of the Reformation with the God-centered culture of the Middle Ages. Luther, the individual who brought this sad state upon much of Christendom, bears the brunt of their indignation.

Before long the average Catholic fills in a mental picture of the German Reformer as a coarse, lustful, proud, vituperous, vain, and rebellious priest who started his own church in order to marry a former nun. Parochial school sisters sometimes feel called upon to remind their pupils that we have no *certain* grounds on which to declare that Judas and Luther are in hell. The more candid reappraisal of the Reformer undertaken by Catholic theologians has not yet reached the laity. Should the average Catholic come upon Karl Adam's description of the low state of the Church in Luther's day and his estimate of the man, he might find it necessary to revise his own caricature. For example, in his slim book *One and Holy* the distinguished German priest writes:

> Yes, it was night. Had Martin Luther then arisen with his marvelous gifts of mind and heart, his warm penetration of the essence of Christianity, his passionate defiance of all unholiness and ungodliness, the elemental fury of his religious experience, his surging, soul-shattering power of speech, and not least that heroism in the face of death with which he defied the powers of the world — had he brought all these magnificent qualities to the removal of the abuses of the time and the cleansing of God's garden from weeds, had he remained a faithful member of his Church, humble and simple, sincere and pure, then indeed we should today be his grateful debtors. He would be forever our great Reformer, our true man of God, our teacher and leader, comparable to Thomas Aquinas and Francis of Assisi. He would have been the greatest saint of our people, the refounder of the Church in Germany, a second St. Boniface.[1]

We have no intention of whitewashing Luther or minimizing his guilt; we do object to a straw Luther as presented in some Catholic apologetics works. We must record his lifelong devotion to the Blessed Mother along with his intemperate outbursts against the papacy and the Jews. We must appreciate the religious motives of the Reformation while not overlooking the nationalistic and economic forces which used the Reformation for their own ends. We must remember that Luther was a conservative who abhorred the excesses of the Anabaptists and Zwinglians as well as the supposed errors and evils of Rome.

Catholic folklore abounds in tales of Luther's undoing: his suicide, his affliction with horrible disease, his deathbed return to the Church. All historical nonsense. Some dismiss the Reformer

---

[1] Karl Adam, *One and Holy* (New York: Sheed and Ward, 1951), p. 25.

by quoting a few choice passages from an unexpurgated edition of *Table Talks*. Others are content to explain the upheaval as the result of Luther's lust for an escaped nun. Respected Catholic historians such as Grisar, Hughes, and Algermissen attempt to correct such caricatures but these distortions continue to exert an unfortunate influence among the laity. In fairness, we should add that the picture of Catholicism painted by some Protestants likewise bears little resemblance to reality.

Today Lutheranism with 73,000,000 adherents is by far the largest component in world Protestantism. This fact is sometimes obscured by the strength of the Baptist and Methodist denominations concentrated in the United States. Many of these Lutherans, especially in the Scandinavian countries, must be classed as inactive or nominal, as must millions of Catholics in France, Italy, Spain, and South America.

To understand Protestantism we must understand Lutheranism; to understand Lutheranism we must know Luther. In order to do this we must try to project ourselves into his age. Catholics occasionally point out what most Protestants seem willing to admit: the Reformation would have been an impossibility in the twentieth century. The conditions in the Church which cried out for reform no longer exist. The refusal to see Luther in the context of his own era magnifies the enormity of his rebellion since Catholics see so little justification for the dismemberment of Christendom.

The modern Church has been singularly blessed by a succession of saintly, capable, and devoted pontiffs. But Alexander VI who is generally conceded to be the worst pope in history occupied the papal throne in Luther's youth.

Not long before Luther's birth three rival popes claimed the allegiance of the faithful, each excommunicating the other and his followers. The Bishop of Rome had resided not in Rome but in Avignon in France for 65 years. To support the luxuries of the papal court new schemes for taxes and revenues had to be devised. The successors of St. Peter installed their children and relatives in the highest church offices, sold ecclesiastical positions to the highest bidders, and lived more like Chinese war lords than spiritual leaders.

Not all the abuses were confined to the papacy. The parish clergy, a huge clerical proletariat in Germany, had lost all ideals of celibacy which had been made mandatory on Latin clergy in the eleventh century. They exacted such large sums for their services that the sacrament of extreme unction was commonly called the rich man's sacrament, too expensive for the dying poor. The upper clergy was composed largely of the sons of royalty for whom lucrative church offices had been purchased. Monasteries grew lax and wealthy and the monks earned the contempt of the people. Among the laity infidelity, illegitimacy, and superstition were rife. The educated classes turned to the pagan writers of Greece and Rome rather than to the Bible or the Church Fathers and fed on a wisdom of hedonism and sensuality.

We must not overstate the case. The age also produced its saints and devout Christians. Not all priests and monks were untrue to their vows. A few bishops called for reform of the manifold scandals. But after all these allowances are made we must admit that the Church of Christ had fallen on evil days.

Into this situation was born a baby boy named Martin Luther after St. Martin on whose feast day he was baptized. The boy knew poverty in his youth but his father's fortunes improved and he was able to study at three prep schools. At 18 he transferred to the University of Erfurt to study, not theology, but law. He won his master's degree in 1505.

At this point the course of Luther's life changed dramatically. While riding in a storm he was hurled to the ground by a bolt of lightning and in terror he cried, "St. Anne, help me. I will become a monk." Evidently the reputation of the monastery he choose was such that a young man would consider it a logical refuge if he wished to consecrate his life entirely to God. Luther joined the strict Hermits of St. Augustine.

No one doubts that Luther determined to be a good religious. In fact, his self-imposed penances went far beyond the rules of the order. Professed in 1506, he was ordained a year later and only then began his study of theology. No religious order today would accept a candidate who sought entrance because of a vow made in fear of his life and certainly no one would be ordained two years after entering as a novice and without theological preparation.

Father Martin was barely able to complete his first Mass as he contemplated the miracle he was about to perform. Subject to extreme states of depression and melancholia, the young friar was obviously a victim of scrupulosity. He would spend as much as six hours in the confessional attempting to recall all his sins. What if he had forgotten to confess some sin? What if he had violated some rule of his order and had forgotten about it? His weary but wise confessor finally told him, "Man, God is not angry with you. You are angry with God. Don't you know that God commands you to hope?" Luther continued to be haunted by the thought that he might lose his soul and efforts by his religious superiors to assuage his fears were useless.

He visited Rome briefly on official business for his order and returned with a lowered estimate of Italian Catholicism. From Erfurt he was transferred to the young university at Wittenberg where he received a doctor of theology degree in 1512. Frederick the Wise had founded this university only 11 years before in a village of about 2500 population. The young priest took over the position of professor of scripture and began an intensive study of the Bible.

His theological invention was taking shape. He was already teaching that through the Fall man's nature was completely corrupted. In essence man is a sinner, inclined only to evil, a possession of the devil. "Sin is not a specific wrongdoing but the basic condition of our personality," decided Luther. All man can do is make a complete act of trust in God who confers justification on him through the merits of Christ.

When God gave mankind the Ten Commandments He knew they could not be observed. They were given to humble man, to break his willful spirit and bring him to a complete act of faith in God's goodness and mercy. For the sake of His Son, Jesus Christ, God casts a cloak over man's sins and man, still a sinner, is justified.

Since every action of man is sinful, good works are sinful and of no avail for salvation even after man is justified. Perhaps Luther knew the traditional Catholic position that good works performed

by man in the state of original sin are of no merit. He now denied
the merit of any and all good works.

Luther tormented himself with the question, "Where can I
find a merciful God?" How could he be assured that he would be
saved? While preparing his scripture lectures he came upon a
passage in Romans which he called the "door to paradise." He
read, "The just man lives by faith." Here was the answer to his
anxiety.

Luther used his conception of justification by faith as the key
to interpret the rest of the Bible. It remains the basis of the experi-
ential Protestant theology of consolation. St. James wrote that "Faith
without good works is dead"; the Reformer dismissed this epistle
as a "straw epistle."

Since Luther considered good works useless to salvation, we
may not assume that he encouraged moral laxity. The just man will
gladly perform good works and avoid evil for the glory of God.
That not all Luther's followers reasoned in the same manner cannot
be blamed entirely on the Reformer. The sacraments as good works
were also superfluous, but since baptism and the Lord's Supper had
been prescribed by Christ they would remain.

The barefoot friar of Wittenberg developed his doctrinal position
while busily engaged in a variety of other tasks. In a letter to a
friend written in 1517 he wrote:

> I really ought to have two secretaries or chancellors. I do hardly
> anything all day but write letters . . . I am at the same time preacher
> to the monastery, have to preach in the refectory, and am even
> expected to preach daily in the parish church. I am regent of the
> house of studies and vicar, that is to say prior eleven times over;
> I have to provide for delivery of the fish from Lietzkau pond and
> to manage the litigation of the Herzberg friars at Torgau; I am
> lecturing on Paul, compiling lectures on the Psalter, and, as I said
> before, writing letters most of the time . . . It is seldom that I have
> time for recitation of the Divine Office or to celebrate Mass, and
> then, too, I have my peculiar temptations from the flesh, the world,
> and the devil.

The sale of indulgences was the occasion of Luther's open protest
but quite incidental to his theological creation. No one denies

that scandalous abuses of all sorts had crept into the granting of indulgences. Luther's own patron, Frederick, boasted a collection of relics said to include a strand of Jesus' beard, a nail from the crucifixion, a piece of the swaddling clothes, and a twig from Moses' burning bush. Those of the faithful who venerated all these relics and made a contribution could amass a total indulgence of 1,909,202 years and 270 days.

Pope Julius II granted a new indulgence in order to obtain funds for the building of St. Peter's in Rome. The preaching of such an indulgence resembled a modern parish mission although the salesmen claimed to guarantee results even though the recipients were not in the state of grace. Frederick forbade the preaching of this indulgence in his province since it would compete with his own collection. But many Wittenbergers crossed the nearby border to obtain its extravagant promises from a Dominican priest by the name of Tetzel. Tetzel employed all the devices of the modern huckster in promoting this indulgence. A representative of the Fugger's banking house sat next to the coffer to collect his share of the proceeds as promised by the playboy archbishop of Mainz.

Luther nailed a list of 95 theses on indulgences to the church door in Wittenberg which was the usual manner in which scholars invited debate. The debate never took place but the theses were widely circulated throughout Germany.

Soon Luther was driven to more radical positions and he launched attacks on papal authority, infallibility, confession, invocation of the saints. He presented himself as the champion of the German people, groaning under the demands of Rome.

At one stage the Reformer may have hoped that his new theology would find acceptance by the Church. Indeed, as we have seen in the preceding chapter, the positive principles of the Reformation are in complete harmony with the teachings of the Church. The Church was forced to condemn the negative principles of extrinsic justification, the wholesale condemnation of good works, absolute predestination, a personal religion which dispensed with the Church itself, and the denial of the role of tradition. Luther sought authority in a council rather than in the pope but he finally settled for the authority of the Bible. We have seen that he ridiculed the Epistle of St. James since it contradicted his pet theory. When he realized that the doctrine of purgatory and prayers for the dead were implied in the Second Book of Maccabees, he threw out that book. The Book of Esther he called a "superfluity of heathen naughtiness" and he relegated the Apocalypse (the Protestant Book of Revelation) to the appendix. He nevertheless insisted that the Bible was the complete and infallible Word of God.

Two sympathetic priests joined Luther at Wittenberg, Carlstad and Melanchthon. Luther had refused to go to Rome at the pope's orders to answer charges of heresy but Carlstad was challenged to a debate by Dr. John Eck at Leipzig. Luther's voluminous writings were receiving wide circulation through the relatively new medium of the printing press and he grew bolder and denounced the pope as the anti-Christ. While he lost the support of some humanists such as Erasmus he won a number of dissatisfied priests, monks, nuns, and lay people to his cause.

Three violent tracts went to the printer in 1520. In these tracts, *The Babylonian Captivity*, *The Freedom of the Christian Man*, and the *Address to the German Nobility*, Luther trimmed the number of sacraments from seven to three (he later eliminated confession as a sacrament) and cut the idea of sacrifice from the Mass.

His revolutionary theology was formally condemned by the faculties of the Universities of Paris, Louvain, and Cologne. When the papal bull threatening excommunication and citing 41 errors finally reached Luther from Rome in 1521 he tossed it on the fire while admiring students sang the *Te Deum*. He was summoned before the civil Diet of Worms by the Emperor Charles V and asked to admit the authorship of his heretical books. Closing his defense the defiant friar declared: "Unless I am convicted by Scripture and plain reason — I do not accept the authority of popes and councils for they have contradicted each other — my conscience is captive to the Word of God. I cannot and will not recant anything, for to go against conscience is neither right nor safe. God, help me. Amen." Assuming his sincerity, his stand on the supremacy of conscience was, of course, strictly orthodox and St. Thomas

Aquinas points out that anyone convinced that the Church is in error is bound to leave the Church. The dramatic phrase "Here I stand, I cannot do otherwise" seems apocryphal.

At Worms Luther stood convicted of heresy but the emperor promised him safe conduct back to his home in Wittenberg. The followers of Luther refused to accept the decision of what they called a rump court. En route a band of masked men kidnaped Luther and delivered him into protective custody at the castle at Wartburg. Frederick arranged this maneuver to forestall possible treachery since Luther was now an outlaw in the rest of Germany by order of the emperor. During his year in the Wartburg Luther completed his translation of the New Testament into German. We should note, however, that before 1518 there had been 14 translations into High German and four into Low German.

Back at Wittenberg his two colleagues assumed the leadership of the snowballing Reformation. Priests, monks, and nuns began to marry; German replaced Latin in the liturgy; images were smashed; Masses for the dead were forbidden. When Luther returned home in the disguise of a bearded knight he upbraided Carlstad for his violence and iconoclasm but otherwise applauded the changes.

When three laymen from neighboring Zwickau visited Wittenberg and began to denounce infant baptism, Luther was horrified. He repudiated any connection with these anarchistic Anabaptists while they, in turn, chided the Lutherans as compromisers. Since Luther maintained the necessity of faith for the reception of a sacrament, he was hard pressed to present a convincing case for infant baptism.

The general disparagement of authority and the radical doctrine of the priesthood of all believers inflamed the German peasants and inspired the bloody peasant revolt of 1524-25. Rather than becoming their leader Luther penned the vicious tract, *Against the Murderous and Thieving Hordes of Peasants*. In this tract he advised, "Let everyone who can, smite, slay and stab secretly or openly, remembering that nothing can be more poisonous, hurtful or devilish than a rebel. It is just as when one must kill a mad dog; if you don't strike him, he will strike you, and the whole land with you." More than 5000 peasants were slain in the hopeless uprising. Luther, the peasant, turned his attention to the princes while the betrayed peasants listened with greater interest to the left-wing Anabaptists.

The marriage of parish priests was one thing but that of monks was quite another. Seeing his Augustinian brethren in Wittenberg taking wives Luther exclaimed, "Good heavens! Will our Wittenbergers give wives to monks? They won't give one to me." But they did. Nine Cistercian nuns arrived at the cloister in search of husbands and Luther acted as matchmaker. After two years one ex-nun remained unmarried, Katherine von Bora. Urged to practice what he preached and to give his father a grandson, Luther finally married the former nun and established his household in the Augustinian monastery. Six children were born to the union and the male succession continued until 1759. To suggest that Luther left the Church in order to marry a runaway nun eight years later is unhistorical and absurd.

Turning from the peasants for his support, Luther came to rely more and more on the German princes as "emergency bishops." Lutherans early disassociated themselves from secular affairs and have traditionally allowed the prince, emperor, president, or dictator to manage state affairs with a minimum of church interference or ethical judgment. The Reformation gave the princes an opportunity to seize coveted church property and to escape the inconveniences of an international Church.

The Diet of Spires in 1529 reaffirmed the verdict of Worms and insisted on liberty for Catholics in Lutheran areas but limited the further spread of the new religion in Germany. The Lutherans protested and this gave rise to the term "Protestant." They had formerly preferred the term "Evangelical" and eventually came to be known as Lutherans despite Luther's wishes: "I beg that my name be passed over in silence, and that men will call themselves not Lutherans but Christians. What is Luther? My teaching is not mine. . . . How does it happen that I . . . have the children of Christ called after my unholy name! Let us root out party names and call ourselves Christians, for it is Christ's gospel we have."

Unlike the Reformed leader, Calvin, Luther left no systematic statement of his theology. His co-worker Melanchthon performed this task and represented Lutheranism at the Diet of Augsburg in 1530 called by the emperor to restore religious unity. Melanchthon prepared a conciliatory confession which softened the more abusive criticism of the ancient church and went so far as to suggest that the adoption of vernacular in the liturgy would solve most of the differences. This Augsburg confession remains the most authoritative Lutheran doctrinal statement. It also branded the Zwinglians and Anabaptists as heretics.

Plagued by insomnia and constipation Luther nevertheless turned his tremendous energies to institutionalizing his new church. He translated the Old Testament and prepared his larger and smaller catechisms. He composed several dozen hymns including "A Mighty Fortress is Our God," the battle hymn of Protestantism. His revised liturgy emphasized preaching and congregational singing.

Toward the end of his life Luther found himself carried along by the revolution he had triggered. One of his young supporters, Philip of Hesse, tired of his wife and appealed to Luther to grant him a divorce. This Luther refused but he suggested that the prince take a second wife as in Old Testament days. Wife No. 2 was to be kept secret but her mother objected and the Reformer then advised recourse to a lie. Luther's conduct during the peasants' revolt and his countenancing of bigamy are seldom defended by even his stanchest admirers.

Many results of his Reformation distressed him. He saw moral standards sink below those of former times and he lamented: "Avarice, usury, debauchery, drunkenness, blasphemy, lying and cheating are far more prevalent now than they were under the Papacy. This state of morals brings general discredit on the Gospel, and its preachers, as the people say, if this Gospel were true, the persons professing it would be more pious." The masses were unable to understand the subtleties of Luther's justification by faith. They discarded the Ten Commandments and the spiritual exercises of the Church and found little to replace them.

As the years went by the Reformer grew intolerant of any who might venture to disagree with him. "He who does not believe my doctrine is sure to be damned," he announced. Toward the end of his life he penned two unfortunate attacks on the Jews and the papacy, illustrated with lewd cartoons. Referring to the Jews he recommended, "That their synagogues be burned, their houses broken down and destroyed, and their rabbis forbidden to teach under pain of death." Luther died in 1546.

Luther had not intended to found another church. In 1519 he would write to Pope Leo X: "Before God and all his creatures, I bear testimony that I neither did desire, nor do desire to touch or by intrigue undermine the authority of the Roman church and that of your holiness." He never considered himself outside the fold of the historic Catholic Church.

The Catholic convert Friedrich Leopold Graf von Stolberg wrote, "The Reformation proceeded originally from a pure intention. I will never raise a stone against Luther in whom I honor not only one of the greatest minds that ever lived but also the profound religiosity which never forsook him." Martin Luther was and is a Catholic priest for eternity; he wore the habit of a friar for 19 years, including three years after his excommunication. Had he not been captivated by the Nominalist philosophy of William of Occam he might have discerned that the Pelagian influence in the Church of his day was what should have been uprooted. Had Luther imbibed his philosophy from St. Thomas Aquinas instead of from the Nominalists he might have filled the role of the Great Reformer and Saint of the German people which Karl Adam depicted.

Where later Reformers attempted to dispense with everything not specifically commanded or authorized by the Bible, Luther preserved whatever was not specifically forbidden by scripture. His religion retains more of the liturgy, church year, vestments, and church architecture than other continental Protestant churches. He halted the destruction of works of art which had been instigated by Carlstad.

Lutheranism soon hardened into a rigid orthodoxy which made the Protestant right of private interpretation inoperative. Conformity or excommunication was the choice after 1580. This orthodoxy went far beyond Luther in rejecting ancient practices such as confession and the veneration of Mary. Meanwhile the Council of Trent effected a true reformation within the Church and the new Jesuit order blocked further Protestant advances and won back Catholic territories. By 1550, however, the new religion was firmly entrenched in Germany, Denmark, Sweden, and Iceland.

Pietism arose as a reaction to Lutheran orthodoxy and gave full vent to emotionalism and subjectivism. The University at Halle sponsored the pietistic movement which encouraged Bible study, hymn singing, and religious literature. Dogma took a back seat and as a consequence the Protestant world was wholly unprepared for the assaults of the Enlightenment after 1770.

The Lutherans in America have often been considered religious isolationists by their fellow Protestants. For many years, they clung to the German and Scandinavian languages; contributed little or nothing to the propagation of the social gospel, liberal theology, prohibition efforts, and the ecumenical movement; educated their children in their own parochial schools. Their continental background gave them a different attitude toward beer drinking, smoking, dancing, and the Sabbath observance. A greater degree of co-operation between Lutherans and non-Lutheran Protestants can be observed today although such groups as the Missouri and Wisconsin Synod Lutherans usually stand aloof.

American Lutheranism constitutes the third largest religious family in U. S. Protestantism. Of the 8,340,000 Lutherans, 3,200,000 belong to the mildly liberal Lutheran Church in America, 2,500,000 to the Lutheran Church — Missouri Synod, 2,450,000 to the American Lutheran Church, and 350,000 to the conservative Wisconsin Synod. In general, Lutherans are scarce in New England and the South and strongest in the Middle West.

In 1960 a merger was consummated by the Evangelical Lutheran Church, American Lutheran Church, and the United Evangelical Lutheran Church taking the name the American Lutheran Church.

Four other Lutheran Churches merged in 1962 to create the Lutheran Church in America. They included the United Lutheran Church in America, the Augustana Synod and the small American

Evangelical Lutheran Church (Danish) and the Finnish Evangelical Lutheran Church (Suomi Synod).

Until recently the Wisconsin Evangelical Synod cooperated with the larger Missouri Synod in many activities such as missions, campus foundations, and publications. Leaders of the Wisconsin Synod now accuse the Missouri Lutherans of doctrinal compromise and have withdrawn fraternal relations. At one time Lutherans in this country were divided into more than 150 separate synods.

The first stable colony of Lutherans in this country was composed of Swedish immigrants in Delaware in 1638 but most of these Swedes eventually became Episcopalians. Henry Melchior Muhlenberg is known as the patriarch of American Lutheranism since it was through his 45 years labor that the scattered German parishes were organized on a permanent basis. Of his 11 children all the men became ministers and most of the women married ministers. One son became a general and served under Washington.

A wave of conservative German Lutherans in the 1840's disrupted American Lutheranism and the breach between conservative and liberals and between north and south was not healed until 1917. The amalgam, the United Lutheran Church in America, heir of colonial Lutheranism, became the largest Lutheran body in the country, the most liberal branch of a conservative theological family, and a member of both the National and World Councils of Churches.

Two Wisconsin pastors in the ULCA were unfrocked for heresy in a widely publicized trial in 1955. The accused ministers openly doubted the virgin birth, the Resurrection and Ascension, the authenticity of Christ's miracles, the efficacy of prayer, the Lutheran doctrine of original sin, and the Real Presence. Apparently private interpretation of the scriptures has its limits.

Several boatloads of "Old Lutherans" from Luther's own province of Saxony landed near St. Louis in 1839. These ultraconservative Lutherans fought the proposed union with the Reformed in their homeland and also waged war against all forms of rationalism. In this country they soon drove their pastor from the community for immoralities and for assuming the powers of a bishop. Fortunately for the group a brilliant organizer, C. F. W. Walther, assumed leadership and can be called the real father of the Lutheran Church-Missouri Synod. The synod was formally organized in Chicago in 1847. Today the Missouri Synod is a nationwide church with its largest membership in Illinois.

The Missouri Synod Lutherans built their own parochial school system from kindergarten to university. They operate 1308 grade and high schools, Valparaiso University in Indiana, and the largest Protestant seminary in the nation, Concordia in St. Louis. They are accustomed to refer to other Lutherans as "so-called Lutherans," label the pope the anti-Christ, fight Masonry and other secret societies, excommunicate backsliders, demand strict adherence to the Lutheran confessions, and refuse to associate with other Protestants in ecumenical efforts. In recent years they have emerged from isolation and have pioneered in aggressive radio, TV, advertising, and church public relations programs. They sponsor "This is the Life" series on television, the "Lutheran Hour" on radio, and were instrumental in producing the film "Martin Luther." The Missouri Synod Lutherans are also known for their outstanding work among the deaf and mentally ill. The Missourans maintain 1135 home and 729 foreign mission congregations and have doubled their membership in the past 25 years.

Another even more conservative group is the Wisconsin Synod which shares most Missouri Synod positions but also bans membership in the Boy Scouts and the Lutheran Men of America. Since 1869 the Missouri and Wisconsin Synods have co-operated in the Lutheran Synodical Conference of North America which included Norwegian, Slovak, and Negro bodies. Recently the Wisconsin Synod has criticized the Missourans as too liberal and has made clear its disapproval of Missouri's common confession with the American Lutheran Church. The small body of Norwegians who affiliated with the Synodical Conference have already withdrawn because of Missouri's alleged laxity.

The American Lutheran Church was formed in 1930 in a union of three German Lutheran branches, the Ohio, Buffalo, and Iowa Synods which had begun between 1818 and 1854. When it merged with two other Lutheran bodies in 1960 Lutherans of German, Danish, and Norwegian backgrounds were united in one Church.

Lutheran pastors receive the benefit of a thorough, classical theological education. A candidate for the Missouri Synod ministry, for example, often begins his studies after completing grade school. He attends one of ten prep schools to take six years of pretheological training and junior college. He then completes two more years of college, two years of theology, one year as a vicar in some larger parish or college student foundation, and a final year of theology before ordination. The course includes Latin, Greek, Hebrew, and German. Concordia Seminary enrolls 1200 ministerial students while a smaller seminary in Springfield, Illinois, trains those entering the ministry later in life.

Lutheran deaconesses undergo special training, staff foreign missions, hospitals, parish offices, and welfare homes. They do not take vows and sometimes wear no distinctive garb but usually serve for life. Some synods such as Missouri operate training colleges for parochial school teachers. The immediate aim of this synod is 50 per cent of its children in parochial schools, a goal which it has already more than half reached.

All Lutheran churches have regulations against membership in lodges but only the Missouri and Wisconsin Synods enforce these regulations strictly. Some ULCA ministers are themselves high ranking Masons. Synodical conference churches carry on active campaigns against secret societies and continually warn their members against affiliation.

Augustana and ULCA have come out flatly in favor of birth control while other synods leave this matter up to the individual. Divorce with remarriage is allowed for such reasons as adultery and desertion because of "hardness of hearts." At its 1956 convention the ULCA decided to permit Lutheran pastors to witness a marriage of any divorced person who shows "repentance."

Lutheran worship is liturgical to a greater degree than that of any other Protestants, except Anglo-Catholics. They observe the church year, wear vestments, follow a set ritual. Their order of worship closely resembles the Catholic Mass from which it was adapted. The Common Service consists of silent prayer, hymn, confession of sin, declaration of grace, introit, Kyrie Eleison, gloria, collect, epistle and gospel, recitation of one of the creeds, hymn, sermon, general prayer, announcements, offering, hymn, the Our Father, and benediction.

The Lord's Supper is observed once a month and seven other times during the year. The preface, sanctus, communion prayer, words of institution, and agnus dei are inserted in the Common Service on these occasions.

Music has always played a prominent part in Lutheran worship and someone has estimated that there are at least 100,000 Lutheran hymns. Their hymnology is enriched by the compositions of Bach, a devout Lutheran.

Either a crucifix or a plain cross will be found on the Lutheran altar which occupies the central position in the chancel. Candles, the Bible, and flowers are often found on the altar, and the altar hangings and minister's stole follow a color cycle which calls for white for Christmas, red for Reformation Sunday (Sunday nearest October 31), violet for Ash Wednesday, etc. Most ministers wear a cassock, surplice, and stole and some use the historic chasuble. During the day some pastors wear a Roman collar and dark suit but most wear ordinary business clothes. They prefer to be addressed as "Pastor" rather than as "Reverend" or "Mr."

European Lutheran churches follow an episcopal polity but those in America have preferred a congregational system which allows the local church to own property, call pastors, and elect church officers but which preserves doctrinal unity.

To most Lutherans the church is invisible, composed of all those believing Christians who are justified through the merits of Christ. Only the Missouri and Wisconsin Synods continue to refer to the visible head of the Catholic Church as the anti-Christ.

Surveying the Protestant panorama, Catholics will see that their Lutheran brethren have retained more of the central Christian doctrines than other Protestants. Modernism made little headway in Lutheran ranks. Relations between Catholics and Protestants in Germany, the homeland of the Reformation, have never been more cordial since the sixteenth century. Unfortunately, this is not the case in the United States. We share so many fundamental Christian principles, demonstrate the same concern for religious training by building parochial schools for our children, stand firmly against the assaults of deism and rationalism, that the antagonism between Catholic and Lutheran in this country is all the more lamentable.

Professor Jaroslav Pelikan of the University of Chicago's Federated Theological faculty recently commented: "We [Lutherans] are theologically specific and theologically concerned. We are not concerned with positive thinking, with hustle-bustle for its own sake. The interesting thing is that while historical differences remain, Lutherans have begun to recognize that they are closer to Roman Catholics in many ways than they are to other Protestants." Pelikan's own *Riddle of Roman Catholicism* has been acclaimed one of the most perceptive contributions to ecumenical understanding in recent decades.

Catholics must be candid enough to admit the real evils which infested the Church during Luther's age. Lutherans must be willing to admit that not a single Reformation-age charge against the Church of Rome could be justifiably made today. Catholics must try to see Luther in true perspective and be willing to shed the popular caricatures of the great heresiarch. Lutherans may well reappraise the papacy as an institution which has proved to be the historic conserver of Christian truths despite the few unworthy wearers of the Fisherman's ring.

Chapter IV

THE PRESBYTERIANS

Calvinism Replaced Bishops With Elders

L<small>IKE</small> the Episcopal Church, the Presbyterian Church takes its name from its form of government. Elected elders rather than bishops rule the presbyterian churches. But the larger church exercises supervision over the congregations through presbyteries or associations of churches in a given area. This representative system strikes a mean between the town meeting democracy of the congregationalists and the autocracy of the episcopalians.

Theologically the Presbyterians also follow the teachings of John Calvin, a French lawyer who systematized non-Lutheran Protestantism in the sixteenth century. Not all Calvinists, for instance the Baptists and Congregationalists, are presbyterian in polity and likewise not all presbyterians, e.g., some Lutherans, are Calvinist in theology. We should keep in mind that presbyterianism refers to a particular representative form of church government while Calvinism refers to a theological emphasis which centered around the absolute sovereignty of God and the helplessness of man and, at least originally, predestination to heaven or hell.

American Presbyterianism is wealthy, sizable, influential, middle and upper class, generally conservative, often fashionable, and largely English, Scotch, and Scotch-Irish. Three denominations, the *United Presbyterian Church in the U. S. A.* (a recent merger of the Northern and the United Presbyterians), the *Presbyterian Church in the U. S.* (south), and the *Cumberland Presbyterian Church* enroll 98 per

47

cent of the 4,327,000 communicants. Presbyterian or Reformed churches predominate in Scotland, Northern Ireland, and Holland and claim large constituencies in Switzerland, South Africa, Germany, and Hungary. Most French Protestants or Huguenots adhere to a Reformed theology. The world total is about 15,000,000 members of Presbyterian and Reformed Churches.

Between 1800 and 1837 the Presbyterian Church was certainly the most influential church in the new nation. In 1837, however, the church split into two factions, Old School and New School, over questions of doctrine and church government, particularly the Plan of Union with the more liberal Congregationalists. These two branches remained apart until after the Civil War and this situation handicapped the growth of Presbyterianism in this country. Meanwhile these branches subdivided over the issue of slavery into northern and southern churches in a rupture which has never healed. Presbyterian insistence on a trained ministry forfeited much of the frontier to Methodist and Baptist preachers.

To trace the beginnings of Presbyterianism we must go back to the early days of the Reformation. While Luther led the revolt in Germany an ex-priest, Ulrich Zwingli, established the new religion in Switzerland. Zwingli began to devour Luther's writings in 1518 and four years later he was denying the value of fasting and clerical celibacy. He petitioned his bishop for a release from the obligations of celibacy and when this was naturally denied he married the widow with whom he had been living. A daughter was born four months after the wedding.

Zwingli soon parted company with the German reformer on the question of the Real Presence of Christ in the Eucharist. This led to the split between Lutheran and Reformed Protestantism which continues to this day. Zwingli held the Lord's Supper to be nothing more than a simple memorial service whereas Luther upheld the Real Presence while denying the doctrine of transubstantiation. The Swiss reformer stripped the churches of all art and music and established a theocracy at Zurich. He was slain in battle in 1531 as he led his followers against the Catholic cantons.

Jean Cauvin, known to us as John Calvin, was the son of a

minor French ecclesiastical official. A year after his father's excommunication Calvin turned from the study of theology to law and in 1533 he embraced the new religious ideas of the Reformation. His reasons for leaving the Catholic Church were never explicitly stated but he became the tireless propagator of the new religion. Fearing persecution he left his native country. At Basle he composed his classic exposition of Reformation doctrine, the *Institutes of the Christian Religion*. He was 27 at the time.

A reformer at Geneva, where he had stopped to spend the night, persuaded him to stay and guide the Protestant community in this Swiss city of about 15,000 population. Calvin agreed and set about establishing what might be termed a religious police state. Modeled after Old Testament theocracies, the Geneva city government employed harsh penalties, espionage, and religious sanctions to enforce a drab and severe religious code. Calvin fulminated against dancing, amusements, luxuries, feast days, indolence, and vestigial Catholic practices. After two years of this regime the citizens rebelled and forced Calvin to leave.

He taught at Strassbourg for three years, married a widow, and finally received a second invitation to come to Geneva. During his exile he had perfected his presbyterian system of representative church government. Older and wiser, Calvin returned and undertook to transform Geneva into a model Protestant community. Thousands of religious rebels from Europe and the British Isles swelled the city's population and returned to their homelands with Calvinistic orientations.

Calvinism furnished the theological foundation for the Huguenots and for the more successful Reformed churches of the Netherlands. John Knox brought Calvinism to Scotland and Scotland has always been the main Presbyterian center. English divines banished by the Catholic Queen Mary found refuge in Geneva and when they returned under Elizabeth they carried their Calvinism with them.

Classical Calvinism based its theology on five points, all of which have been drastically modified by modern Presbyterianism: (1) predestination or election; (2) limited atonement; (3) total depravity; (4) the irresistibility of grace; and (5) perseverance of the saints. In other words, Calvin taught that man's nature since the Fall is totally depraved. God elects some men to salvation and damns others to hell. Christ died only for the elect, who cannot resist God's grace and cannot backslide once they have received this grace of election.

"We assert that by an eternal and immutable counsel, God has once for all determined, both whom He would admit to salvation, and whom He would condemn to destruction," wrote Calvin. Calvinists generally relied on passages from St. Augustine to substantiate their views of absolute or double predestination. They deduced that unbaptized babies were certain to be cast into hell and the American theologian and preacher Jonathan Edwards asserted, "Hell is paved with the skulls of unbaptized children."

The pure Calvinist impulse to reaffirm the absolute sovereignty of God and to expose the idolatry of acting as though God and man existed on the same plane was often misdirected. By 1741 Edwards was presenting the following picture of God the Father to his congregation: "The God that holds you over the pit of hell, much as one holds a spider, or some loathsome insect, over the fire, abhors you and is dreadfully provoked; His wrath towards you burns like fire; He looks upon you as worthy of nothing but to be cast into the fire; He is of purer eyes than to bear to have you in His sight; you are ten thousand times so abominable in His eyes, as the most hateful and venemous serpent is in ours."

The Catholic Church approaches the question of predestination with greater trepidation than Lawyer Calvin. The Council of Trent called predestination "a hidden mystery." Catholicism upholds the truth that salvation is primarily God's work and His grace but that man is not totally depraved. After justification he may offer the merits of good works for his salvation. Man possesses free will, and whether a man is saved or damned he arrives at this state through the exercise of his free will. God condemns no one to hell; man condemns himself to hell by his sins. Calvinism finds itself in the position of implicating God with sin since, if God damns a soul to hell, He must also force that soul to sin to deserve hell. Catholic doctrine denies that unbaptized infants, incapable of actual sin, are condemned to hell if they die. The Church's common teaching is that such souls enjoy a state of natural happiness in limbo.

Whereas Luther claimed to preserve whatever was not specifically forbidden by the Bible, Calvin sought to reject everything which was not positively commanded. He divested the Reformed worship service of all beauty when he discarded vestments, altar, images, paintings, organs, and hymns. God could be praised only by His own words, therefore, Calvin forbade any hymns but the psalms themselves. Today Presbyterians acknowledge Calvinistic excesses and have reintroduced Christian art and symbolism into their architecture, chancels, hymns, and liturgies.

Calvin adopted a position on the Eucharist slightly closer to Luther's than was Zwingli's, but like Luther he upheld a mystical rather than a substantial Real Presence. The Calvinist receives the bread and wine as a guaranty of the grace flowing into his soul from Christ in heaven.

Calvinism encouraged education, sobriety, thrift, political as well as religious democracy, philanthropy, capitalism, Bible reading, and the somber Sabbath. The Bible became an infallible rule of conduct and the Calvinists accorded relatively greater emphasis to the Old Testament than did other Christians.

Max Weber and R. H. Tawney have suggested the positive relationship between Calvinism and the rise of capitalism. Calvinism stressed the secular vocation, lifted the bans against interest, offered investment opportunities to the many Protestant refugees in Geneva, and pointed out that the elect might well be identified by their material prosperity since God would favor His elect.

In striving to give all possible honor to God Calvin eventually presented a God who arbitrarily damned souls to hell and forced men to sin, who condemned innocent babies to eternal torment, who denied free will to both the elect and the reprobate. His followers today generally regard predestination as a "hidden mystery." The expected reaction against the harsher aspects of Calvinism came from the Dutch theologian Arminius who re-emphasized free will and later inspired Wesleyan theology.

Plagued by headaches and indigestion, Calvin nevertheless kept up an exhausting daily routine. In 1553 he consented to the burning of the Spanish Unitarian, Michael Servetus. Humorless, cold, and ruthlessly logical, he had few close friends but was greatly respected. He died at the age of 54 and shares with Martin Luther the title Father of the Protestant Reformation.

Protestantism never managed to make much headway in Calvin's native France. The politically inspired St. Bartholomew's Day massacre in 1572 involved the slaughter of 30,000 Huguenots. The Edict of Nantes -in 1598 granted them freedom of worship but when it was revoked by Louis XIV in 1685 thousands of French Protestants, many of them skilled artisans, fled to other lands. The Revolution decimated Protestant as well as Catholic churches and today French Protestants number fewer than one million.

The Reformed faith took deep root in the Netherlands and the royal family of Holland and a majority of the people belong to one of the two main Reformed churches. The Catholic population of Holland has increased to nearly 40 per cent in recent decades. Dutch colonists carried the Reformed Church to North America, South Africa, and the Dutch East Indies.

On the continent about 600,000 Germans hold the Reformed faith in a nation which is largely Lutheran and Catholic, and the once powerful Hungarian Reformed Church has sustained losses in that unfortunate nation.

John Knox had been a Catholic priest, Protestant preacher, exile in England, and galley slave in the French navy before reaching Geneva. What he learned from Calvin during three years in that city he taught in his native Scotland, opposing the Catholicism of Mary Queen of Scots and the Anglicanism of the English. He helped dethrone Mary and maneuvered the Scottish parliament into establishing Presbyterianism as the state religion. Periodic attempts were made to overthrow Scottish Presbyterianism and substitute an episcopal system. Charles II sniffed, "Presbyterianism is not a religion for gentlemen." The church suffered a number of schisms over the issues of monarchy and lay patronage but a union of all major branches was effected in 1929 in the Church of Scotland.

Scotch colonists settled confiscated lands in Northern Ireland or Ulster and soon that area of the island was mainly Scotch. These Scotch-Irish took their Presbyterianism with them to the Catholic island. Today Ireland, including the six northern counties, is one fourth Protestant, mainly Presbyterian. Between 1729 and 1809 a steady stream of Scotch-Irish emigrated to America and one such immigrant, the Rev. Francis Makemie, is considered the father of Presbyterianism in this country. The Scotch-Irish influenced the course of American Presbyterianism more than any other nationality.

In England the Church of England was pestered by two groups: the Puritans and the Separatists. Both wished to purify the state church of such popish practices as the sign of the cross, the use of vestments and images, kneeling for prayer, feast days, etc. The Separatists, however, believed that the Anglican church was hopeless; they felt compelled to separate from this church and found another, purer church. The Puritans were convinced that they could remain Anglicans and bring about their reforms from within. Calvinism pervaded both parties and most but not all of the Puritans were also Presbyterians, with a sprinkling of Congregationalists.

Eventually the Puritan party gained power in England and the episcopacy was abolished. "No bishop and no king" was their motto. Parliament called together 151 clergymen and laymen, most of whom were Presbyterians, to formulate a confession of faith. The delegates remained in session for five years at Westminster, threw out the Book of Common Prayer, and prepared the Westminster Confession of 1648, a Directory of Worship, a Form of Government, and a Larger and Shorter Catechism. Fourteen years later the Puritan Commonwealth under Cromwell gave way to the monarchy and the Anglican hierarchy was restored.

The Westminster Confession remains the standard of faith for American, Scottish, and English Presbyterianism but its statement on predestination has been modified from its original form: "By the decree of God, for the manifestation of His glory, some men and angels are predestined unto everlasting life, and others foreordained to everlasting death. . . . The rest of mankind, God was pleased . . . to pass by, and to ordain them to dishonor and wrath for their sin, to the praise of His glorious justice."

Presbyterianism in England crumbled in the eighteenth century as a result of government disabilities, Arian and Unitarian heresies, and a poorly trained ministry. Only later Scottish immigration saved Presbyterianism from extinction there and even now the denomination counts only 100,000 adherents in that country.

Puritan ministers brought Presbyterianism to America where they soon followed the Separatists out of the Church of England. Some switched to Congregationalism in the Massachusetts Bay Colony but others remained Presbyterians. Makemie organized the first presbytery, an essential of that form of polity, at Philadelphia in 1706. Disagreement over the place of revivals in the church and interpretations of the Confession led to the New Side-Old Side division which lasted from 1741 to 1758.

Presbyterians were almost 100 per cent behind the colonists in the American Revolution. In fact, the Revolution was known by many in England as the "Presbyterian Rebellion." This attitude was in contrast to that of the Loyalist Methodists and Anglicans.

The two Calvinist denominations, Presbyterian and Congregationalist, entered into a Plan of Union whereby congregations on the western frontier could maintain affiliations with both denominations. Although this Plan usually worked to the advantage of the Presbyterians, an Old School party within Presbyterianism complained of Congregational influence. This led to the schism of 1837 which was not healed until after the Civil War. In 1920 the Welsh Calvinistic Methodists joined what was then known as the northern *Presbyterian Church in the U. S. A.*

Slavery was not the sole reason for the schism of the southern branch, now known as the *Presbyterian Church in the U. S.,* with 917,000 members. The southerners also disliked the liberalism of their northern brothers. They have remained more conservative than the northern church and are concentrated in 16 southern states. Fraternal relations are cultivated between the northern and southern Presbyterian churches and ministers and members freely switch affiliation. Negro members of the Presbyterian Church in the U. S. are segregated in colored churches and presbyteries.

Revivalism led in 1810 to the secession of the Cumberland presbytery which had begun to ordain preachers lacking the proper educational qualifications. The Cumberlanders organized their own church when they were officially dissolved by the Kentucky synod. They preached an Arminian rather than a pure Calvinist doctrine but no greater a departure from Geneva Calvinism than that now held by the northern church. Most of the Cumberlanders rejoined the parent church in 1906 but 83,000 members are reported by the *Cumberland Presbyterian Church* which refused to enter the reunion. The parallel *Cumberland Presbyterian Church in U.S.* and *Africa* enrolls another 30,000.

The 257,000-member *United Presbyterian Church of North America* represented an 1858 merger of two strict Scotch Presbyterian churches. Both had withdrawn from the Church of Scotland. Particularly before 1925 this denomination had been known for its espousal of classical Calvinism, opposition to secret societies, exclusive use of the psalms in worship, and closed communion. It supported six colleges including Muskingum, Westminster (Pa.), and Monmouth.

Completion of the merger of the northern Presbyterians and the United Presbyterians was announced in 1958. The new 3,242,000-member church is known as the United Presbyterian Church in the U. S. A. Overtures for a similar merger with the southern branch have been turned down as recently as 1956 but an eventual union is anticipated within a decade.

While Episcopalians have fussed over ritualism and Methodists debated the evils of smoking and drinking, Presbyterians have stoked the fires of theological controversy. They stood on the firing line in the leading fundamentalist-modernist battles which shook American Protestantism from 1910 to about 1925.

Two wealthy Presbyterian laymen in Los Angeles published the tracts which outlined the "fundamentals" of the Christian faith. More than 3,000,000 copies of *The Fundamentals*, the articles of war against modernism, the social gospel, and evolutionary theory, were distributed in 1910 and the years following. Presbyterian evangelist, the Rev. Dr. (Westminster college) Billy Sunday, enlivened tent and tabernacle with his colorful denunciations of modernists, saloon keepers, birth controllers, and Socialists.

Dr. Harry Emerson Fosdick, a Baptist, occupied the pulpit of New York's First Presbyterian church. His frankly modernist position and specific denial of the virgin birth prompted the General Assembly to invite him to become a Presbyterian (under its jurisdiction) or give up his position as pastor of a Presbyterian church. He followed the latter course and continued to expound his liberal theological views at Riverside church.

Modernism continued to upset Presbyterian conservatism long after the main battle ended. A small group of conservatives followed Prof. J. Gresham Machen of Princeton out of the mother church. Machen, one of the ablest advocates of fundamentalism and one of its few real scholars, organized the Presbyterian Church of America but the courts made him adopt another name for his church, the *Orthodox Presbyterian Church*.

Shortly thereafter some of the Machen schismatics disagreed with him on total abstinence and millennialism and set up their own *Bible Presbyterian Church* now known as the Evangelical Presbyterian Church. Rev. Carl McIntire, leader of this faction, also bitterly opposed the Federal Council of Churches as modernist and organized his American Council of Churches and later the International Council of Churches.

Presbyterianism has traditionally been strong in the Middle Atlantic states of New York, New Jersey, and Pennsylvania but it also enrolls large memberships in Ohio, Michigan, Indiana, Illinois, Iowa, and California. Presbyterians have participated in conferences called to consider the so-called Blake-Pike proposal to merge the Episcopalian, Presbyterian, Methodist, United Church of Christ, and several other denominations.

Forty-four colleges and universities are related to the northern church and 16 others to the southern church. Presbyterian seminary curricula still include Hebrew and Greek and more theology than most Protestant denominations offer their ministerial candidates.

Princeton and McCormick in Chicago are two leading seminaries. It has also been estimated that 85 per cent of Presbyterian young people of college age are attending college.

The whole number of the elect comprise the invisible church according to Presbyterian thought; the visible church consists of "all those throughout the world that profess the true religion, together with their children, and is the Kingdom of the Lord Jesus Christ." The following description of the visible head of the Roman Catholic Church was revised by the northern Presbyterians in 1903: "There is no other head of the Church but the Lord Jesus Christ. Nor can the pope of Rome in any sense be head thereof; but is that anti-christ, that man of sin, and son of perdition, that exalteth himself, in the Church, against Christ, and all that is called God."

On the matter of predestination and free will today's Presbyterian stands much closer to the original Catholic position than did Calvin. You would have to look to the tiny Presbyterian sects to hear absolute or double predestination preached. The drastic modification of the Westminster Confession is indicated in the 1903 interpretation of the northern church: "Concerning those who perish the doctrine of God's eternal decree is held in harmony with the doctrine that God desires not the death of any sinner, but has provided in Christ a salvation sufficient for all . . . men are fully responsible for their treatment of God's gracious offer . . . his decree hinders no man from accepting that offer . . . no man is condemned except on the ground of his sin."

Presbyterians do not consider baptism necessary for salvation but do urge that infants and adults receive the sacrament. The usual form is sprinkling. The current theory about the fate of unbaptized infants who die in infancy differs from Edwards' grim description of hell's pavement. Presbyterians now assume that death in infancy is a sure sign of election and the soul of the infant will spend eternity not in hell or limbo but in heaven, even though unbaptized.

Divorce on grounds of adultery and desertion was allowed by the Westminster Confession under certain conditions. But in 1953 the northern church extended this to "grounds explicitly stated in Scripture or *implicit* in the gospel of Christ." (Italics mine.)

Each Presbyterian congregation elects about a dozen ruling elders and a teaching elder all of whom are ordained church officials. The teaching elder is the minister but theoretically he holds a position on a par with the other elders. The Session, comprised of the pastor and the ruling elders, is supervised by the presbytery or regional body to which it belongs. At least five Sessions are needed to form a presbytery which is composed of all the ministers and one ruling elder from each church. The presbytery examines and ordains candidates for the ministry, installs and removes ministers, settles doctrinal and disciplinary questions, checks the records of local churches, starts new churches, and the like. Except in the case of national or racial groupings, the presbyteries are plotted on geographical lines.

The Synod performs the same function for the presbyteries which the latter perform for the churches. Most Synods are organized along state lines with at least three presbyteries in each synod. In the northern church, for example, there are 40 synods and in the southern church, 14. The member presbyteries elect an equal number of ministers and ruling elders to the synod which meets once a year.

The General Assembly tops the national Presbyterian structure and includes an equal number of pastors and elders from each presbytery. The powers of the Assembly include the right to suppress heresy and schism, reorganize synods, settle doctrinal and disciplinary controversies, and ratify mergers with other denominations.

Members of Presbyterian churches in the United States need not subscribe to the Westminster Confession or any other creed. Such a declaration of belief is required of ministers, ruling elders, and deacons but even in these cases ingenious interpretations may be devised by modernist sympathizers. If we were to rank Protestant denominations according to theological liberalism, we would probably put the Presbyterians somewhere between the Congregationalists, Disciples, and Methodists, on the one hand, and the Lutherans, Episcopalians, and Baptists on the other.

Presbyterianism has always made its greatest appeal to activist

Anglo-Saxons. Unchurched Americans looking for a church home may decide to affiliate with the Presbyterian church which they see as less nationalistic than the Lutheran, more fashionable than the Baptist, more democratic than the Episcopalian, less blue-nosed than the Methodist, and more traditional than the Disciples.

As we have seen, traditional Calvinist principles carry little weight in twentieth-century Presbyterianism. Predestination, for example, may be the first thought a Catholic observer associates with this church but it has become an historical curiosity for the average Presbyterian layman. The drab and barren Calvinist worship is being enriched by a return to the practices of the ancient church. Here more so than in many denominations we find a huge gulf between the classical formulation and present-day beliefs.

Chapter V

THE EPISCOPALIANS

Comprehensive Christianity: Calvinism and Catholicism

A ROMAN CATHOLIC who happened to visit an "Anglo-Catholic" church some Sunday morning would find himself in a familiar setting. He would observe the holy water fonts, the confessional booth, the stations of the cross, statues, and the sanctuary lamp. The officiating Episcopalian priest wears the traditional Christian vestments, the alb, stole, cincture, and chasuble or cope. The sermon at this Holy Communion or Mass might concern the seven sacraments, fast and abstinence regulations, or the Real Presence of Christ in the Eucharist. Except for the use of English in place of Latin the visitor might easily imagine himself in his own parish church.

But were he to continue his Episcopalian itinerary, he might be puzzled at his next stop. This second Episcopal church, three or 300 miles away, might resemble a typical Protestant chapel in architecture, ecclesiastical furniture, vestment, and liturgy — little different from a Congregational or Methodist church. The minister would be vested in surplice and stole and the main worship service would be Morning Prayer rather than a communion service or Anglican Mass. The congregation might be hearing a sermon on justification by faith alone or the sole sufficiency of the scripture or the two Christian sacraments as opposed to the seven sacraments of the Catholic Church.

A third Episcopal church might resemble the first or second in appearance and liturgy but the sermon would soon disclose a rationalist or modernist slant which would find an equal welcome in Unitarian circles.

Our Catholic visitor would have seen representative parishes of the three main parties in Anglicanism: the High Church or "Anglo-Catholic," the Low or Evangelical, and the broad or Modernist. The Church of England and its American counterpart, the Protestant Episcopal church, embraces a wider spectrum of doctrine and practice than any major Protestant communion.

Claiming to be both Catholic and Protestant, it combines the ritual and polity of Catholicism with a moderately Calvinistic theology. Episcopalians assert that they resist the "additions of Romanism and the subtractions of Protestantism." Episcopal divines do not claim that theirs is the only Catholic Church but that it constitutes one of four branches of the Catholic Church: Roman Catholic, Eastern Othodox, Anglican, and Old Catholic. In its original formulation in the middle of the nineteenth century, this branch theory included only the first three bodies but the subsequent Old Catholic schism added a fourth branch.

Unlike most Protestant sects, Anglicanism values the apostolic succession, the episcopacy, and the priesthood. Anglicans are happy to acknowledge the authority of the pope as the Bishop of Rome but deny that his authority extends beyond the boundaries of his own diocese.

Anglican claims to Catholicity, however, must be rejected by the Roman Catholic Church which views Anglicanism as one of many movements which have passed from schism to heresy. Pope Leo XIII was forced to declare Anglican orders invalid in 1896 although the Church has always recognized the validity of Orthodox and Old Catholic orders.

Anglicanism differs from the products of the Continental Reformation in that the motives for the separation of the Church of England from Rome were admittedly political rather than religious. No one suggests that Henry VIII severed the English ties with Rome and set himself up as head of the national church for spiritual reasons. Neither theological disputes nor a demand for the elimination of abuses played a big part in the English revolt.

One consequence of the purely political motivation has been that the Anglican church retains more Catholic beliefs and forms than either the Lutheran or Reformed churches. And since the Oxford Movement of the past century the Church of England has witnessed a revival of Catholic practices which has brought large sections of the establishment closer to Rome than at any time since the reign of Queen Elizabeth. Sad to say, many who have labored for the return of Catholic truths to Anglicanism have faced both the taunts of Protestant-minded churchmen and the jibes of some Catholics who see the revival as simply imitative.

Forty monks accompanied St. Augustine to Britain on a missionary journey commissioned by Pope Gregory. He found a handful of Christians in Wales and Western England, remnants of the Christian community which had flourished in Roman times, who had been pushed into corners of the island by pagan Angles and Saxons. St. Augustine became the first Archbishop of Canterbury.

For nearly 1000 years the Church in England recognized the supremacy of the bishop of Rome as did the rest of Western Christendom. For example, Venerable Bede wrote in A.D. 735: "The Pope bears pontifical power over the whole world." In the eleventh century St. Anselm of Canterbury declared, "It is certain that he who does not obey the Roman Pontiff is disobedient to the Apostle Peter, nor is he of that flock given to Peter by God." In 1154 an Englishman, Nicholas Breakspeare, was elected pope.

Episcopalians have good reason to object to Catholic controversialists who attempt to prove that their church was founded by the lustful Henry VIII. The monarch would have been an uncomfortable Episcopalian. A fair theologian himself, Henry penned a volume on the Seven Sacraments and a refutation of Lutheran errors which won him the title from the pope of "Defender of the Faith." English kings still bear this papal title.

Validly married to the Spanish princess Catherine of Aragon, the king became enamored of Anne Boleyn, a lady in waiting. Anxious to marry Anne and provide a male heir for the throne, the king asked for an annulment but the pope hesitated and refused.

His archbishop of Canterbury, Thomas Cranmer, took it upon himself to declare the marriage to Catherine invalid and Henry announced himself to be the sole head of the Church of England in 1534. The Act of Supremacy stated that: "The Bishop of Rome hath not by Scripture any greater authority in England than any other foreign bishop." Sir Thomas More, the Lord Chancellor, among others, was executed for refusing to recognize this spiritual supremacy of the king.

Although he suppressed some 616 monasteries (to get needed funds) and murdered hundreds of bishops, monks, nobles, and women, the king never departed from orthodox Catholic teachings except for the question of papal supremacy. He insisted on communion under one species, auricular confession, clerical celibacy, requiem masses, and belief in transubstantiation. No Catholic wishes to present Henry as a Christian model but he did hold fast to dogmatic positions and he quashed efforts to Protestantize the national church. Cranmer was obliged to pack his secret Lutheran wife and children back to Germany.

Henry VIII removed the English church from obedience to the Roman See but he never tampered with doctrine. Priests continued to offer true Masses and bishops ordained true priests during his rule. For the common man Catholic life continued much as before the administrative quarrel. England was in schism not heresy. Rather than being the first Anglican, Henry was a disobedient and wicked Catholic.

The Protestant party captured the English church during the subsequent seven year reign of the tubercular boy king Edward VI, the son of Henry and Wife No. 3, Jane Seymour. Members of the Reformed faith flocked to England from the continent with their novel doctrines of justification by faith alone, two sacraments, the sole sufficiency of the Bible. Priests took wives, the Mass was abolished, and churches were stripped of works of art. Cranmer's Book of Common Prayer cut the sacrificial heart out of the Mass and the revised ordination rite made no mention of the sacrificial powers of the priest.

Matthew Parker, a married cleric with Lutheran sympathies, was consecrated (1559) according to the defective Edwardian ordinal of 1552. Through Parker, all Church of England bishops claim to trace their apostolic succession. The defective form was employed, from the accession of Queen Elizabeth until 1662. By the end of this period all validly consecrated Anglican bishops had died and the apostolic succession was broken.

Queen Mary, the daughter of Henry and Catherine, reigned until 1558 and vowed to return the church to its Catholic heritage. For a period of almost five years from 1554 the English church was reunited with Rome and the Holy Father sent Cardinal Pole as his delegate to consolidate the reunion. The Protestant innovators were exiled and Cranmer was burned at the stake. Mary's efforts to re-establish the ancient faith failed and earned her the title "Bloody Mary" in Protestant history texts.

Elizabeth, the daughter of Henry and Anne, again cut the ties with Rome. She abolished the Mass and reintroduced the oath of supremacy although she called herself the Supreme Governor rather than the Supreme Head of the church. She stabilized what has become known as Anglicanism and could more logically be considered the founder of the Church of England than her notorious father. The Thirty-nine Articles, trimmed from 42, formed the doctrinal standard for the national church, now definitely in the Protestant camp. Queen Elizabeth and all members of the Church of England were excommunicated by Pope Pius V, an action which Cardinal Newman and other Catholic writers have considered a blunder which only bolstered anti-Catholicism in the nation.

Successes over the hated Spanish and the destruction of the Armada, political astuteness, and economic prosperity contributed to the queen's popularity. The new religion shared the credit for the nation's good fortune. As critical of the dissenting Presbyterians and Congregationalists as of the Papists, the queen suppressed all non-Anglicans by force.

Eventually the Puritans, Anglicans who wished to purify their church of lingering popish practices, established a dictatorship under Oliver Cromwell. In the restoration Charles II again made the Anglican church supreme.

The various Baptist, Congregational, Quaker, and Presbyterian sects would plague the established church and in the eighteenth century the Wesleyan revival would lead hundreds of thousands out of the Anglican fold. Today in England the Anglicans and Roman Catholics each number about 3,000,000 active members and the Methodists claim 739,000. Most Englishmen do not attend church and cannot be considered even nominal Christians. It has become commonplace to refer to the "post-Christian era" in England today.

A century after the start of the Wesleyan movement the Church of England experienced a different sort of revival. The Oxford Movement called for a return to Catholic traditions, a renewed sacramental life, a greater appreciation of the church, the episcopacy, and the priesthood. John Henry Newman and other Oxford men sparked the movement which revitalized Anglicanism and gave birth to the High Church or Anglo-Catholic party. Newman himself submitted to the Catholic Church in 1845, inspired several others to follow him into the Church, and died a cardinal at the age of 89.

British colonists brought Anglicanism to American shores in the Virginia settlement in 1607. Completely dependent on the mother church and the Bishop of London, the American branch had no bishop or diocesan organization for 177 years. Candidates for the priesthood had to risk smallpox and shipwreck to return to England for ordination and the colonials were unable to receive confirmation until after the American Revolution. That an episcopal church without bishops showed little vitality should not be surprising.

At the outbreak of the Revolution most Anglican clergymen fled to England and Canada since they had taken an oath of loyalty to the king. Before the outbreak of hostilities the Church of England had been supported by taxes in seven Southern colonies. In Virginia, for example, the law stipulated an Anglican clergyman's salary at "1,500 pounds of tobacco and 16 barrels of corn." With this financial support gone, its clergy scattered and discredited, and its name closely associated with the recent enemy, the Church of England in the American colonies faced serious postwar problems.

The remaining Anglicans selected Samuel Seabury to be bishop. He spent a year in England seeking consecration but the law forbade consecration of a bishop who was not a British subject. In desperation, Seabury turned to the outlawed Scottish Episcopal Church which granted him consecration in 1784. Three years later the Archbishops of Canterbury and York did consecrate two Americans. A General Convention in Philadelphia in 1789 united the Anglicans in America into the *Protestant Episcopal Church*.

Few immigrants after the Revolution professed the Anglican faith and the church was unable to hold its own on the frontier against the aggressive Methodist and Baptist preachers. By 1830 only 30,000 Protestant Episcopal communicants could be counted and these were clustered on the Atlantic seaboard. During the Civil War the Southern bishops organized a Confederate church but after the war the two branches were reunited.

As in England the High Church movement introduced more ritual and beauty into the liturgy. The use of incense and the question of vestments enlivened the ritualist controversy with Bishop John Henry Hobart of New York and William Augustus Muhlenberg, a convert from Lutheranism, upholding the High Church position. Between 1825 and 1855 thirty Episcopalian priests entered the Catholic Church.

Phillips Brooks, recognized as the greatest preacher in the Episcopal church, guided the Broad movement from his pulpit in Trinity church, Boston. This party represented modernism and rationalism in the Unitarian stronghold but has remained relatively small compared to the Anglo-Catholic wing.

A group of low churchmen seceded in 1873 to found the *Reformed Episcopal Church*, the only serious schism in Episcopalian history in this country. They abhorred all ritual, and deleted such words as "priest, altar, sacrament, and holy communion" from their revision of the Book of Common Prayer. This sect has declined in membership and now numbers fewer than 7700 members.

The typical Episcopalian minister can be called a Prayer Book clergyman who follows a middle course, avoiding the extremes of Anglo-Catholicism, evangelicalism, and modernism. The Thirty-nine articles, which are relegated to the appendix in the Book of Common Prayer, do not bind either priest or layman. At ordination Episcopal priests must declare: "I do believe the Holy Scriptures of the Old and New Testaments to be the Word of God, and to contain all things necessary to salvation; and I do solemnly engage to conform to the Doctrine, Discipline, and Worship of the Protestant Episcopal Church in the United States of America."

Most Episcopalians would consider that the Apostles' and Nicene creeds reflect their creedal beliefs, but they may attach unorthodox interpretations or reservations to these historic creeds. Anglicans are accustomed to appeal to the teachings of the undivided Church, the Church which existed before the East-West schism in 1054. Despite the ordination declaration the Anglican priest is unlikely to hold the Bible to be the sole rule of faith. He will probably add the tradition of the undivided Church and the use of reason to the Scriptures as rules of faith. All but the Anglo-Catholics concur in the Reformed or symbolic interpretation of the Eucharist. Anglicans do not use the term "purgatory" but they believe in a state of purification which they may call the Church Expectant. Some Anglican theologians entertain universalist views and express doubts that God's mercy may be reconciled with an eternal hell.

In contrast to the plainly Protestant positions of most of their Episcopalian brethren, the Anglo-Catholics stress the Catholic heritage. Anglo-Catholicism is aggressive and articulate, which may lead some Roman Catholics to overestimate its strength within the Protestant Episcopal Church. The head of the American Church Union, the chief Anglo-Catholic organization, estimates there are 200,000 Anglo-Catholics out of a total of 3,269,000 Episcopalians but adds that perhaps 1,000,000 more may support specific Anglo-Catholic positions.

A midwestern "biretta belt" of Anglo-Catholicism embraces the dioceses of Fond du Lac, Eau Claire, Milwaukee, Chicago, Quincy,

Springfield, and Northern Indiana. The Long Island diocese also figures prominently in the movement and Anglo-Catholic parishes may be found in New York and other Episcopal dioceses. Nashotah House in Wisconsin trains many Anglo-Catholic priests.

Anglo-Catholics emphasize the seven sacraments, the Real Presence, fast and abstinence, auricular confession, the Eucharistic fast, prayers and requiem Masses for the dead, retreats, invocation of the saints. They say the rosary, make the sign of the cross, genuflect, address their priests as "Father."

The papalist Confraternity of Unity, with an executive board of 16 Anglican priests, is "composed of members of the Anglican communion who believe that the See of Rome is the Center of Unity for all churches. . . . Members are asked to pray daily for reunion with the Holy Apostolic See."

The Guild of All Souls promotes the celebration of requiem Masses and prayers for the dead. The American chapter of the Living Rosary of Our Lady and St. Dominic encourages Episcopalians to recite the rosary while the Confraternity of the Blessed Sacrament of the Body and Blood of Christ directs the attention of Anglicans to the real presence.

Although usually outvoted in the General Convention, the Anglo-Catholics have long urged that the word "Protestant" be dropped from the official title of the church. They have managed to scuttle attempts at merger with the Presbyterians and perennially condemn open communion and open pulpits. They have recently been asking for permission to reserve the communion elements on the altar.

Anglo-Catholicism revived religious orders in Anglicanism after a lapse of 300 years. Eleven Episcopalian orders for men and 14 for women seek to follow the evangelical counsels of poverty, chastity, and obedience. These include the Holy Cross Order, the Society of St. John the Evangelist, and Episcopalian Franciscans, and Benedictines; and the Sisterhoods of St. Mary, the Holy Nativity, St. Margaret, St. Anne, and Poor Clares. Besides the sisters, Episcopalian deaconesses assist rectors in parish work or in any activity entrusted to them by a bishop. Anglican canon law recognizes the religious vocation of those men and women who bind themselves by vows in a religious community. The priests and monks conduct missions and retreats, engage in charitable and parish work, publish magazines and tracts, while the Episcopalian sisters generally operate girls' academies. One such Anglican community, the Society of the Atonement, entered the Catholic Church in a body in 1905 and now numbers more than 500 priests, brothers, and sisters.

With rules closely modeled on those of the Society of Jesus and the Congregation of the Mission (Lazarists), the Society of St. John the Evangelist was the first successful religious order for men in the Church of England. Popularly known as the Cowley Fathers, these Anglican religious came to the United States in 1870, five years after the founding of their community in England. Their spiritual formation centers around the Mass, the Divine Office, confession, and daily meditation.

Anglo-Catholics often find themselves in the awkward position of reinforcing the authority of Episcopal bishops whose views they consider heretical. One Episcopal bishop may encourage, another may tolerate, and another forbid such Anglo-Catholic practices as the use of incense and holy water in his diocese. The average Episcopalian seems to view the Anglo-Catholics with a mixture of suspicion and amusement. Many of them, of course, are completely unaware of the nature of Anglo-Catholicism and may not even have heard of Anglican religious orders.

Few Anglo-Catholics in the United States go as far as the English Papalists who acknowledge the supremacy of the pope, use the Roman missal, and pray openly for reunion but hold out for corporate reunion since they believe in the validity of Anglican orders. The recent recognition of Church of South India orders has disillusioned some High Churchmen. This Indian experiment is an amalgamation of Methodist, Presbyterian, Baptist, and Anglican churches. When these Papalists see their church admitting Rome's charge that Anglicanism holds non-Catholic views of the Church, sacraments, and priesthood they find their present position untenable. Some of the estimated 2000 Papalist clergymen in England may be expected to resolve their dilemma by leaving the Church of England.

Bishops govern the 74 dioceses and 13 mission districts in the United States. They are elected by the clergy and laity of the diocese with the approval of the other bishops and a majority of the standing committees. Compulsory retirement for bishops is set at 72. Every three years the House of Bishops and the House of Deputies convene in the General Convention. The latter House includes clerical and lay delegates.

The worldwide Anglican communion of 40,000,000 Christians comprises a number of independent sister churches such as those of England, Wales, Scotland, Ireland, Canada, Australia and Tasmania, New Zealand, Burma and Ceylon, South Africa, the West Indies, and the United States. Besides these are the semiautonomous churches of China, Japan, East and West Africa, and scattered dioceses and missions. The Anglican church is largely confined to England and to former English colonies.

Every ten years the Archbishop of Canterbury invites all 300 bishops to meet at his residence, Lambeth Palace. The decisions of the Lambeth Conference do not bind independent churches or individual Anglicans. Therefore, some Anglo-Catholics continue to condemn contraception and the remarriage of divorcees after the Conference sanctioned these practices.

The king or queen of England is technically head of the Church of England (he or she automatically becomes head of the Presbyterian Church of Scotland after crossing the border from England). Actually the prime minister appoints the Archbishop of Canterbury and the prime minister may be and has been a Unitarian, Baptist, and Presbyterian, and could conceivably be a Roman Catholic or Jew. Not a Christian monarch but a non-Christian parliament rules the Church of England. When the church presented revisions of the Book of Common Prayer in 1927–28 the House of Commons simply refused to accept the proposed revisions and the churchmen were helpless. The word "obey" was, however, deleted from the wedding ceremony.

The German church historian von Döllinger characterized the Anglican establishment in the following words: "There is no church that is so completely and thoroughly as the Anglican the product and expression of the wants and wishes, the modes of thought and cast of character, not of a certain nationality, but of a fragment of a nation, namely, the rich, fashionable, and cultivated classes. It is the religion of deportment, of gentility, of clerical reserve."

Certainly in the United States the Episcopal church counts a distinguished roster of communicants, among them George Washington, Alexander Hamilton, James Madison, John Marshall, Henry Clay, Patrick Henry, Daniel Webster, Admirals Farragut and Dewey, Robert E. Lee, Washington Irving, James Fenimore Cooper, Francis Scott Key, and Franklin D. Roosevelt.

Here as elsewhere the Episcopal church caters to those in the upper class and this class orientation limits its social ministry. Its settlement houses and home missions attract some of those in the poorer economic status. As in colonial times it finds its chief strength on the Eastern seaboard.

The English background of most of its clergy and laity might be expected but its present clergy lists include such names as Cherbonnier, Chavez, De Christofaro, Hoffenbacher, Kitagawa, O'Grady, Scarinci, and Wittkofski.

Entrance into the old Federal Council of Churches was opposed by the Anglo-Catholic party which delayed Episcopalian participation in the Council until 1940. When the Protestant Episcopal church did join the Council, the Council showed its appreciation by electing the presiding bishop of the church as its head.

Close relations are cultivated between the Episcopal church and the Polish National Catholic, Eastern Orthodox, and Old Catholic churches. Intercommunion is also observed with the Philippine Independent church (Aglipayan) which traces its orders through Anglicanism, and with the Church of Sweden, a Lutheran body which preserved the episcopacy.

In the past ten years a number of Polish National Catholic and Orthodox bishops have served as co-consecrators in Protestant Episcopal consecrations. A possibility exists that some Episcopalian priests have come to possess valid orders, not from the Anglican succession but from the apostolic succession of these schismatic bodies. Some Episcopal priests have obtained ordination from non-

Anglican sources in order to guarantee their priesthood. Such a situation presents interesting ecumenical possibilities; however, the Catholic Church has not precisely defined the role of the co-consecrator nor examined officially the orders of the Polish National Catholic church.

Throughout its history in America the Episcopal church has refused to follow the Puritanical path of other Protestant churches and sects. Like the Lutheran church it has declined to join campaigns against liquor, tobacco, gambling, dancing, the theater, and the like.

The Episcopal church has established relatively few colleges for its size: Hobart, Kenyon, St. Augustine, Trinity, and University of the South. However, these are first class institutions. On the other hand, the church supports dozens of academies and prep schools, including some of the best known in the country. Twelve seminaries train Episcopal clergy.

Despite Anglicanism's failure to attract its English constituency to regular church attendance and its vacillating stand on many moral issues, the church demonstrates its vitality by the caliber of its recent converts: T. S. Eliot, Paul Elmer More, and W. H. Auden.

The growth of its religious orders for men and women promises to give Episcopalianism a dedicated band of missionaries and educators. Often called the "sleeping giant of U. S. Protestantism," the Episcopal church is giving some signs that the giant is awakening.

Outsiders experience great difficulty in appreciating Anglican comprehensiveness. A variety of devotions and rites such as you find in Catholicism, Western and Eastern, is one thing; toleration of mutually exclusive theological views is another. A generous "room for all" attitude has preserved the Episcopal church from serious schism in this country but it has also undercut any clear and authoritative Christian message. Episcopalianism seems to be presenting not one Christian message but several contradictory messages.

Chapter VI

THE METHODISTS

"All the World Is My Parish."
— *John Wesley.*

W<small>HAT</small> began as a revival of tired eighteenth-century Anglicanism has become the second largest single Protestant church in the United States. Since the 1939 reunion of the three main Methodist bodies, *The Methodist Church* has embraced 99 per cent of the estimated 10,000,000 white Methodists.

A few years ago *Life* magazine described the Methodist Church in these words: "In many ways it is our most characteristic church. It is short on theology, long on good works, brilliantly organized, primarily middle-class, frequently bigoted, incurably optimistic, zealously missionary and touchingly confident of the essential goodness of the man next door."[1]

John Wesley, Methodism's chief founder, emerges as one of the noblest and most appealing figures in Protestantism. Catholics as well as Protestants admire his genuine piety, zeal, and organizational abilities. As the Catholic scholar Moehler has said: "Under other circumstances he would have been the founder of a religious order or a reforming pope."

No theologian himself, Wesley founded a church which assigns to dogma a relatively minor role. If any attribute fits Methodism from Wesley's day to this it is activism. The founder once remarked, "The distinguishing marks of a Methodist are not his opinions of any sort. His assenting to this or that scheme of religion, his

---

[1] *Life*, Nov. 10, 1947.

embracing any particular set of notions . . . are all quite wide of the mark. Whosoever imagines that a Methodist is a man of such or such an opinion is grossly ignorant of the whole affair." Since 1924 American Methodists have been excused from subscribing to any statement of belief or creed. Instead they promise "loyalty to Christ."

Ranked with Luther and Calvin as one of the Big Three of the Protestant reform, Wesley differed from the other two in that the milieu in which he labored was not a Catholic but a Protestant land. Many of his admonitions have been forgotten and certain developments in twentieth-century Methodism would certainly distress him, but we must turn to Wesley to gain an insight into this huge American denomination and the reasons for its phenomenal success on this continent.

John and his youngest brother Charles were born in a Church of England parsonage at Epworth. His mother, Suzanna, had been one of 25 children and John was her fifteenth and Charles her eighteenth. (Methodist Bishop G. Bromley Oxnam recently decided it was "sinful" for a married woman to refuse to practice birth control.)

Life in the rector's large family was orderly and scholarly and John in particular valued the guidance of his strong-willed mother. Eventually both sons entered Oxford where they organized a Holy Club in the amoral university atmosphere. Rules for the Club included fasting on Wednesdays and Fridays, Bible reading, diligent study, two hours of daily prayer, frequent communion, almsgiving, and visiting the poor and imprisoned. Adolescent scoffers labeled the members Bible Moths and Methodists because of their regular habits of prayer and strict self-discipline. John's favorite devotional book was *The Imitation of Christ* by Thomas à Kempis.

When the Holy Club, forerunner of Methodism, was disbanded the brothers volunteered for a mission to recently settled Georgia. Both had been ordained Anglican priests and adhered to the High Church party which later nurtured the Oxford Movement. Their hope was to convert the heathen Indians in Oglethorpe's new American colony.

During the sea voyage to America Wesley saw the lack of faith in his own heart as he witnessed a band of Moravians calmly singing psalms and hymns during a raging storm. These spiritual descendants of John Huss, the Czech heretic burned three centuries earlier, had also been sent from their German headquarters to spread Christianity in the New World.

Wesley spent two unhappy years in Georgia. He found the Indians indifferent to the gospel. He himself was involved in the first of a series of unfortunate love affairs. Finally a judicial body accused him of various church offenses such as insisting on confession before Holy Communion as dictated by his unbending High Church conscience. He returned home to England disappointed and frustrated.

Still fascinated by the simple faith of the Moravians, he made contact with their missionaries in London. From them, especially from Peter Bohler, he accepted the doctrines of justification by faith alone and of instantaneous conversion.

One evening in 1738 Wesley attended a prayer meeting in a small chapel on Aldersgate Street. A lay preacher was reading Luther's preface to the Epistle to the Romans. "I felt my heart strangely warmed. I felt I did trust in Christ, Christ alone for my salvation; and an assurance was given me that He had taken away my sins, even mine, and saved me from the law of sin and death," Wesley later related. This experience at 8:45 p.m. on May 24, 1738, marks the beginning of the Wesleyan revival in Protestantism. The young Anglican priest now felt he had received the same faith which he had admired in the Moravian missionaries.

Few Anglican churches would admit the Wesleyan enthusiasts to their pulpits. Undeterred, the brothers took to the open air and began to preach in the fields, barns, and private homes. They sought out the neo-pagan miners, factory workers, slum dwellers rather than the wealthy and offered them a warm, emotional message which had never come from the cold established church. They were joined by the eloquent George Whitefield, a Holy Clubber and the converted son of a saloon keeper, who had also labored as a missionary in Georgia but with greater success.

All three of the first Methodist preachers instructed their converts to remain within the Church of England. They had no desire to found another sect. Methodists were urged to receive the sacraments in the established church although they might gather to study scripture, testify, sing hymns, and hear sermons in Methodist classes. They were encouraged to become a leaven in the Anglican church, a sort of Protestant Third Order. Since few clergymen joined the revival, Wesley reluctantly consented to the use of licensed lay preachers.

Theology received scant attention. Practical religion was the goal. If any theological principle received emphasis, it was the insistence on man's free will in opposition to Calvinist predestination. This represented a return to Catholic doctrine which flatly denied that God elected some to salvation and damned others to hell.

Their doctrinal views approximated those of Jacob Arminius (1560–1609), a Dutch theologian, who contradicted the absolute predestination taught at Geneva. Arminianism insisted that Christ died for all men, that He offers His grace to all men rather than to a body of the elect. As predestination has been relegated to the shelf in modern Presbyterian and Reformed theology, the sharp differences between Methodists and Calvinists have been blurred.

Assurance of salvation became another original Methodist tenet. Wesley taught that a man who has experienced a second blessing or entire sanctification can be absolutely sure he will reach heaven. Such a man can lose all inclination to evil and gain perfection in this life. Wesley never claimed this state of perfection for himself but he insisted that the attainment of perfection was possible for all Christians. Here the English reformer parted company with both Luther and Calvin who denied that man would ever reach a state in this life in which he could not fall into sin. Today the Wesleyan doctrine of perfection has been soft-pedaled by The Methodist Church but finds champions in the smaller Methodist bodies and the Holiness sects spawned by Methodism.

Since Wesley claimed a conversion which he could pin point to the day, hour, and minute, he assumed that all genuine conversion is the instantaneous operation of the Holy Spirit. At one time Methodists expected all converts to testify to a miraculous and instantaneous conversion. This requirement has been abandoned. Adults joining The Methodist Church today need not relate their spiritual experience nor admit to having such an experience.

From the night of the Aldersgate meeting until his death at 88 Wesley followed a back breaking schedule of preaching, writing, traveling, and organizing his Methodist classes. Initially he was assisted by his Moravian friends and he even made a trip to their headquarters at Herrnhut to observe their way of life at firsthand. Within a few years he had broken with the Moravians over the practice of "stillness." In stillness the brethren suspended all work, study, and prayer and waited for a special blessing from God. The Wesley brothers also disagreed with Whitefield when he turned to Calvinism and began to mix Methodism and predestination.

Once asked by what authority he dared to preach in the open fields as a Church of England priest, Wesley replied, "To save souls is my vocation; all the world is my parish." He preached 42,000 sermons and covered an estimated 250,000 miles on foot and horseback throughout the British Isles. The democratic structure of Methodism was admittedly a façade during his lifetime since he ruled his society as an ecclesiastical dictator.

Never a successful suitor, he finally married a shrewish widow with four children. Quarrels and humiliations marked the match and they separated. He learned of his wife's death only after the funeral and it has been said that his only child was Methodism.

John's relations with his more conservative brother became strained as he drifted further from the High Church orbit which Charles never left. While Charles devoutly believed in the Real Presence and the apostolic succession, his older brother came to accept a symbolic interpretation of the Eucharist and attempted to ordain priests himself. Among Charles's 6500 hymns are the popular "Hark, the Herald Angels Sing" and "Jesus, Lover of My Soul." He has been called the poet of the revival, John, the organizer, and Whitefield, the orator.

Critics commonly charged the Wesleys with being Jesuits in disguise bent on subverting the established church to the interests

of the papacy. Certainly the Wesleys restored the positive principles of the Reformation to English and continental Protestantism
and stripped Protestantism of its negative features. They opposed
extrinsic justification, predestination in the Calvinist sense, and
the depreciation of good works. To this extent the revival may
be considered a return to the traditional Catholic positions.

Furthermore, they urged fasting and abstinence, daily prayer and
devotions, frequent communion. The Wesleys believed in the seven
sacraments which have been trimmed to two by their modern
heirs. Both honored celibacy, John more after his unhappy marriage than before. They accorded an importance to good works
which was foreign to Lutheranism. They not only taught that man
is changed by justification and sanctification but that he could attain perfection — a far cry from Luther's "sinful and sinning" Christian. Most of these Catholic inclinations were diluted and lost as
Methodism accommodated itself to the conditions of the American
frontier.

The first authorized Methodist missionaries were dispatched to
the colonies in 1769, only ten years before the American Revolution and fully 150 years after the other denominations had staked
out their claims. Francis Asbury stands as the greatest figure in
American Methodism and to his foresight and energy must be
credited much of the amazing growth of this tardy denomination.
Like Wesley he spent a great part of his life in the saddle. He perfected the system of circuit riders, celibate lay preachers who brought
religion to the people in isolated cabins and frontier towns. Equipped
only with Bible, hymn book, and a set of sermons they preached
six days a week, urging all who would listen to "flee from the wrath
to come." Their main audience were the poor and underprivileged.
They conserved the effects of their conversions by setting up classes
under class leaders.

Methodism suffered a near fatal setback during the Revolution
even though it gained some numerical strength. Many colonists
looked on Methodism as an English importation and their sus-
picions were buttressed by two pamphlets in which Wesley disowned the agitation for independence. "We Methodists are no

republicans and never intend to be," wrote Wesley. All but two Methodist preachers were Tories who fled to Canada or England during the war.

Discredited by their pro-British attitude during the conflict, the Methodists retained strength below the Mason and Dixon line and recouped losses by concentrating on the expanding frontier. Here their zealous lay preachers could outnumber the college-trained Congregationalist, Episcopalian, and Presbyterian ministers. Here their proclamation of man's free will made more sense to the independent frontiersman than the fatalism of Calvin. When Bishop Asbury began his preaching Methodism counted scarcely a few hundred members in the American colonies; at his death he could survey a thriving church of 200,000 souls.

As in England, the Methodists were directed to receive baptism and Holy Communion from Episcopalian priests. Naturally they soon petitioned to receive the sacraments from the same Methodist preachers who visited their homes and conducted their worship services. The Bishop of London refused to ordain preachers in the colonies so in 1784 Wesley assumed the power to ordain ministers himself. When he ordained two men and sent them to America Methodism moved from the status of a revival movement in Anglicanism to that of a separate church.

He justified his action by claiming that bishops and presbyters were identical in the primitive church, at least at Alexandria, and that therefore priests like himself could lawfully ordain other priests. He then consecrated Thomas Coke as superintendent for the Methodists in the United States and he in turn consecrated Asbury. Both men assumed the additional title of bishop over Wesley's ineffective protest. Brother Charles disassociated himself from these actions and declared, "I can scarcely believe it that in his eighty-second year my brother, my old, intimate friend and companion, should have assumed the episcopal character, ordained elders, consecrated a bishop, and sent him to ordain our elder preachers in America." "My brother has put an indelible stigma upon his name," he added.

The Christmas conference of 60 preachers in 1784 is taken as the founding of the *Methodist Episcopal Church*. Wesley died proclaiming his loyalty to the church of which he was a priest: "I live and die a member of the Church of England, and none who regard my judgment will ever separate from it."

Wesley had prepared an abridgment of the Anglican Thirty-nine Articles which was accepted as a doctrinal statement by the Americans. They added another article to Wesley's 24 which recognized the independence of the colonies. Among other doctrines the articles affirmed justification by faith, the sufficiency of the scriptures, and the baptism of infants. "The Romish doctrine concerning purgatory, pardon, worshipping and adoration, as well of images as of relics, and also invocation of saints, is a fond thing, vainly invented, and grounded upon no warrant of scripture, but repugnant to the Word of God," according to the Wesleyan articles. The sacrifice of the Mass was termed a "blasphemous fable and dangerous deceit." Other sources of Methodist belief are Wesley's *Notes on the New Testament* and 53 collected sermons.

A demand for greater lay participation in church government led to the formation of the *Methodist Protestant Church* in 1830. Slavery drove a deeper wedge into Methodism in 1844 when the Southerners seceded and formed the *Methodist Episcopal Church, South*. Reunion of the three branches was not effected until 1939 although no doctrinal issues were involved. At this time the Southern faction was pacified by constructing a segregated Central Jurisdiction for 340,000 Negro members regardless of place of residence. The five white jurisdictions were mapped out on a geographical basis. This racial compromise struck many Methodists as a betrayal of Christian brotherhood and the 1956 General Conference adopted a constitutional amendment to dissolve the Negro jurisdiction gradually.

The great majority of Negro Methodists are found in separate denominations outside The Methodist Church, such as the *African Methodist Episcopal Church*, the *Christian* (formerly *Colored*) *Methodist Episcopal Church*, and the *African Methodist Episcopal Zion Church*. Together they enroll about 2,400,000 members. Both the A.M.E. and A.M.E. Zion churches were organized before 1800 by Negroes who resented discrimination by their white coreligionists. The C.M.E. church gathered the Negro remnant of the Methodist Episcopal Church, South, after the Civil War and remains the smallest of the three major Negro bodies with 444,000 members. These Negro bodies follow the same theology and polity as The Methodist Church but little intercourse exists between white and Negro churches and no move to unite these bodies has received serious attention.

By the middle of the nineteenth century most Methodists had become fairly prosperous and conservative. Methodism has followed the typical pattern from sect to church even though from the beginning it lacked two sectarian characteristics: congregational government and adult baptism. The upper middle class now dominates The Methodist Church, once the church of the English workingman.

A dozen tiny Methodist sects totaling only 135,000 members include the fundamentalist *Free Methodist Church* which still emphasizes entire sanctification and elects superintendents instead of bishops, and the equally strict *Wesleyan Methodists*, pre-Civil War abolitionists and secret society antagonists. A proposed merger of these two similar bodies has been scuttled by the Wesleyans.

No religious body of Christians outside the Catholic Church is so highly and efficiently organized as The Methodist Church. Organizational problems and the social gospel receive the attention which other churches direct toward theology and liturgy. Laymen play a large part in Methodist projects and a layman with any special talent can find a suitable niche in Methodism.

Someone has commented that the background of the British labor movement is more Methodist than Marxist. The American workingman, however, may be pardoned if he views Methodism as more interested in taking away his glass of beer and cigarette than in boosting wage scales and strengthening labor organizations.

National committees in the church are set up for missions, the local church, education, evangelism, lay activities, Christian social relations, temperance, world peace, social and economic relations, hospitals and homes, chaplains, and pensions. Methodism is big business with over $3,000,000,000 invested in 40,000 churches and institutions.

Full authority in church matters rests with the General Conference. This body, consisting of equal numbers of locally elected laymen and ministers, meets every four years. Laymen were first admitted in 1872; before this the complaint of the Methodist Protestant faction was probably justified. General Conference decisions are incorporated in the 890-page *Discipline* which roughly corresponds to the Code of Canon Law.

A wide range of theological views is tolerated within Methodism. In general, we may say that The Methodist Church follows closely after Unitarianism and Congregationalism in doctrinal liberalism; there are prominent Methodists who are fundamentalists and others who are as modernist as anyone in the Unitarian church. The southern churches are more conservative as are the Free, Wesleyan, and other branches of Methodism.

Personal moral standards rule out alcohol and tobacco although lay members who indulge are no longer excommunicated. Ministers must pledge total abstinence. At one time Methodism in this country also banned dancing, card playing, all forms of gambling, and the theater but these are now tolerated. Methodists led in the formation of the Women's Christian Temperance Union and the Anti-Saloon League and take a large share of the credit for the 18th Amendment and the Great Experiment. The Methodist Church still officially lobbies for national prohibition, condemns beer and cigarette advertising on radio and TV, tries to ban beer from army and navy establishments. Incidentally a Methodist now heads one of the nation's largest breweries.

Planned parenthood was endorsed by the 1956 General Conference. "We believe that planned parenthood practiced in Christian conscience, may fulfill rather than violate the will of God," reported the delegates. Methodism thus became the largest Protestant denomination to sanction birth control although the Augustana Lutheran Synod had previously declared itself in favor of the practice. Speakers for the birth control resolution at the General Conference suggested that Methodist approval would help counteract Catholic influence in Massachusetts and Connecticut, the only two states which have anti-birth control laws. These laws were enacted years ago by Protestant majorities in these states and have been upheld by Catholic voters.

Among Protestant denominations Methodists take first place in missions, hospitals, and colleges. Some of their 78 colleges and universities have all but severed their ties with the denomination but others remain definitely Methodist: Syracuse, Boston, Emory, Duke, and Southern Methodist. The church operates 360 schools and institutions of higher learning overseas. Methodists established the Goodwill Industries in 1907 to help handicapped persons help themselves by repairing and selling old furniture and clothes. Seventy-two hospitals in the United States are run by The Methodist Church.

Relatively few Methodist ministers receive adequate theological training compared to Catholic, Lutheran, Episcopalian, Presbyterian, and Congregational clergymen. Methodism still depends to a large extent on lay preachers whose training is received via correspondence and short courses. A ministerial candidate may attend any of the ten seminaries maintained by the church, among which are Garrett Biblical Institute, Drew, and Boston.

About 350 women are serving as Methodist ministers but few have become pastors. The 1956 General Conference accorded full clergy rights to women. The 800 deaconesses in this country receive a fixed salary, regular leaves of absence, and provision for retirement. The Methodist deaconess movement has experienced little growth in recent years but deaconesses operate a number of hospitals and homes.

Bishops are elected and their main duties are administrative. The 67 American bishops ordain ministers, appoint them to parishes, and supervise church activities in their areas. The bishops are elected at the General Conference, consecrated by three bishops, and expected to retire at 72. The Council of Bishops serves as the executive branch of Methodism just as the General Conference is the chief legislative branch. Methodists hold that the difference between a bishop and an ordinary minister is purely one of administrative responsibility.

Wesley prepared a revised liturgy from the Book of Common Prayer but it was never widely adopted. Methodists are liturgical individualists who resist all attempts to impose a uniform pattern of worship on the local congregation. As in most Protestant denominations a trend toward beauty in the worship service has reintroduced gowns, candles, crosses, a central altar.

A typical form of worship would be: call to worship, hymn, prayer of confession, silent meditation, words of assurance, Lord's Prayer, anthem, responsive reading, gloria patri, affirmation of faith, scripture lesson, pastoral prayer, offertory, hymn, sermon, prayer, invitation to Christian discipleship, doxology, benediction, silent prayer, and postlude. An alternate form is used when the Lord's Supper is observed. Four forms of Sunday worship and two forms for the Lord's Supper are presented in the Discipline but the local church need not follow these liturgies.

Weekly communion was one of Wesley's frequent spiritual prescriptions but few Methodist churches today observe the Lord's Supper oftener than quarterly or monthly. The communicants kneel at the altar rail, receive bread and grape juice in a communion service which is considered symbolic as in the Reformed tradition.

Methodists deny that baptism produces sanctifying grace or takes away sin. The sacrament may be administered by sprinkling, pouring, or immersion although sprinkling is most widespread. Infants as well as adults are baptized. Confirmation, which is not believed to be sacramental, is conferred by ministers as well as bishops.

The great bulk of Methodists reside in the United States. Within a few years after the founder's death British Methodism split into half a dozen sects. These groups developed a nonepiscopal form of church government and never emphasized the Puritan concern for personal morals which has preoccupied their American cousins. The world's 20,000,000 Methodists co-operate in the World Methodist Conference.

Successful itself in reuniting the three main Wesleyan bodies, The Methodist Church takes an active and prominent part in the ecumenical movement. It acted as host to the World Council of Churches meeting in Evanston and Bishop Oxnam has held high office in the pan-Protestant organization.

Methodism is distantly related to a score of other denominations, Arminian in doctrine and sometimes claiming the authentic mantle of Wesley for themselves: The Salvation Army, the Evangelical United Brethren Church, countless Holiness sects, and the General Baptists.

In many respects the Wesleyan revival represented a distinct reversal of Protestant direction in the eighteenth century. Wesley's emphasis on free will, his insistence on the need for good works, his doctrine of conversion, his encouragement of fasting and abstinence, frequent communion, the value of a personal devotional life set early Methodism on a path verging toward Rome.

Wesley himself, however, knew little of Catholic doctrine and his picture of the sacraments and the theology of the Church was often a caricature. His estrangement from the High Church position of his youth and the transplanting of Methodism to the American frontier carried the movement more directly into the Protestant camp. Modern Methodism exhibits slight appreciation of Wesley's Catholic heritage.

THE EVANGELICAL UNITED BRETHREN

The reluctance of American Methodist bishops to sanction preaching in the German language led to the formation of two independent German Methodist denominations: the United Brethren in Christ and the Evangelical Church. These two bodies, similar in doctrine, polity, and national origin, merged in 1946 at Johnstown, Pennsylvania, to form the Evangelical United Brethren Church.

Both partners to the 1946 union had dickered with the Methodists on plans of union in the nineteenth century but these plans never materialized. A merger of the E.U.B. Church and The Methodist Church is a real possibility since no serious doctrinal questions stand in the way. The E.U.B. Church reports 749,000 members and has traditionally been strong in Pennsylvania.

Philip Otterbein studied for the Reformed ministry in Germany and came to America in 1752. He began to preach Arminian doctrines and to conduct revivals and prayer meetings with Martin Boehm, a Swiss Mennonite preacher. Had there been no language problem their converts would have been absorbed into Methodism. As it was they formed their own United Brethren Church in 1800 with themselves as bishops. A minority seceded in 1889. The 20,000 members of the *United Brethren in Christ* (*Old Constitution*) oppose secret societies and participation in war.

A development parallel to that of the United Brethren led to the founding of the Evangelical Church, once called the Evangelical Association. In this case Jacob Albright, an ex-Lutheran, began to preach in eastern Pennsylvania but his plan for a German Methodist branch was vetoed by the Methodist hierarchy. In 1803 he organized a separate church whose adherents were variously known as Albright people or Brethren or German Methodists. The greatest period of expansion of this body was during the administration of Bishop John Seybert, elected in 1839. A serious schism disrupted the denomination from 1894 to 1922 when the two factions reunited in the Evangelical Church.

Both the United Brethren and the Evangelicals generally confined their evangelism to the German population in this country. Of course, most of their converts came from Lutheran, Reformed, or Mennonite backgrounds. At the time of the merger in 1946 the United Brethren reported 450,000 members and the Evangelicals about half that number. They have not grown much in numbers since then.

Seven bishops elected for four year terms administer as many geographical areas. This limited term for their bishops is probably the chief difference between the E.U.B.'s and the Methodists. Members must avoid liquor, gambling, narcotics, and tobacco. Education has never received much attention but the combined denomination supports eight small colleges and three seminaries. This sizable but rather colorless denomination has worked out a polity which combines episcopal, presbyterian, and congregational elements.

Chapter VII

THE BAPTISTS

"No Human Founder, No Human Authority, No Human Creed."

BAPTISTS carry the Protestant principle of justification by faith alone to its logical conclusion. Since infants are incapable of such an act of faith, they cannot receive the grace of baptism. Hence, only adults able to make a profession of faith in Christ may be admitted to baptism.

Likewise, since the Baptists deny the sacramental character of baptism in favor of a symbolic interpretation, they see immersion as the most dramatic symbol of burial and rebirth in Christ. Immersion is certainly the ancient form of baptism and was practiced by the Latin rite of the Catholic Church until the twelfth century. The modern Baptists deny that baptism removes the stain of original sin and that baptism by a non-Baptist Christian may be valid.

To define a Baptist, we may say that he is a follower of Jesus Christ who has been baptized by immersion and belongs to a local congregation which is identified by the name Baptist. Some Baptists would add that he must be committed to the Baptist principles of religious liberty.

Religious liberty and freedom of conscience have perhaps characterized the Baptists more than their concern about the first sacrament. Whereas the Episcopalian and Presbyterian acknowledges the authority of the larger church and the Congregationalist recognizes the authority of the local community of Christians, the Baptist denies any spiritual authority over the individual. The local congregation is a law unto itself and receives no directives or liturgies or regulations from denominational headquarters.

The Baptist family, numbering 21,400,000 adult members, constitutes by far the largest American Protestant denomination. Every third Protestant in the United States is a Baptist. About half of the Baptists are Negroes and the bulk of Negro and white members live in the South. The emergence of this radical, left-wing sect into a position of numerical superiority in this country has influenced American Protestantism in the direction of individualism, anti-ritualism, and sectarianism.

Most Baptists belong to one of the four largest groups: the *American Baptist Convention* (called Northern Baptist until 1950) with 1,521,000 members; the fast growing *Southern Baptist Convention* with more than 10,000,000; the *National Baptist Convention of the U. S. A., Inc.,* original Negro body, with 5,000,000; and a 1916 offshoot of the latter organization, the *National Baptist Convention of America,* which reports 2,669,000. Twenty-three other Baptist groups are represented in this country, many of them claiming only a handful of adherents.

Some Baptists like to claim Christ or St. John the Baptist as their founder, but history does not tell us of any organized Baptist groups until the early seventeenth century. Their spiritual ancestors, once removed, were the Anabaptists of Reformation times who despaired of the theological conservatism of Luther, Zwingli, and Calvin. They yearned for a church of saints not a church of saints and sinners. These Anabaptists called for a voluntary association of adult Christians rather than a state church into which all citizens were born and baptized. These early radical reformers also agitated for separation of Church and State, complete sovereignty of the local congregation, communism, pacifism, and Biblical literalism. Persecution by both Protestants and Catholics drove them into stranger paths of theology and into immoralities. By 1535 the Anabaptist movement had been largely suppressed by force except for a remnant gathered by the ex-priest Menno Simons.

A refugee congregation of English separatists in Amsterdam accepted the doctrine of believer's baptism from the Mennonites around 1607. John Smythe and Thomas Helwys shepherded this first English Baptist congregation in Holland but Smythe himself left to join the Mennonites. A handful returned to England with Helwys and carried their Baptist principles with them. As these pioneer Baptists pondered the symbolic meaning of baptism, they began to prefer immersion rather than the pouring mode used by the Mennonites. The first church to baptize by immersion was a London congregation in 1638. Theologically most of the original English Baptists were Arminian, but Baptists of this persuasion now form a small minority since most Baptists have adopted a more or less Calvinist theology.

Roger Williams, the founder of the first Baptist church in America, remained a Baptist for only four months. A Nonconformist clergyman, he left England in 1630 and sought religious freedom in the Puritan Massachusetts Bay Colony. Instead of freedom he found himself accused of heresy and was exiled. Indians gave him shelter and he founded a settlement of his own at Providence. In 1639 he had become convinced of the Baptist position and was rebaptized, but within a few months he resigned his pastorate of this first Baptist church in the New World. Williams continued to search for religious truth until his death.

Little expansion was undertaken during the first century of the Baptist movement in America. The sect would register its tremendous gains in the late eighteenth and the nineteenth centuries by an appeal to the lower classes, the Negro, the frontiersmen, and the Southerner. Thousands of unschooled Baptist preachers carried the gospel to the settler in his frontier cabin. These preacher-farmers found a rich soil on America's frontier for their principles of separation of Church and State, church democracy, simple worship services, and freedom of conscience. They offered no creeds but the Bible itself. Defections by the Disciples and the Adventists amounted to nothing more than temporary setbacks to Baptist growth.

The Baptists brought the Christian gospel to white man and Negro. Today most American Negroes are either Baptists or Methodists. Negro Baptists number 7,500,000 and the Abyssinian Baptist church in Harlem with 12,000 members is the largest Protestant congregation in the world. A disagreement over the management of denominational publications led to a split of the main Negro Baptist body in 1916.

Often called the problem child of American Protestantism, the Southern Baptist Convention is ultraconservative, nonco-operative, and isolated. Statistics indicate it is the fastest growing major denomination and 1000 new members are baptized every day. This denomination has grown from 325,000 in 1845, the year of its secession from the northern group over the issue of slavery.

In 1963 the Southern Baptists overtook The Methodist Church to claim the title the largest single Protestant church in the nation. Its aggressive evangelistic campaigns, its well-organized Sunday School program, and its frank espousal of the "old-time religion" help to explain its success. Billy Graham, a Southern Baptist minister, succeeded Billy Sunday as America's best known revivalist. Notwithstanding their geographical label the Southern Baptists are engaged in a religious invasion of the North. Besides establishing numerous churches outside the South the Southern Baptists support 1300 foreign missionaries especially in Brazil, Japan, and Nigeria. They have declined to join the National and World Councils of Churches and usually boycott Southern ministerial associations.

The liberal American Baptist Convention participates in ecumenical activities, harbors modernist theologians in its seminaries and colleges, and tolerates unimmersed and even unbaptized members of local churches. Colgate-Rochester and the University of Chicago divinity schools actively foster liberalism among northern Baptists. The American Baptist Convention ordains women and admits non-Baptists to communion in contrast to standard Baptist customs. Their 600 foreign missionaries concentrate on evangelism in the Orient and South America. Racial segregation, modernism, and a willingness to enter into interdenominational activities divide the northern and Southern Baptists and any merger seems remote.

Protesting modernism in the former Northern Baptist Convention, a group of Baptists organized the *General Association of Regular*

Baptist Churches in 1932. The number of churches affiliated with this conservative association has increased from the original 22 to more than 1000. Their original indictment of the parent body charged that the Northern Baptists honored members who denied the inspiration of the Bible, the divinity of Christ, the redemption, and the resurrection.

The 193,000 *Free-Will Baptists* continue to oppose Calvinist predestination with their slogan of "free grace, free salvation, free will and free communion." Of Welsh origin, many Free-Will Baptists in the north were absorbed into the American Baptist Convention in two mergers, one in 1910 and the second in 1950. The Negro counterpart, the *United Free-Will Baptist Church*, claims 100,000 members.

The *Landmarkers*, members of the American Baptist Association, add a strong premillennial conviction to a thoroughgoing fundamentalism. This group of 650,000 Baptists experienced a doctrinal schism in 1950 which led to the formation of the *North American Baptist Association* which now reports 330,000 members in southern and midwestern states.

Primitive Baptists, also known as Hardshell, Old School, and Antimission Baptists, oppose Arminian compromises with Calvinism, instrumental music in worship services, and church societies. As usual, white and Negro groups support separate denominations with a total Primitive Baptist constituency of about 150,000.

Nine tenths of the world's Baptists reside in the United States. This means that the largest Protestant denomination in this country occupies a relatively small niche in world Protestantism which is overwhelmingly Lutheran, Anglican, and Reformed. Fear of compromising local church autonomy has also kept most Baptists, including those in the huge Southern Baptist Convention, from exerting a proportionate influence in local ministerial associations and the National and World Councils of Churches. An undetermined number of Baptists, perhaps half a million, live in Soviet Russia and 200,000 are reported in England. Baptists in mission fields include 350,000 in India, 110,000 in Brazil, 142,000 in Burma, and 95,000 in the Belgian Congo. There are about 145,000 Canadian

Baptists. The 21,000,000-member Baptist World Alliance meets every five years. It was established in London in 1905 but now maintains headquarters in Washington, D. C.

Many, if not most, Baptist clergymen are poorly trained. A local congregation may choose to ordain a grade school graduate as minister and the loosely-knit national bodies have little to say about it. Of course, as in all denominations the trend toward more formal seminary training may be observed among Baptists. In the more stable branches of the Baptist family the local church submits the name of a candidate for the ministry to a committee composed of members of several churches. If approved, the ordination is performed by a council. In some Negro groups the number of ordained ministers is nearly double the number of active ministers.

The increasing use of symbolism and ritual which is obvious in most Protestant denominations has found fewer proponents among the Baptists. Symbols in Baptist architecture and church decoration are limited to the cross, Bible, anchor, banner, globe, and gate. Few Baptist preachers wear any type of vestment or gown, and no set liturgy is prescribed. Most churches baptize in shallow pools in the church proper although some use rivers and streams in mild weather. Communion may be administered on a monthly, quarterly, or annual basis. What other denominations consider sacraments, the Baptists consider simple ordinances with no supernatural significance.

Most Christian churches, including the Catholic Church, admit the validity of other modes of baptism. Eastern rite Catholics continue the ancient form of immersion and a Catholic may be validly baptized by immersion or pouring. The sacrament need not be administered by a Catholic, much less a Catholic priest, in order to be valid.

As early as the first century, however, the Church began to baptize infants. Origen writes: "The Church received from the Apostles the tradition of giving baptism to infants." The New Testament admittedly does not command the baptism of infants but the Catholic sacramental view of baptism assumes the desirability of baptizing infants. Luther was driven to ingenious explanations for his acceptance of justification by faith and infant baptism. According to Protestant principles it would seem that the adult baptism of the Baptists, Disciples of Christ, Mennonites, Seventh-day Adventists, Brethren, and Jehovah's Witnesses is more consistent.

Except for the modernists in the northern branch, the Baptists preach a Christianity based firmly on the divinity of Christ and the central facts of His incarnation and redemption of mankind. They accept the doctrines of the Trinity, the virgin birth, original sin, heaven, and hell. In some areas they have carried Protestant principles to conclusions which the original Reformers hesitated to draw. Unlike some denominations which have catered to the upper classes, the Baptists have worked with the humble people and have developed an amazing spirit of personal evangelism. Estimates have placed two thirds of American Baptists in the lower economic class and at least one Baptist out of three is colored.

Hans Herzl, only son of the founder of Zionism, turned from Judaism to the Baptist faith and finally became a Catholic in 1924. After his final conversion he wrote, "I came to know them (the Baptists) as a sect of good, zealous Christians whose life was lived in the spirit of the Holy Scriptures."

Chapter VIII

THE DISCIPLES OF CHRIST

"No Creed But Christ"

P<small>LEDGED</small> to the twin objectives of Christian unity and the restoration of the church in its New Testament form, the *Disciples of Christ* represent the most successful indigenous Christian denomination in the United States. During its relatively short 125 years this church has grown to become the sixth largest Protestant denomination in the country.

Paradoxically the unity-minded Disciples movement simply added another denomination to the roster of Protestant churches and sects. In fact, later disagreement over the precise nature of New Testament Christianity led to the schism of the conservative *Churches of Christ*. Another schism within the Disciples looms over the horizon. Thus the Campbellite restoration movement has already contributed two more denominations to the crowded American religious scene.

Closely akin to the much larger Baptist denomination, the Disciples also insist on baptism of adults by immersion. This insistence on adult baptism by a particular mode separates them from the vast majority of Protestants and doomed their efforts at a reunion of Christendom to an early failure. Disciples observe the Lord's Supper every Sunday while Baptists usually hold a communion service only four times a year. This difference between 52 and four communion services a year seem to be the main obstacle to a merger of the Disciples and the American (Northern) Baptists.

Disciples pride themselves on being members of a creedless church. "No creed but Christ" is a familiar maxim, and they will admit to their fellowship and to their communion table all baptized persons who wish to participate. Neither the Apostles' nor the Nicene creed finds any place in the liturgy and no Disciple, minister or layman, need affirm belief in any specific Christian dogma. As a result you will find Disciples who approach unitarian positions and others who would be logically classified as fundamentalists, although most of those in the latter category would likely gravitate toward the Churches of Christ. "Study your Bible and believe what you wish" would be typical Disciples' advice to a potential convert who expressed some reservations about a point of traditional Christianity such as the virgin birth, Christ's miracles, a literal heaven and hell.

The sectarian de-emphasis of any clergy-laity distinction continues to characterize the Disciples to a greater extent than most Protestant bodies. Lay elders and deacons may baptize, serve the communion elements, and preach; for legal reasons only an ordained minister may perform marriages. The Disciples of Christ minister is simply an elder among elders, hired and fired by the local congregation. He may be called "Reverend" by outsiders but Disciples themselves observe no ecclesiastical amenities when referring to their professional, full-time clergy. More and more pastors of the larger churches in the denomination now possess college and seminary degrees but most Disciples ministers lack this training. Women are accorded full clergy rights but few are serving as pastors.

The Disciples movement grew out of a coalition of a number of nineteenth-century "back-to-primitive-Christianity" revivals, but the denomination owes its greatest debt to the Campbells, Thomas and Alexander. Thomas, the son of an apostate Catholic, came to the United States from Ireland early in the century and became minister of a small Seceder Presbyterian church in western Pennsylvania. His liberal views and invitations to non-Presbyterians to partake of the Lord's Supper scandalized his colleagues and in 1809 he and his followers withdrew from Presbyterianism and formed the nondenominational Christian Association of Washington county, Pennsylvania.

That same year his son Alexander arrived in this country and joined his father as a free lance preacher. Both declared their guiding principle to be: "Where the scriptures speak, we speak; where the scriptures are silent, we are silent." Both Campbells thought it was possible and desirable to strip Christianity of all post-New Testament accretions. Every doctrine must be preceded by a Biblical "Thus saith the Lord." Father and son offered this common denominator Christianity as an antidote to rampant sectarianism.

Whereas the Christian Association was more of a fellowship than a church, the Campbells took the next step and organized a separate church at Brush Run, Pa., several years later. They had also been persuaded that adult baptism by immersion was the only valid baptism. They themselves were immersed in 1812. Their newly proclaimed stand on baptism drew them closer to the Baptists and they affiliated with that denomination in a union that lasted for 17 years.

Son Alexander, who had assumed leadership from his father, edited the *Christian Baptist* magazine in whose pages he denounced creeds, clergymen, church organs, mission societies, seminaries, Sunday Schools, Catholicism, and other "nonscriptural" innovations. Over the years the Campbells, champions of the doctrine of free will, grew restive in the Calvinist Baptist fold. They also objected to the labeling of the Baptist church as a "denomination" since they called their own movement a "restoration" and "brotherhood." In 1830 the Campbells severed their Baptist ties and from then on the Campbellites were known by the term "Disciples of Christ."

Meanwhile in Kentucky and Ohio an ex-Presbyterian minister with unitarian tendencies, Barton W. Stone, was urging Christians to discard all divisive doctrines and unite in one "Christian" body. Other anti-Calvinists in New England were forming similar fellowships of "Christians."

Shortly after withdrawing from the Baptists the Disciples entered into a union with the bulk of Stone's "Christians." Those "Christians" in the East who refused to enter the merger continued their corporate existence until 1931 when they fused with the Congregational church in the Congregational Christian church. By this time the doctrinal views of the 100,000 "Christians" were indistinguishable from unitarianism.

The "common sense" approach of the Disciples, the ability of their evangelists, and the wide scope afforded laymen contributed to the denomination's success on the American frontier. Two preachers, Walter Scott in Ohio and Pennsylvania and "Racoon" John Smith in Kentucky, won thousands of converts. The first foreign missionaries were dispatched to teach, preach, and practice medicine among the Jews in Jerusalem. An early Disciples leader, Sidney Rigdon, is credited by some scholars as being the real founder of Mormonism.

By 1860 the Disciples movement counted 200,000 members although statistics of the early Disciples and Christian groups are unreliable. Since Campbell approved of neither slavery nor abolition his church managed to avoid schism during the Civil War. By keeping intact during the conflict the Disciples won an advantage over the sundered Baptists, Methodists, and Presbyterians.

Alexander Campbell, contentious and vain, delighted in challenging clergymen of rival denominations to debate current theological issues. He was bitterly critical of all ministers and priests, whom he accused of being the "cause of all division, superstition, enthusiasm, and ignorance of the people." In 1837 he engaged in a lengthy debate with Roman Catholic Bishop John Purcell of Cincinnati. So strongly anti-Catholic was the Disciples founder that he might be called the "Judge" Rutherford of his day. He proposed several schemes to unite all Protestants against the Roman menace and the "Grand Papa" as he called the Holy Father. The American Protestant Association, a nineteenth-century version of the Ku Klux Klan, received his warm support.

His 60 theological volumes interest no one today except perhaps Disciples ministerial candidates. He railed against mission societies but became head of the first national missionary board. He denounced seminaries and higher education and ended his career as president of Bethany College. He accused the clergy of greed and avarice and died the wealthiest man in West Virginia, a successful businessman, sheep raiser, and author. He scorned instrumental

music, Sunday Schools, choirs, and Bible societies as unscriptural
and eventually incorporated all these devices into his own sect.

He renamed his *Christian Baptist* magazine the *Millennial Harbinger* and his extreme millennial views sometimes embarrass his
twentieth-century spiritual children. The Protestant churches must
drop all sectarian barriers because the end of the world was nigh,
warned the editor. Later he mellowed on this issue as on many
others and he finally predicted that the Second Coming could be
expected about A.D. 2000.

Many of his followers failed to notice his many reversals of
position; they remembered only his earlier injunctions. By 1906
the conservative and progressive wings had split into the *Churches
of Christ* and the *Disciples of Christ*. Today the two branches are
separate denominations with no formal and little informal fellowship or co-operation. If anything, the breach is widening as the
Churches of Christ harden into a rigid Biblical literalism and
fundamentalism and the Disciples drift toward rationalism and
unitarianism.

The outsider is understandably confused by the use of similar
names. Disciples churches rarely include the term "Disciples" in
their church name. They are commonly known as First Christian
church, Main Street Christian church, etc. Some Disciples churches
also use the term "Church of Christ" but no Churches of Christ
church is ever identified as a "Disciples" church. The Disciples *Yearbook* lists some unusual church titles: Plumber's Landing, Weeping
Mary, Rock of Ages, Gum Neck, The Last Chance, Sinners Union,
Dripping Springs, and Little Bethlehem.

Each congregation is completely autonomous. Each church interviews prospective ministers, hires, and fires without supervision by any
conference or administrative body. The individual church may be
high or low liturgically, fundamentalist or rationalist in theology.

Local churches may choose to join district and state conferences
and most Disciples churches belong to the voluntary Christian
Churches (Disciples of Christ), International Convention with headquarters in Indianapolis. All who attend the annual convention
may vote and nothing the convention recommends binds an in-

dividual church or Disciple. This convention is a mass convention rather than a representative assembly. Local churches may or may not contribute funds for the support of the convention.

Practically all of the world's 2,000,000 Disciples live in the United States, although small memberships may be found in Australia, the Belgian Congo, and England. In this country the strength of the Disciples church is concentrated in half a dozen states: Indiana, Missouri, Illinois, Ohio, Kentucky, and Texas. The denomination is all but unknown in New England, the Atlantic seaboard, the deep South, and the intermountain area. New York City has only one Disciples church. A traditional suspicion of higher education stunted the denomination's expansion in this area although Butler, Drake, Phillips, Texas Christian, and College of the Bible are Disciples institutions. They support two other divinity houses: one at the University of Chicago and another at Vanderbilt. A number of unaccredited Bible schools also train ministers for Disciples churches, especially those which resist modernist infiltration. For a denomination of 1,943,000 members in the United States their one hospital, six homes for the aged, and six orphanages reveal only a slight interest in social welfare institutions.

Two Disciples were instrumental in founding and editing the *Christian Century*, now the leading interdenominational Protestant journal of opinion. They were W. E. Garrison and Charles Clayton Morrison. President James A. Garfield was a former Disciples preacher and poet Vachel Lindsay was also a member of the sect.

Disciples have always been active in the National and World Councils of Churches. They claim a measure of credit for easing tensions among Protestant factions which clouded the religious picture in Campbell's day. They sponsor a Council on Christian Unity to promote ecumenical relations and continue to dicker on union with the American Baptists.

Most Disciples churches are equipped with a built-in pool for immersion baptisms. A Disciples minister's manual suggests a supply of leaded robes for men and women, heated water, and banks of flowers around the pool and warns that "humiliating experiences can be related of shallow baptistries." Adults transferring from another denomination are considered associate members until they make their profession of faith and submit to re-baptism by immersion. Campbell's plans for a unified Christian church were doomed as soon as he declared the infant baptisms of the great Protestant denominations, Lutheran, Anglican, and Reformed, to be unscriptural and invalid.

The fundamentalist Churches of Christ keep no records and are even more loosely organized than the Disciples since they have no annual convention, and no local, state, or national associations. Membership figures may be subject to inflation but this group claims 18,500 churches and 2,250,000 members. They are strong in Tennessee, Kentucky, Alabama, Arkansas, and Oklahoma. Few of their ministers have gone beyond high school and few members are drawn from the middle or upper classes.

All music is a *capella* since they find no mention of organs in the Bible (or, for that matter, hymn books, pews, electric fans, and the English language). Their periodicals are carefully identified as "unofficial" and their colleges as "nonsectarian." Churches send funds to individual missionaries but they condemn mission societies as unbiblical. Some of their foreign missionaries have received newspaper publicity by their provocative activities in Catholic countries such as Italy and Colombia. While the Disciples have soft-pedaled most of Campbell's outspoken anti-Catholicism, the Churches of Christ are very critical of the churches of Rome.

Theology interests neither branch of the Campbellite movement. The traditional Christian doctrines receive slight attention and it appears that most Disciples reject original sin. The church has no catechism outside of the Bible itself and no authority exists to decide what is essential Christianity and what is not.

A second schism in the Disciples movement seems a certainty. In many communities there are already three distinct churches which trace their histories to the Campbells' activities. The third branch, for want of a better name, is sometimes referred to as the Church of Christ Number Two. It scores the modernism of the Disciples of Christ and has its own convention, colleges, journals, yearbook, and missionaries — everything but a name. At present these dissenters are included in the total of 1,943,000 Disciples in this country but they may account for as many as 500,000.

Like many another religious reformer Campbell protested that he did not want to found another church. Today two churches with all the apparatuses of separate denominations owe their beginnings to Campbell and Stone. Tomorrow there may be three such denominations. The attempt to duplicate first century Christianity attracted thousands of sincere people by its simplicity and "common sense" approach but it has met the same success as would attempts to reproduce first-century economics or politics. Twenty centuries of Christianity cannot be ignored or disowned. A quibble over church organs and mission societies rent the infant denomination dedicated to Christian unity. Campbell's polemical labors added two, perhaps soon three, more bodies to the Protestant panorama: a liberal majority drifting toward humanism and rationalism and a conservative minority hardening into fanatical bibliolatry.

Chapter IX

THE UNITED CHRISTIANS

Congregational Christians, Evangelical and Reformed Merged in 1957

ALTHOUGH a number of denominational mergers have been completed in recent years, most of these could be termed family reunions rather than marriages. Churches which had divided over some issue such as slavery or language came together to form a united church once more. Other churches which represented almost identical constituencies found common grounds for forming a single denomination.

In this respect the formation of the *United Church of Christ* in June, 1957, was unique in American Protestantism. *Congregationalism*, a product of English Separatism, came to these shores with the Pilgrim Fathers and became a virtual state religion for the New England Yankees. On the other hand the *Evangelical and Reformed Church*, a fusion of two German Calvinist bodies in 1934, found its adherents among the descendants of German immigrants in Pennsylvania and the Middle West. Congregationalism rested upon the complete autonomy of the local congregation and refused to recognize the power of any bishop, synod, or council over the congregation. The Evangelical and Reformed Church operated under a modified presbyterian system of church government. Congregationalists refused to bind members or churches with creeds while the Evangelical and Reformed were committed to uphold the Heidelberg Confession, Luther's Shorter Catechism, and the Augsburg Confession.

Opposition by a minority of Congregationalists blocked the merger through court action for five years. Enemies of the union contended that they would be untrue to their most distinctive Congregational belief by uniting with a presbyterian church such as the Evangelical and Reformed. They lost their case and the proponents of union obtained large majority approvals in their respective church councils.

To understand this new religious synthesis called the United Church of Christ, we must examine the backgrounds of its two diverse components. This youngest Protestant denomination numbers more than 2,000,000 communicants in the United States and represents the same type of ecumenical approach whose counterpart we find in the older United Church of Canada and the Church of South India.

For the origins of Congregationalism we must look to the Separatist movement in England and for the Evangelical and Reformed Church to continental Calvinism and to attempts in Prussia to blend Lutheranism with Calvinism.

"No bishops" had been the battle cry of English Presbyterians who preferred a representative form of church polity which nevertheless exercised a measure of control and supervision over member congregations. This did not satisfy everyone. More radical wings of the Separatist movement denied any authority over the local congregation. "No head, priest, prophet, or king save Christ" was their motto. Each church, composed of the predestined elect, should be free to frame its own creed or no creed and to choose its own minister and church officers. Furthermore, they agreed with the more moderate Puritans that all vestiges of popery be driven from the church. These radicals came to be known as Independents or Congregationalists.

Persecution drove many Congregationalists to tolerant Holland, among them the future Pilgrims. Perhaps the most flourishing community was that at Leyden under the pastorate of the gentle John Robinson. This congregation had been organized by poor people of the hamlet of Scrooby who finally sought refuge in Europe's religious sanctuary.

As time passed these English Separatists found economic conditions harsh in their new home and they saw their children adopting the customs of a foreign land and intermarrying with the Dutch. They wished to preserve their English heritage. A group decided to sail to the New World where they could re-establish their religious community but the majority remained in Holland with their pastor. They arranged transportation through some merchant adventurers; by the time they set sail from England on the Mayflower the majority of the 101 passengers were non-Separatists. When they sighted Cape Cod in 1620 the adult males among the Separatists signed the Mayflower Compact but once ashore the distinctions between the Congregationalists and the "Strangers" disappeared.

Starvation, cold, and disease faced the Pilgrim Fathers but they buried their dead and labored to build their colony at Plymouth. Half the settlers died within six months. Later wealthy Puritans, originally non-Separatists, landed at nearby Salem. Between 1628 and 1635 more than 20,000 Puritans arrived at the Massachusetts Bay Colony and they eventually exchanged their own presbyterian preferences for the congregationalism of their Pilgrim neighbors. The two settlements merged in 1691 and Congregationalism became the established religion of the New England colonies.

Only church members could vote (1708 voters out of 15,000 settlers in the Massachusetts Bay Colony). Everyone was required to pay taxes for the support of the established church. This special status was not abrogated in Connecticut until 1818, in New Hampshire until 1819, and in Massachusetts until 1834.

While it may not be entirely fair to say that the Pilgrims came to this country to worship God in their own way and make everyone else do likewise, they certainly were not champions of religious freedom. They came to the New World to find freedom for themselves rather than to provide it for others. Persecuted in England they became self-righteous persecutors in America. Dissenters were firmly invited to leave. Four Quakers were hanged on Boston Commons. Heresy and witchcraft were vigorously extirpated and Puritan treatment of Roger Williams and the Baptists, Anne Hutchinson, the Quakers, and any episcopal sympathizers is well known. The Salem witchcraft trials of 1692 found a theocracy in religious frenzy. Nineteen men and women were hanged in Salem for trafficking with the devil.

The Puritan theocracy forbade dancing, card playing, smoking, mince meat pies, the observance of Christmas, and all musical instruments save the drum, trumpet, and jew's-harp. "No one shall travel, cook victuals, make beds, sweep house, cut hair or shave and no woman shall kiss her children on the Sabbath Day," declared the Puritan divines. But just as the Congregational heirs of Puritanism jettisoned strict Calvinism for theological liberalism, so they also abandoned Puritan morality to the Methodists, Baptists, and Holiness sects.

Calvinism originally formed the theological basis of Congregationalism although the Congregationalists minimized formal creeds and confessions. Then as now the local congregation could compose a creed of its own, adopt the Apostles' Creed, or remain creedless. A current manual for new members of the Congregational Christian Church by the Rev. L. Wendell Fifield explains, "No member is ever told that he must believe any specific religious tenet in order to be a good church member." Apparently this means that belief in God, the divinity of Christ, the resurrection, miracles, and the like is optional.

An observer in the early nineteenth century would probably have assumed that Congregationalism or the "New England Way" would continue to be the largest and one of the most influential churches in the nation. That it lost this pre-eminence to become one of the smaller major denominations was the result of several factors.

Early in the 1800's Congregationalism split into two parties: Trinitarian and Unitarian. The Unitarians lopped off all but one of Boston's 14 congregations, captured Harvard and the original Pilgrim church at Plymouth, and dominated the religious scene in eastern Massachusetts. Today many Congregational churches may be considered Unitarian themselves in everything but name, and the union of the Unitarian-Universalist Church with the United Church of Christ is a remote possibility.

Another reason for Congregationalism's decline was the Plan

of Union which was devised in 1801 to minimize denominational competition in the West but which usually worked to the advantage of the Presbyterians. Before its repudiation in 1852 the Plan is said to have resulted in a loss of 2000 Congregational churches outside of New England to the better organized Presbyterians. Up to the 1957 merger Congregationalism remained primarily a New England institution with smaller memberships in New York, Ohio, Illinois, Iowa, and California.

Reliance on state recognition and support led to complacency in Congregational ranks and the upstart Methodists and Baptists forged ahead to become the leading Protestant denominations in the country. Like the Presbyterians and Episcopalians, the Congregationalists insisted on an educated clergy and lacked the trained man power to compete with the Methodist circuit riders and the Baptist preachers.

Congregationalism has always demonstrated a concern for higher education; church members founded Harvard, Yale, Dartmouth, Bowdoin, Amherst, Smith, Williams, Oberlin, and 40 other colleges most of which have since passed from church control. When Harvard capitulated to Unitarianism the Congregationalists founded Andover seminary to inculcate orthodox Calvinism. The educational level of Congregationalists, clergy and laity, has traditionally been among the highest of all Protestant groups.

In 1931 the Congregationalists merged with the 100,000-member *Christian Church*, otherwise known as the Baptist Unitarians. This group denied the divinity of Christ and rejected all creeds since it arose from the same religious ferment which produced the creedless Disciples of Christ and Churches of Christ. The first overtures for a merger were made in 1895. The new church was known as the *Congregational Christian Churches*. An even smaller group, the *Evangelical Protestant Church of North America*, made up of Germans and Swiss, had been absorbed by Congregationalism in 1925.

Theoretically the power of the local Congregational church was unlimited. It could fix doctrine and ritual, hire and fire ministers, choose its own officers. Theory and practice differed and there are those who maintain that a Congregationalist had no more freedom than a Methodist and Lutheran. Strict educational and moral standards for the ministry were enforced and a church had to be accepted by the churches in its district before it could use the title "Congregational." Group pressure can sometimes bring about more uniformity and conformity than elaborate governmental structures. Beyond the local churches were the Associations, the Conferences, and the General Council. The decisions of these regional, state, and national bodies had no binding power on the congregations. The problem of preserving the essentials of Christianity in a Congregational polity was never solved and in many cases the essentials were not preserved. A few Congregational churches could be characterized as fundamentalist but most taught a mixture of liberalism, modernism, sentimentalism, social gospel, and unitarianism.

As in the Evangelical and Reformed Church, women were ordained to the ministry but generally served smaller rural churches. At the time of the merger about 4 per cent of Congregational ministers were women. A Congregationalist leader estimated in 1956 that half the Congregational ministers had been recruited, educated, and ordained by other Protestant churches. In fact, 170 Congregational churches were served by ministers who retained their standing in other denominations. Ministers who embraced Congregationalism were not required to undergo reordination.

Early Congregational worship and architecture were severely plain: lengthy sermons, Bible reading and psalms, unadorned meeting houses. Christmas was called a popish holiday and its observance cost the celebrant five shillings. Today Christmas finds a place in the Congregationalist year as well as the Puritan's own contribution to the calendar, Thanksgiving Day. Organs and hymns were gradually introduced and the service was shortened from three hours to one. An altar, cross and candles, cassock, surplice and stole which would have scandalized their Puritan ancestors are accepted by modern Congregationalists.

At the time of the merger with the Evangelical and Reformed Church the Congregational Christian Churches counted 1,342,000 adult members, mostly in New England. Each Congregational Christian church is free to accept or reject the union with the E and R Church.

So far 230 Congregational Churches have refused to join the merger; they have formed the National Association of Congregational Churches.

The Evangelical and Reformed Church itself was the youngest of the major denominations since it traced its beginning as a single church to a union in 1934 of two German-Swiss Calvinist churches. As separate churches the Reformed Church antedated the century-old Evangelical Synod by almost 300 years.

Not all areas in Germany which had abandoned the ancient faith accepted Lutheranism. Certain sections such as the Palatinate adopted a Reformed theology in the Heidelberg Confession of 1563. This confession attempted to strike a middle course between Lutheranism and Calvinism which differed mainly on the doctrine of the Real Presence.

A number of Palatinates left their homeland for America after the devastation of the Thirty Years' War. A Reformed minister, Michael Schlatter, organized these scattered German settlements in Pennsylvania but the American church remained under Dutch control until 1793. In the early 1800's two groups led by Philip Otterbein and John Winebrenner seceded and started churches of their own: the United Brethren in Christ and the Church of God.

A merger of two German Reformed synods in 1863 and the wider use of the English language strengthened the Reformed Church in the United States (not to be confused with the Reformed Church of America, a Dutch body). Units of the Hungarian Reformed Church were absorbed in 1924.

The other party in the 1934 union, the Evangelical Synod of North America, represented the 1817 union of Reformed and Lutherans in Prussia. King Frederick William III desired religious unity in his realm and decreed the union as a solution of religious differences between the Reformed and the Lutheran majority. He chose the 300th anniversary of Luther's revolt for the royal decree.

Members of this synthetic United Evangelical Church of Prussia began to enter the United States almost a century after their Reformed cousins. They formed their church in 1840. Although most of the charter members were Lutherans this church has drifted far from orthodox Lutheranism and its absorption into the United Church of Christ is evidence of the extent to which it had accepted liberal and modernist assumptions.

Both participants in the 1934 merger were organized by German immigrants; both employed the German language in their pioneer days; both preached a liberalized Reformed theology; both were governed by a presbyterian polity. At the time of the merger in Cleveland the Reformed Church counted 348,000 members and the Evangelical Synod, 281,000. An unusual feature of this action was that the two denominations united first and worked out the details later. Church boards were not consolidated until 1941.

Three of the most distinguished Protestant theologians in the United States were ordained Evangelical and Reformed ministers: Reinhold and H. Richard Niebuhr and Paul Tillich. The Niebuhrs grew up in an E and R parsonage and Tillich transferred his membership from the German church. Almost all Evangelical and Reformed ministers have completed four years of college and three years of seminary training.

Pennsylvania and Ohio were the Evangelical and Reformed strongholds; a large proportion of the members resided in these two states and three others: Indiana, Illinois, and Missouri. In this respect E and R membership complemented the New England strength of Congregationalism.

An extensive social welfare program was sponsored by the E and R Church including 18 homes for the aged, ten hospitals, and ten children's homes. These institutions will continue to be operated by the United Church of Christ. Some of these establishments are conducted by deaconesses who take no lifelong vows but usually devote their lives to charitable work in this Protestant Sisterhood. The denomination also operated eight colleges. It numbered 774,000 members the year before the 1957 merger.

Evangelical and Reformed liberalism will find a congenial companion in the Congregational Christian Churches. The new United

Church of Christ is governed by a modified presbyterianism along E and R lines. Some Congregationalists will no doubt continue their historic opposition to any authority over the local church.

The United Church will be more of a national church than either of the former denominations although it has scarcely any adherents in the South. As a matter of fact the growth of the separate parties to the merger has hardly kept pace with the natural increases in population in this country.

Unlike many denominations which have abandoned their city parishes in the face of invasions by Puerto Ricans, Negroes, and Southern hillbillies, the United Church refuses to retreat entirely to suburbia. In Brooklyn, Chicago, Harlem, and even in San Francisco's beatnik colony the church attempts to meet the challenges of metropolitan living.

The United Church may be expected to continue the theological liberalism which characterized the parent churches. The union of two such diverse churches may give impetus to other unions and reunions within American Protestantism such as the perennial Presbyterian-Protestant Episcopal, Methodist-Evangelical United Brethren, Baptist-Disciples proposals.

Congregationalism, in practice, has meant much less congregational autonomy than the name would suggest. Two of the most centralized denominations in the nation, the Lutheran Church-Missouri Synod and the Seventh-day Adventist, are actually congregational in theory but this has not precluded a high degree of control. Congregationalism will now be better exemplified in the Baptist, Disciples, and Holiness churches since the church which once made local independence paramount sacrificed this principle for the sake of union in 1957.

Chapter X

THE QUAKERS

Follow the Inner Light

Q<small>UAKERS</small>, members of the *Religious Society of Friends*, often consider themselves representatives of a third form of Christianity, neither Catholic nor Protestant. At other times they concur with many non-Quakers who see Quakerism as Protestantism carried to its logical conclusion.

Luther rejected the pope, the visible church, five of the seven sacraments, the value of tradition as a rule of faith, the sacrificial element in worship. Calvin dispensed with the rule of bishops, minimized the role of music and art in worship. Congregationalists did away with centralized church government of any kind and Baptists damned infant baptism as unscriptural.

The Quakers dispensed with all sacraments, all ritual, any professional ministry. On the other hand, the familiar Protestant formulae; total depravity, justification by faith alone, and the sole sufficiency of the scriptures are foreign to Quaker thought. Further, the Quakers declare that the ultimate religious authority rests in no church, individual, tradition, or Bible but within each individual.

An understanding of the Quaker's Inner Light is essential to an understanding of this radical but influential phase of the English Reformation. By the Inner Light which each man must follow the Quakers do not mean conscience. Conscience itself is illumined by the Inner Light. This Inner Light is rather the immediate influence of the Holy Spirit, that which is of God in each soul. Like most mystics the early Quakers found themselves helpless to express their experiences in words.

The Friends have never been numerous and there are probably about as many in the world today as there were in 1700. In the United States, now the chief Quaker center, they count 115,000 members which is approximately the same number reported in the 1906 religious census when the nation's population was half what it is today. For a variety of reasons Quakerism has become a static sect with little appeal to moderns.

Most of the customs and mannerisms which once set them apart from the world as a "peculiar" people have disappeared. The group mysticism of the English lower classes has become a respected denomination for the middle class American. Their witness against war and their active interest in social questions continue and they have won the universal admiration of their countrymen.

Like Luther and Wesley, the founder of the Quakers had no intention of founding another church or sect. George Fox, born in 1624, had little opportunity to attend school or study. He was apprenticed to a shoemaker at the age of 12 but developed a dissatisfaction with his religious life and that of his Puritan neighbors. One day as a youth of 19 he was shocked at the sight of two clergymen engaged in a drinking bout at a fair. In a vision he said he heard the voice of God tell him: "Thou seest how men give themselves over to vanity. Forget about them. Keep aloof from them and in the future be as a stranger to them."

He decided to break with home, friends, church, and trade and he began four years of wandering about England. Fox came to the conclusion that man arrives at truth not by study or Bible reading or listening to sermons but by following the Inner Light whereby God speaks directly to each soul. Of what use, then, is learning and ritual and church organization? Quakers take the year 1649 as their founding date.

The young enthusiast found many converts for his views among the dozens of sects which dotted the English countryside: Seekers, Ranters, Baptists, and mystics of all types. He found many who disliked the Anglican establishment and kindred spirits who had reacted against the harshness of Calvinism.

The Quaker founder believed that God granted the Inner Light to all; Fox had no place in his system for elect and reprobate. He denied that man was depraved and he set up perfection and freedom from all sin as a spiritual goal. Even the atonement was rejected since the Quakers believed that no one, not even God, could atone for another's sins. They reverenced the Bible but considered it a Word of God and not the Word of God.

Imprisoned for a total of six years, Fox endured dogged persecution throughout his life. Once condemned to death for his religious views he missed execution only through the intervention of powerful friends. Nevertheless he maintained a full schedule of preaching and won many followers, especially in northern England.

On one occasion he was brought before a judge and accused of blasphemy. Fox startled the magistrate by shouting, "The time has come for even judges to quake and tremble before the Lord." "Oh," mocked the judge, "so you are quakers, are you?" The name stuck although it has never been officially adopted and the term Friends is sometimes preferred. Fox's converts had previously called themselves "Children of Light" and "Friends of Truth."

Quaker ideas of social equality contributed to their persecution in seventeenth-century England. They refused to acknowledge any special privilege among men which meant that they would doff their hats to no human and address no one with the then complimentary "you." Instead they used the plain "thee" and "thou." They opposed taking oaths on Biblical grounds and as implying a double standard of truth, one for the market place and one for the courtroom. Objecting to the pagan origin of the days of the week they renamed Sunday "First Day," Monday "Second Day," and so on. Simple dress, simple speech, sober habits were prescribed. Participation in war was strictly forbidden. Music, art, fiction, and the theater fell under Quaker ban. As a result of their attitudes more than 13,000 Quakers were imprisoned and hundreds died in prison during the Stuart Restoration and the reign of Charles II.

At their meetings for worship neither preaching nor ritual had a place. The only ritual was silence. Quakers waited quietly for inspiration from God and occasionally one or another of the assembled Friends would stand to testify or present a religious thought. Since they abhorred ritual of any kind they neither baptized nor observed the Lord's Supper.

Pioneer work in the social field was undertaken by the Quakers and millions of people have benefited from their efforts. They were among the first to urge proper care for the poor, aged, and insane; they fought slavery and battled for just treatment of the American Indians; they promoted temperance, prison reform, and equality of the sexes.

Two other names besides Fox are associated with Quaker history in a special way: Robert Barclay, the theologian of Quakerism, and William Penn, the founder of Pennsylvania.

Barclay was Fox's Melanchthon. He drew up the systematic presentation of Quaker doctrine. A Presbyterian in his youth, Barclay was sent to Paris to study under his Catholic uncle who taught at a Jesuit college. The Jesuit Fathers taught Barclay scholastic philosophy, Catholic theology, the Church Fathers, Latin, and French. Fearing his conversion to popery his parents withdrew him from the college. Back in England he finally joined the new Quaker movement in 1666 and employed his Catholic-sponsored education in the interests of this mystical sect. His chief work was *Apology for the True Christian Divinity*.

Penn, son of an English admiral, had embraced the principles of Quakerism and planned to establish a haven for his persecuted brethren. The king owed Penn's father a large sum of money and was happy to settle the debt by chartering a tract of land in the New World to Penn in 1681.

The first Quaker missionaries to America, two women, had been condemned as witches and sent back to England within five weeks of their arrival. The Massachusetts Puritans resisted and harassed the revolutionary Quakers in every way possible. Four intrepid Quakers who followed the women were hanged on Boston Commons and their coreligionists were imprisoned, whipped, and tortured.

Penn arrived in his colony in 1682 and found Swedes, Englishmen, and Dutch already settled. He assured them that they would be governed by their own laws as before. Following his religious convictions he soon concluded a model treaty with the Indians. He granted freedom of worship to all Christians, including Catholics, and laid out the streets of his City of Brotherly Love, Philadelphia.

Meanwhile, in England the Act of Toleration of 1689 released the Quakers from some of the harsher penalties and by the time of Fox's death two years later there were at least 50,000 Friends in the British Isles (twice as many as in 1956).

Quakers prospered in the American colonies and by 1700 Quakers owned not only Pennsylvania but New Jersey and Delaware, controlled Rhode Island and the Carolinas, and had strength in New York and Maryland. They constituted the greatest single religious community in the New World at this time.

Eventually the Quakers lost not only preponderance in the colonies but shrank to comparative numerical insignificance in American religious life. They lost political control of Pennsylvania in 1756 when they voluntarily relinquished their seats in the state assembly rather than vote for war against the Shawnee and Delaware Indians. Schisms, doctrinal disputes, lack of trained leaders, quietism, defection, periodic membership purges, and a reluctance to proselytize contributed to the Quaker decline.

Quietism infected the movement for many decades. This enervating philosophy, which has appeared in many religious systems, teaches that God operates in man only when man silences all his usual activities: prayer, study, and work. Its infection of Quakerism might have been anticipated. As a result of this philosophy, planning, organization, and foresight are neglected. Such Catholic Quietists as Molinos, Fenelon, and Madame Guyon were popular among the Quakers. Membership dipped from 60,000 in 1700 to 17,000 half a century later.

The sect depended almost entirely on birthright members who might grow indifferent to the original Quaker message. At other times purges crossed hundreds of names from the membership rolls. No replenishing evangelistic campaigns were conducted.

But the most serious organizational disruption of Quakerism sprang from the schism of Elias Hicks. A modernist theologian bordering on unitarianism, Hicks apparently rejected the divinity of Christ and the existence of original sin. He led a large group of rural Quakers from the main body in 1827. The Hicksites never adopted Hicks' theology in toto but this split handicapped Quaker activities for nearly a century until the original differences melted away. A smaller group called the Evangelical Friends or Wilburites broke away in 1837 in the expected conservative reaction.

It was not easy to be a Quaker. They were expected to wear a distinctive garb (see the Quaker Oats package), oppose all wars, refuse to swear oaths, adopt peculiar habits of speech, ignore the traditional Christian holidays, and marry within the group. The periodic purges expelled backsliders. Even today no orthodox Quaker gambles, plays the stock market, or drinks.

Quakers early opposed slavery in all its forms. Led by the gentle John Woolman they dismissed all slaveholders from their ranks and threw their weight behind the abolitionist crusade. Today they continue to fight segregation and racial intolerance.

Eventually compromises diluted Quakerism. The silent meeting often gave way to a programmed meeting differing only slightly from a simple Protestant service. Next came professional pastors. Those groups with programmed services came to be known as Friends Churches in contrast to the original Friends Meeting.

Officially the Quakers continue to oppose war but as more young Quakers volunteered for military service the attitude toward soldier-members softened. Estimates put 8000 Quakers in the armed forces during World War II, 1000 as noncombatants, 1000 as conscientious objectors, and 100 in prison. Those who did serve in the military services were no longer ostracized as they would have been in the earlier days of the sect.

The peculiarities which once set Quakers apart from the rest of the community have become private family customs.

The monthly meeting for worship and business is the basic unit of Quaker polity. This meeting convenes for silent or programmed worship, keeps records of births, deaths, and marriages, appoints committees, and conducts the necessary business. These meetings come together in quarterly meetings and they in turn comprise the yearly or Five Years meetings of which there are 28 in the United States and Canada.

Largest Quaker body is the *Five Years Meeting of Friends* with headquarters in Richmond, Indiana. Its 68,000 Friends include some in Africa and the West Indies. The Hicksite tradition is preserved in the *Religious Society of Friends, General Conference,* with 28,000 members and main offices in Philadelphia. Six other groups are identified by the areas they serve: Kansas, Ohio, Oregon, Philadelphia, Pacific and Central states.

Not majority rule but unanimity is sought in Quaker deliberations. The clerk of the meeting records the "sense of the meeting" and dissenters are persuaded rather than outvoted. Women have the same rights as men in Quaker government.

Representatives of the various Quaker branches formed the American Friends Service Committee in 1917. Since then the committee has spent millions of dollars on war and disaster relief work, rehabilitation, and care of conscientious objectors. Many non-Quakers contribute to the committee's financial support. Together with the Friends Service Council (London) it received the Nobel Peace Prize in 1947.

The sect operates ten small but distinguished colleges including Swarthmore, Earlham, Friends University, and Whittier. Quaker pastors receive training at a number of interdenominational seminaries.

Quakerism remains strongest in Indiana, Pennsylvania, North Carolina, Kansas, and California. Of the world's estimated 163,000 Friends, 115,000 reside in the United States and fewer than 1000 can be found in continental Europe. The London and East Africa meetings with 20,000 apiece account for the bulk of non-American Friends.

Well-known American Quakers have included John Greenleaf Whittier, Herbert Hoover, Johns Hopkins, Rufus Jones, Paul Douglas, and Richard Nixon. When Communist courier Whittaker Chambers left the party he turned to the Friends for spiritual direction.

Quakerism flourished during the lifetimes of its original trium-virate: Fox, Barclay, and Penn. Since then it has accomplished much in the way of social action and philanthropy but it has hardly held its own membership-wise. Millions of Americans applaud Quaker activities but never seriously consider joining the sect and no one ever asks them to do so. Schisms and compromise marked the Quaker decline. Wearing a standard Protestant garb in most parts of the country the sect seems to have little chance of reversing the trends of the past two centuries.

Quakerism has produced some admirable and saintly personalities in its 300 years. We must note with regret that their prejudice against all ritual has deprived birthright Friends of the grace of Christian baptism. The attempt to present mysticism on the group plan seems to have run its course.

Chapter XI

THE PERFECTIONISTS AND PENTECOSTALS

"Holiness Unto the Lord"

SEVERAL dozen sects comprise the Holiness movement (popularly known as Holy Roller) which grew out of post-Civil War revivals. These revivals stressed Wesley's doctrine of entire sanctification or Christian perfection which had been quietly eased out of the regular Methodist churches.

Today these numerous Holiness groups are characterized by emotionalism, swingy gospel hymns, faith healing, strict morality, premillennialism, revivals, and camp meetings. We can distinguish two branches of the Holiness movement, a right and a left wing, perfectionist and pentecostal.

Included in the perfectionist wing are the *Church of the Nazarene*, the *Church of God (Anderson, Indiana)*, the *Christian and Missionary Alliance*, and the *Pilgrim Holiness Church*. The pentecostal wing embraces those groups which maintain that speaking in tongues, glossolalia, is a necessary and natural accompaniment of the baptism of the Holy Spirit. These sects range from the 514,000-member *Assemblies of God* to weird backwoods cults which specialize in snake and fire handling. Many of the groups in this category include Pentecostal in their official titles but others, such as the *Church of God* (scores of varieties) and Negro groups, are not so identified.

All these groups from the Methodistic Church of the Nazarene to the most primitive hillbilly cult believe they have restored the

Biblical and Wesleyan doctrine of entire sanctification to its proper and central position in the Christian life.

According to the theology of holiness or, as it has been termed, the theology of the Holy Ghost, a Christian can receive a subsequent blessing after justification which frees him from all sinful desires. His nature is then freed from all depravity wrought by original sin. Whereas repentance is considered the prime requisite for baptism, consecration is the main requisite for holiness. All Christians are called to this holiness experience, an instantaneous transformation wrought by faith.

No one denies that Wesley, departing from the pessimism of Luther and Calvin regarding human nature, taught the doctrine of holiness and that his teaching on this subject has all but been disowned by modern Methodists. Many would deny that Wesley's teaching was carried to the extremes of some Holiness enthusiasts in the United States. By the end of the Civil War the doctrine was seldom mentioned in Methodist circles. When the postwar revivals renewed interest in holiness the devotees of the Latter Rain movement first formed prayer groups within the existing churches and eventually broke away to form their own congregations.

More radical or ecstatic elements claimed that the gifts showered on the Apostles at Pentecost were necessary signs of holiness. They especially encouraged congregational babbling or speaking in tongues which the Nazarenes, for example, have never countenanced. Pentecostals generally feature divine healing and preaching on the Second Coming to a greater degree than their Perfectionist brethren.

A recent Pentecostal revival meeting in a medium-sized Indiana community illustrates the appeal of these groups. In this case an evangelistic team from Texas was imported to stage a six night revival and healing campaign under the auspices of the local Pentecostal church.

About 200 people had assembled in the armory when the master of ceremonies began the hymn fest with piano accompaniment. A young lady in an orange blouse sang a solo entitled "Wicked Life." After half an hour of lively singing the M.C. asked that all those willing to contribute five dollars for the expenses of the meeting step forward to receive special prayers. No one did but he repeated the invitations for those with one dollar, fifty cents, and finally small change.

After several more gospel songs which the audience seemed to know by heart, the M.C. introduced the white-suited evangelist. His 40-minute sermon berated the larger churches for neglecting divine healing and for wasting money on medical missionaries and drugs. His talk was interrupted ritually time and again with "Amen," "Hallelujah" and "Praise God."

Finally he invited all those seeking healing to raise their hands and then to stand while everyone else was to bow his head and resist the temptation to peek. They were then asked to come to the platform; seven or eight people complied. Among the complaints were deafness, sore legs, fallen arches, and internal disorders. A white-haired lady of 80 and a lad of nine were among the petitioners.

"I command you, Satan, in the name of Jesus Christ to leave this woman," screamed the perspiring evangelist as he slapped his palm on a woman's forehead. Most of those participating mumbled that they felt better and had been miraculously cured. The 80-year-old grandmother showed no signs of regaining her hearing and the young healer calmly told her daughter that her mother evidently was not a true Christian and lacked genuine faith. A gentleman with fallen arches hobbled up to the front of the auditorium, submitted to the exorcism, praised God that he had been cured, and hobbled back to his seat. During the healing service a number of those in the audience rocked on the seats with closed eyes and upraised hands and uttered frequent ejaculations.

After the healing, the evangelist himself led several familiar hymns and then asked all who wished to be prayed for to hold up their hands. As with those who wished healing they were then urged to stand up and step forward. About 30 responded. They retired to the anteroom and the air was soon filled with groans, shrieks, and moans. The meeting closed with a hymn. The preacher pointed out that some of his books could be purchased under the "Saved By His Blood" banner in the rear of the hall. He announced that the next night's sermon topic would be "What Dr. Kinsey Dare Not Put in His Book." The service had lasted about two hours.

Obviously people who demand this type of religious experience will not find it in the established churches. They find it in thousands of storefront churches, revival tents, and camp meetings.

One of the largest Perfectionist bodies of the Holiness movement, the Church of the Nazarene, represents a merger of a number of smaller sects whose members were drawn from Methodism. These congregations sprang up around the country between 1890 and 1900 and the formal organization was completed at Pilot Point, Texas, in 1908. The original merger brought together 10,400 members and this church now claims 315,000 members in more than 4,500 congregations. Sociologists see in the Nazarene church an excellent example of a body in transition from sect to church. Within another generation or two it will no doubt take its place along with the Baptist, Methodist, Congregational, and Presbyterian churches as a "respectable" established church. The word "Pentecostal" was deleted from the church name in 1919 and all Nazarene colleges have dropped the "Holiness" designation from their names.

The Church of the Nazarene closely resembles Methodism in theology, polity, and worship. Once it attains full "church" status the church might well consider a merger with The Methodist Church of which it is an offspring.

All Nazarene ministers and local church officials must testify that they have experienced instantaneous entire sanctification. They believe in divine healing but do not disparage or ignore medical science. Their moral code exemplifies the Puritan attitudes of most Holiness sects. For example, their general rules for church membership condemn "profaning the Lord's Day, either by unnecessary labor, or business, or patronizing or reading of secular papers, or by holiday diversions." Another section bars "Songs, literature and entertainments not to the glory of God; the theater, the ballroom, the circus, and like places; also, lotteries and games of chance; looseness and impropriety of conduct; membership in or fellowship with oathbound secret orders or fraternities."

Nazarenes invariably rank high in the per capita donation to the church among Protestant denominations. A recent year revealed a per capita (not per family) donation of $142. General superintendents take the place of Methodism's bishops and are elected to four year terms. The sect operates six small liberal arts colleges in addition to Bible schools and a graduate theological seminary; headquarters are maintained at Kansas City, Mo. Ministers are ordained after completing a four-year college Bible course but many now enroll for graduate work at the seminary, which opened its doors in 1945.

A first cousin of the Church of the Nazarene, the *Pilgrim Holiness Church* was organized as such in 1922 as a result of a union of the International Holiness Church and the Pilgrim Church of California. Actually the beginnings go back to the International Apostolic Holiness Union, organized in 1897 in Cincinnati. This sect reports 33,500 members in the United States and Canada and engages in mission work in Africa, Mexico, South America, and the West Indies. Headquarters are now in Indianapolis. This sect admits women to the ministry on an equal basis with men.

Both the Free Methodist and Wesleyan Methodist churches have continued to uphold entire sanctification and should be included as part of the Holiness movement.

Sunday School attendance of the *Church of God* (Anderson, Indiana) exceeds church membership: 250,000 in Sunday School compared to 142,000 communicants. Now highly organized, this sect was begun as a protest against church organization and shares a distaste for the term "denomination" with the Disciples of Christ. It prefers to be called the Church of God Reformation Movement but adds the geographical location of its headquarters to distinguish it from the innumerable Church of God sects. Daniel S. Warner, a thrice married Winebrennarian preacher, began this sect in 1880. His second wife attempted to wrest control of the sect from the founder but he managed to retain control and obtained an uncontested divorce. Headquarters were moved to Anderson in 1906 where the church also maintains a college and publishing house. Like the Nazarenes, the members of this church are moving in the direction of church status. A full-time professional ministry, growing emphasis on education, and development of church organization accelerate this evolution.

Although most Holiness leaders came from Methodist and Baptist backgrounds, the founder of the *Christian and Missionary Alliance* was a former Presbyterian preacher, A. B. Simpson. Members of other Protestant denominations support the evangelistic work of this organization much as they lend support to the Salvation Army. Like the Army, the Christian and Missionary Alliance has developed into a denomination itself with a particular emphasis on skid row and foreign missions. It reports 60,000 members in more than 1000 congregations.

No one could compile a complete list of pentecostal sects since they come and go, merge and split, assume new titles. Ultra-fundamentalist like the more conservative Perfectionists, the Pentecostals preach the literal infallibility of the Bible, the virgin birth, the trinity, original sin, the divinity of Christ, the atonement and resurrection, heaven and hell and other Christian beliefs and Protestant additions. Their appeal is frankly to the poorer classes and they find their chief support in rural areas of the South, West, and Middle West.

What distinguishes the Pentecostals from the Perfectionists is the experience of speaking in tongues. This usually appears after several days of intense revivalism during which the preacher describes past occurrences in which the Holy Spirit is said to have bestowed this gift. After the proper preparation the congregation is ready for the phenomenon. Someone at the height of a gospel hymn sing or excited sermon will begin to mutter strange sounds and break out in a flood of meaningless words. The Holy Spirit has descended, the preacher praises God, the worshipers gather around the fortunate brother. Perhaps the minister will try to interpret the tongues as a message from God.

We find that the *Assemblies of God* comprise the largest organized body in Pentecostalism with 514,000 members. As usual a number of groups banded together to form the present sect. They met at Hot Springs, Arkansas, in 1914, and worked out an organization which preserved the autonomy of the local churches.

True to Pentecostal principles they insist that all Pentecostal gifts found in the New Testament must be duplicated in the twentieth-century church. The sect supports 760 missionaries and enrolls 992,000 children in its Sunday Schools. Members are expected to tithe, submit to immersion baptism, abstain from liquor and tobacco, and avoid secret societies. Affiliated branches cater to members of German, Polish, Ukrainian, and Latin American nationality.

Another large group of churches preaching pentecostalism is made up of those bearing the name *Church of God*. They range from fly-by-night storefront churches with a handful of adherents to sects with a membership in the tens of thousands. Altogether probably 300,000 people belong to one of the many Churches of God. Five such churches maintain headquarters in Cleveland, Tennessee, and trace their origin to A. J. Tomlinson. Tomlinson, a Bible salesman, served as general overseer of the original Church of God from 1903 to 1923 when he was impeached and set up another Church of God. After his death his sons, Homer and Milton, headed separate Churches of God, one with headquarters in Queens Village, New York, and the other in Cleveland, Tennessee. The latter body was first called "The Church of God Over Which M. A. Tomlinson Is General Overseer" but this has been shortened to *Church of God of Prophecy*.

A Negro cook on the Sante Fe Railroad claimed a revelation that the Negroes are descendants of the lost tribes of Israel. The 38,000 members of the resulting *Church of God and Saints of Christ*, who are also known as Black Jews, observe the Jewish Sabbath and high holydays and use Hebrew terminology.

Among the larger groups which include the designation "Pentecostal" in their church titles are the *United Pentecostal Church* (175,000 members), the *Pentecostal Holiness Church, Inc.* (55,-000), the *Pentecostal Church of God of America, Inc.* (109,000), and the *Pentecostal Assemblies of the World, Inc.* (45,000). A Pentecostal Holiness evangelist and healer, Oral Roberts, of Tulsa, Oklahoma, appears weekly on 147 TV stations and 600 radio stations. He claims to have been healed of TB and stuttering himself and now conducts gigantic healing revivals in one city after another with his 14,000-seat tent and revival troupe. His income is reported to be $100,000 a year.

Perhaps the most colorful personality in the Pentecostal movement was "Sister" Aimee Semple McPherson, foundress of the *International Church of the Foursquare Gospel*. In her heyday Sister Aimee would enter her 5300-seat Angelus Temple in Los Angeles wearing football togs and riding a motorcycle. Thrice married, she never used the surname of her last husband, David L. Hutton, a Temple choir baritone.

A native of Canada, she was converted at the age of 17 and married the Baptist preacher who had converted her. The pair went as missionaries to China but her husband Robert Semple died of malaria in Hong Kong and she returned to the States. She embarked upon a career of evangelism, married a grocer by the name of Harold McPherson, and came to California in 1920. Her Temple was dedicated three years later as 1000 voices sang "Open the Gates of the Temple." Sister Aimee employed every device of oratory, lighting, costuming, publicity, dramatics, and crowd psychology to gain attention and win converts. The newspapers devoted headlines in her disappearance in 1926. Two men lost their lives diving for her body in the ocean. Finally she turned up and related that she had been kidnaped and tortured but managed to escape from a hideout in the desert. At her death in 1944 her followers contributed $100,000 worth of flowers including a 600-foot floral cross. Twelve pallbearers took 20 minutes to carry the 1200 pound bronze casket a few hundred yards to her grave at Forest Lawn cemetery.

Her son, Rolf, assumed the office of president of the International Church of the Foursquare Gospel which his mother had incorporated in 1927. L.I.F.E. Bible College next to the Angelus Temple has graduated 5000 Foursquare ministers and radio station KFSG is operated by the sect in Los Angeles. The sect survived Sister Aimee's career and death and its growth from 21,000 members in 1936 to 84,000 in 1962 in this country indicates that it will continue to expand. More than 960 Foursquare missionaries are working in 28 nations, especially in South America.

In general the Perfectionists and Pentecostals are isolated from the mainstream of Protestant church life. Their doctrines, membership, and church organization are as unfamiliar to the average Methodist and Lutheran as to Catholics. They are unlikely to join the local ministerial society or co-operate in interdenominational projects. Their preachers do not hesitate to lambast the established churches for deserting the "old time religion." Nevertheless these Holiness groups claim a combined constituency of at least 1,500,000 and they have been registering much greater membership increases than the older churches. Their adherents contribute far more per capita than do other Protestants even though they represent a lower income bracket. Their foreign mission programs rival those of the very largest denominations in number of workers and converts. They probably spend more time in church than most Protestants since the Sunday evening, midweek service, and revival remain features of almost all Holiness groups.

As members of these many sects attain a degree of financial security and social position, they exert a liberalizing influence on the sect. Some leave the Holiness sect for a Methodist or Baptist church which carries more prestige in the community. Others remain in the sect and help transform it into a church-type organization.

As time goes on seminaries and colleges are founded, a full time minister replaces the part-time preacher, local congregations acquire property and leave their rented quarters, ministers with college and professional training move into the top positions, some of the sect's young people leave farming and factory work for white collar positions, the worship service calms down. Over a period of several generations the original protest against the established churches becomes a curious bit of denominational history. Other groups arise to offer what the sect-turned-church no longer countenances.

Most of these Holiness sects hold fast to traditional Christian doctrines which their Modernist brethren have explained away. On the other hand, they make few intellectual demands on their members and their peculiar doctrines of entire sanctification, divine healing, and speaking in tongues carry them far from Catholic truth.

Chapter XII

THE SEVENTH-DAY ADVENTISTS

A Prophetess Combines Fundamentalism and Recrudescent Judaism

---

At first glance Seventh-day Adventists seem to be simply conservative Protestants who emphasize the Second Coming of Christ and go to church on Saturday instead of Sunday. Closer examination reveals several basic departures from traditional Protestant theology and practice.

While Catholics and Protestants agree that man's soul is immortal, Adventists insist that man is mortal. Man does not have a soul; he *is* a soul. At death the soul enters a state of deep sleep or unconsciousness until the Second Coming when those who have been saved through the gospel will receive the gift of immortality. The wicked are resurrected one thousand years later at the close of the millennial reign of Christ and are annihilated by fire together with Satan.

Therefore, while the righteous may receive the gift of immortality and the wicked may be brought back to life briefly before their cremation, man's nature is basically mortal. Justin Martyr championed the view that the souls of the just enter heaven only after the resurrection and echoes of this heresy may be found in present-day Eastern Orthodoxy.

Members of the Adventist sect believe that the followers of Christ will be raised from the dead and reign with Him in heaven for a millennium. During this time the earth will be depopulated, a wilderness and prison for the devil.

Adventists attribute the belief that people go to heaven or hell immediately after death to the infiltration of pagan mythology into Christianity. They attempt to prove from the Bible that the dead are asleep until the Second Coming.

At the close of the millennium Christ and His faithful will return to the earth, witness the resurrection and destruction of the wicked, and establish a New Jerusalem in a purified earth.

Catholics and Protestants, on the contrary, teach that man has both a body and a soul. His soul is immortal. At death each man is judged and assigned to heaven, hell, or purgatory (Protestants generally reject the idea of a place of temporary punishment and purification).

The Catholic Church teaches that the Second Coming of Christ will precede the Last Judgment. The millennium is not a literal 1000 years but indicates the entire period between the Incarnation and the Last Judgment. At the resurrection man's soul is reunited with his body with special characteristics of glory for the saved. The earth will be destroyed.

Adventists propagate their peculiar eschatological doctrines with an aggressiveness and sense of urgency which has brought them a good measure of success. To many they appear as prophets of gloom and doom. Embarrassed by several awkward date-setting episodes in their pioneer days, they carefully avoid such pitfalls today. Their revivalists and preachers, however, produce all types of natural catastrophies, wars, A- and H-bombs, modern inventions, and moral lapses as evidence that mankind is living in the latter days.

Total abstinence from liquor and tobacco is not only recommended but considered a sure test of Christian faith. Any who have not eschewed cigarettes and beer are refused baptism and adherents who lapse into such habits are promptly excommunicated. The movement likewise commands observance of the Jewish dietary laws, forbidding the eating of pork and other unclean flesh itemized in the Old Testament. In fact, most Adventists are vegetarians.

The Seventh-day Adventist and Mormon churches are the two

best known denominations which base their financial structure on the tithe. Adventists expect each member to tithe his gross income since this is the divine plan for church support as revealed in the Bible. Adventism adopted tithing in 1858. The basic tithe or 10 per cent goes to the support of the ministry. Over and above this a second offering provides for church buildings, maintenance, parochial schools, publishing plants, missions, relief work, etc. Many Adventists contribute 20 per cent or more of their income to the church; all members in good standing tithe. Although Adventism counts few wealthy devotees, an Oregon businessman recently turned over his $10,000,000 lumber company to the church.

Statistics consistently show the Adventist church at the head of the list of Protestant denominations in per capita contributions. A recent year indicated a per capita contribution of $212, probably ten times that of American Catholics.

Their observance of the seventh-day Sabbath has become more of an obsession than a matter of preference. Their literature insists time and again that man's most important responsibility in this life is the correct choice of God's seal (the Saturday Sabbath) or the beast's sign (Sunday). Those who changed the Christian observance from the Judaic Saturday to Sunday are branded as tools of Satan. Christians who persist in keeping Sunday as the Lord's Day become accomplices in this nefarious plot to disobey God's own commandment.

Since history plainly records that the Catholic Church changed the Christian observance in memory of Christ's resurrection on Easter Sunday, Adventists cherish a particular hatred of the popes and "Romanism." However, Protestants find themselves far more vulnerable to Adventist attacks on this score since they hold the Bible to be the sole rule of faith. "Search your Bible from Genesis to Revelation and show me any authorization for a Sunday Sabbath observance," taunts the Adventist.

Here Adventism dramatizes Protestant dependence on Catholic tradition. At least two Protestant leaders saw the inconsistency of this position and observed the original Sabbath: Melanchthon and the Moravian's Count Zinzendorf.

Catholics point out that the word Sabbath means "rest" and the third commandment commands man to rest every seventh day and to offer special worship to God. The Jews chose Saturday for their Sabbath while the early Christians chose Sunday. Writing in the fourth century St. Augustine comments, "The Apostles and their contemporaries sanctioned the dedication of Sunday to the worship of God."

Adventists, preoccupied with what they consider the letter of the law, reason that since all other Christian churches have tampered with God's commandment without Biblical leave, these churches must be apostate. Thus the Seventh-day Adventist church alone constitutes the remnant church in these last days. This charge in the face of today's "live and let live" ecumenism arouses bitter feeling among other Protestants. Some of the harshest anti-Adventist tracts circulate among fundamentalists who would otherwise find common cause with the Adventists.

As we indicated, a special place of dishonor is reserved for the Church of Rome by Adventist writers. The stock Bible prophecies from the Book of Daniel and the Apocalypse (Revelation) are trotted out and identified with Catholicism. The naïve nature of much of this libel may be surmised from the following arithmetical exercise from a popular Adventist handbook *Highways to Truth* by Arthur E. Lickey. The author points out that the beast mentioned in Revelation 13:18 wears the mysterious number 666. He continues: "A leading title for the pope is the Vicar of the Son of God. In Latin this is Vicarius Filii Dei. Adding up the numeral letters in this title we have: V-5, I-1, C-100 (A and R no value), I-1, V(U)-5 (S and F no value), I-1, L-50, I-1, I-1, D-500 (E no value), I-1. This totals 666, the number the Bible gives for the beast."[1] We would be spoiling the writer's fun if we added that others engaged in this numerological pastime have matched the number 666 with Caesar, Hitler, Napoleon, and even Franklin D. Roosevelt.

Next to the Catholic Church, the Lutheran Church-Missouri Synod and the Christian Reformed Church, the Seventh-day Ad-

---

[1] Arthur S. Lickey, *Highways to Truth* (Washington, D. C.: Review and Herald Publishing Association, 1952), p. 468.

ventist sect operates the largest parochial school system in the United States. They try to set up a school wherever six pupils are gathered. Worldwide the sect conducts 4892 church schools and academies with more than 260,000 students. It manages to educate about half of its young people in church institutions. On the higher education level in this country it controls 11 small coeducational colleges, a theological seminary, Potomac University, and an accredited medical-dental college in Los Angeles and Loma Linda, Calif.: the College of Medical Evangelists. Adventists make enormous sacrifices to provide religious training for their young people from kindergarten to college and even to medical and dental school.

Adventism is booming. Worldwide membership recently passed the 1,150,000 mark with about 330,000 Seventh-day Adventists in this country. The extraordinarily generous support from the tithe enables the sect to finance a missionary, publishing, and educational effort out of all proportion to its numbers. The extensive school system graduates thousands of loyal and Bible-indoctrinated followers.

It all began during the early decades of the past century when some Protestant clergymen and laymen began to dabble in Bible prophecy. Many calculated that the Second Coming was at hand and would certainly occur during their lifetimes. Someone has estimated that 300 Anglican ministers and twice that number of Nonconformists in England were heralding the immanent personal return of Christ in the 1820's and 1830's. This enthusiasm found converts in England, the continent, and the New World.

William Miller, a War of 1812 veteran, a converted deist and Baptist farmer-preacher, spearheaded the American version. Like all slide-rule prophets Miller concentrated on the Books of Daniel and Revelation. His chief discovery was that the 2300 days referred to in Daniel 8:13, 14 meant years. Figuring from the year 457 B.C., the date of the commandment to restore Jerusalem, he announced that the Second Coming could be expected in 1843. He began preaching this news in 1831.

People flocked to the movement from the old line Protestant churches and hundreds of ministers enrolled under Adventism's banners. But 1843 came and passed. The date was revised to Oct. 22,

1844. By this time at least 50,000 people were known as Adventists, and Miller issued a call that his followers come out of "Babylon." By Babylon he meant the other Protestant communions. Many sold their possessions, settled their affairs, and awaited the Great Day. The press helped to publicize the event. But Oct. 22, 1844, also came and passed.

Disillusioned, thousands abandoned religion entirely as a monster hoax; others drifted sheepishly back to their former church homes in "Babylon." Miller died lonely and forgotten, expelled by the Baptists in 1845. But a tiny band of diehards in Washington, New Hampshire, remained true to Adventism and reopened their Bibles to see what had gone wrong. They were First-day Adventists.

This group of New England Millerites formed the nucleus of the present Seventh-day Adventist sect. They insisted, despite rather convincing evidence to the contrary, that the 1844 date was correct. Finally one of their number hit upon the explanation that the error was not in the date but in interpreting the date in terms of an earthly event. What really happened on Oct. 22, 1844, was that Christ had cleansed the heavenly sanctuary. This cleansing involves determining who will merit immortality and has been going on since 1844.

A master stroke, this ingenious apology rescued the wobbly movement from complete collapse. Satisfied that they had not been deceived by Miller, they rekindled their Adventist hopes and also resolved never again to set a specific date for the Second Coming.

All the leaders in the reorganized Adventist cult such as Joseph Bates, James White, and his wife Ellen White (nee Harmon) had been closely associated with the pre-1844 Millerites. Of this trio Mrs. White became the undoubted leader. Never a church officer or minister, she claimed supernatural powers and was and is considered a prophetess by Seventh-day Adventists. She dictated many of her 20 books and 3000 articles while in a trance and her writings are held to be inspired. She is said to have written 24 million words.

Mrs. White, a Methodist in her early youth, guided the SDA church for nearly 70 years, dying in 1915. She has been elevated to a role comparable to that of Mrs. Eddy in Christian Science with

Miller her Quimby. Here again Adventists cross swords with fellow fundamentalists who reject Mrs. White's visions and inspiration altogether.

By 1855 the sect had gained enough adherents in Michigan to establish a national headquarters in Battle Creek. Here they opened their first health sanitarium which has since passed from church control. The present name of the sect was adopted in 1860 and in 1903 headquarters were shifted to Takoma Park, a suburb of Washington, D. C. The General Conference, highest governing body, was organized during the Civil War.

From a visiting Seventh-day Baptist the Adventists picked up their second distinctive doctrine. Prophetess White confirmed this doctrinal standard by announcing that an angel had shown her the tablets of the Ten Commandments with a great halo of light surrounding the defiled Fourth (Catholic Third) commandment.

The 1906 religious census reported a SDA membership of 62,111. Fifty years later this enrollment had quadrupled in this country with even greater gains outside continental United States. Few denominations have done as well. The sect registers its largest membership in California, Oregon, Michigan, Washington, and New York.

Standards of personal conduct among Adventists are strict. Of course, no Adventist may drink or smoke. Other prohibitions include card playing, dancing, attendance at the movies or theater, costly or immodest apparel, jewelry, and lodge membership. Use of coffee, tea, and pepper is discouraged.

They observe the Sabbath from sundown Friday to sundown Saturday. Adventists attend church most of Saturday morning and abstain from all buying, selling, and unnecessary labor. Most food is prepared Friday before the Sabbath begins as in Orthodox Jewish households. Bible reading and study of church publications are recommended for the rest of the Sabbath.

Converts are instructed in the essentials of Adventism, and must promise to tithe, observe the Sabbath, and practice total abstinence before they are admitted to baptism. Baptism of adults by immersion is the rule.

Their worship service resembles that of other nonliturgical Protestant denominations. A foot washing ceremony in an adjoining room precedes the quarterly observance of the Lord's Supper. To Adventists as to others in the Reformed tradition this constitutes merely a memorial service; all those attending are invited to the communion table. Only grape juice is used. Incidentally, Adventists refuse to observe Easter which they call a pagan and unscriptural holiday.

Seventh-day Adventists have a habit of conducting proselytizing campaigns incognito. Advertisements in the daily newspaper ask "Will New York Be Destroyed by an H-bomb?" or "Does Russia Rule the Vatican?" Adventist sponsorship of the revivals goes unmentioned. Their widespread "Voice of Prophecy" radio program and "Faith for Today" TV series are also presented sans Adventist credit lines. Such approaches antagonize many Protestant ministers in the communities where they are used.

No church sponsors a more ambitious foreign mission program. Adventist medical, educational, and religious work is now carried on in 198 countries by some 39,000 salaried workers. The only nations not penetrated by indefatigable SDA evangelists are Afghanistan, Crete, and Vatican City. An ex-priest by the name of M. B. Czechowski inaugurated Adventist evangelism in Europe in the nineteenth century. Today three out of every four Seventh-day Adventists reside outside the United States which indicates the success of this missionary endeavor. For example, the entire population of Pitcairn Island of *Mutiny on the Bounty* fame has embraced the sect. Since the Adventists reveal a pronounced anti-Catholic bias they often find themselves in difficulties in Latin America, their principal mission field.

Health reform became a plank of the Adventist platform following a revelation to the prophetess in 1863. Members show a concern for health seldom found among other fundamentalists. In their chain of 114 hospitals and sanitariums and 82 clinics. Adventist doctors, nurses, dietitians, X-ray technicians, and dentists care for more than 2,000,000 patients each year. SDA institutions graduate 90 physicians and 450 nurses annually. Although they emphasize drugless healing and hydrotherapy they do not neglect surgery or modern drugs such as penicillin. *Life and Health* magazine features popular health articles with a SDA twist regarding alcohol and tobacco.

A flood of literature pours from 42 Adventist printing presses of which 34 are overseas. About 75 new book titles are issued yearly besides 348 periodicals in 198 languages. A quarterly magazine entitled *Liberty* advocates separation of Church and State and serves as an organ of the National Religious Liberty Association. Adventists oppose tax-supported welfare measures for parochial school pupils, including their own. Their publications regularly blast Blue Laws urged by fellow Protestants but paradoxically they also call for national prohibition.

Adventist scholars are thoroughly antievolutionist and have supplied this school with some of its most respected controversialists such as Prof. George McCready Price. They believe the earth was created in six literal days.

Seventh-day Adventists are not pacifists and do not seek exemption from military service. They call themselves "conscientious co-operators" rather than "conscientious objectors" since they do not dodge army service but only object to bearing arms. To prepare their young men for medical duty the sect operates 35 training programs each year. About 12,000 Adventists served as medical corpsmen during World War II and an Adventist corporal is one of the few noncombatants to receive the Congressional Medal of Honor.

Local church government is technically congregational. Actually the district conference appoints pastors and co-ordinates area activities and the General Conference wields great power. Pastors are called "Elder." Seminary training is not required for ordination but many receive a bachelor's degree in theology from a church college which serves the purpose. Women serve as grade school and Bible class teachers.

Adventists do not consider themselves bound by a creed. Nevertheless the annual *Yearbook* includes a statement of "Fundamental Beliefs of Seventh-day Adventists." They reject predestination and seem to stress man's co-operation in the work of justification more than most evangelicals.

Not all Adventists whose faith survived the Millerite debacle were attracted to Seventh-day Adventism. Four other Adventist sects, of which three are moribund and minuscule, are listed in religious directories. The *Advent Christian Church* which upholds the conscious state of the dead and the eternal punishment of the wicked and the observance of Sunday counts 30,000 members in the United States. The other tiny sects are the *Church of God (Abrahamic Faith)*, *Life and Advent Union*, and *Primitive Advent Christian Church*.

The SDA doctrines of soul-sleep after death and the annihilation of the wicked have been appropriated by Jehovah's Witnesses whose founder, Russell, received his introduction to millennialism in Adventism. However, Seventh-day Adventists differ from their Watchtower cousins in a number of respects, among which are the Saturday Sabbath, the character of the millennium, military service, voting and civic responsibilities, and the tithe.

Catholics may respect the Seventh-day Adventists for the sobriety of their lives, their missionary zeal, their generosity toward their church, their health contributions, their insistence on providing religious training for their children. At the same time the Catholic must reject their scriptural selectivity and juggling and deplore their crude attacks on the Church and other Christians. Many Adventists seem to have crossed over the line which separates the zealous from the fanatical.

Most Christians reject the dual doctrines proclaimed by the name Seventh-day Adventist since "The Sabbath was made for man, not man for the Sabbath" (Mk. 2:27) and they recall "Be not easily moved . . . neither by spirit, nor by word, nor by epistle as sent from us, as if the day of the Lord were at hand" (2 Thess. 2:2).

Chapter XIII

OTHER PROTESTANTS

American Protestantism Comprises More Than 210 Churches and Sects

Every second American Protestant is a Baptist or Methodist and 80 per cent of the Protestant Christians in this country belong to the 13 largest denominations. Nevertheless we find hundreds of smaller groups which are classified as Protestant for census and tabulation purposes. Actually, some of these are Protestant only in the sense in which they are not Catholic: Mormonism, Christian Science, Unitarianism, Spiritualism, and others. Many are subdivisions of denominational families such as the Two-Seed-in-the-Spirit Predestinarian Baptists and the Lumber River Annual Conference of the Holiness Methodist Church. Scores of sects belong to the Holiness and Pentecostal family and some are religious curiosities such as the "House of God, Which is the Church of the Living God, the Pillar and Ground of Truth, Inc." and the "House of David."

This chapter will examine a number of significant but smaller churches in the Protestant tradition. These include the Moravians, the Swiss and Dutch Mennonites, the Reformed and Christian Reformed, the Brethren or "Dunkers," the militant members of the Salvation Army, and the Swedish Mission Covenanters. All of these churches represent more or less distinct traditions and could not conveniently be grouped with other denominations.

THE MORAVIANS

One of the two Protestant bodies which predate the Reformation, the Moravian Church received its inspiration from the Bohemian heretic John Huss. (The other pre-Reformation Protestants are the Waldensians in northern Italy, who are few in number in the United States.)

Huss died at the stake in 1415. He appealed to the authority of the Bible alone, rejected the doctrine of purgatory and the invocation of the saints, and demanded the cup for the laity. His followers disagreed among themselves after his execution but a small group organized themselves in 1457 as the Unity of the Brethren or Unitas Fratrum. They wielded influence in Bohemia, Poland, and Moravia for more than two centuries. By the time Luther was nailing his Ninety-five theses to the Wittenberg church door this Bohemian Protestant church numbered about 175,000 members in 400 congregations.

The Counter-Reformation and the Thirty Years' War all but obliterated the Hussites, most of whom were absorbed into the Catholic, Lutheran, and Reformed churches. A few diehards kept alive Hussite beliefs and traditions and this underground church found a distinguished leader in the educator John Amos Comenius (1592–1670).

Count Nicholas Ludwig von Zinzendorf, a Lutheran layman, sponsored the Moravian revival in the eighteenth century. He turned over a corner of his Saxony estate to a nucleus of the Unitas Fratrum, nominally Catholic, with the thought that they would act as a leaven in the Lutheran establishment.

Eventually the Moravians at Herrnhut became a separate church and chose Zinzendorf as their bishop. The first large scale Protestant missionaries, they worked among Negro slaves on St. Thomas Island in the West Indies and among the Indians in Georgia. As we have seen, a band of Moravian missionaries traveling to the New World impressed John Wesley, the founder of Methodism, with their piety and faith. Moravianism multiplied its influence on Protestantism through Wesley and the Wesleyan revival.

Bethlehem and Nazareth in Pennsylvania and Salem in North Carolina became centers for American Moravianism. Zinzendorf himself visited this country in 1741 and for many years Moravian settlements in America were closely supervised from the German headquarters. Changes in the middle of the nineteenth century brought autonomy in church government to the American members. To this day the *Moravian Church in America* remains relatively small with about 56,000 members concentrated in half a dozen Eastern states. A later immigration of Czechs and Moravians in 1850 led to the formation of the 6000-member *Unity of the Brethren*.

Moravians are known for their liturgical worship, especially their outdoor Easter morning service. They follow the ancient church year, consecrate bishops with limited powers, emphasize mystical experience over doctrine, and support 13 foreign mission stations.

THE MENNONITES

Once the Reformation sundered the unity of Western Christendom, more radical groups than the Lutherans and Reformed urged a complete return to what they considered primitive Christianity. Chief among these sects were the various Anabaptist bodies which insisted that infant baptism was unscriptural. Adults who had been baptized as infants had to submit to rebaptism, hence the name Anabaptist.

One such Anabaptist sect in Zurich branded Zwingli a slow poke in 1525 and demanded a more thorough reformation and it is to this group that the Mennonite movement traces its origin. Elsewhere on the continent Anabaptists were persecuted by Protestants and Catholics and eventually got a bad name for fanaticism and excesses growing out of the latent antinomianism of their radical leaders. Menno Simons, a Catholic priest for 20 years, left the Church to join the conservative Anabaptist wing. He systematized its organization and theology and provided such outstanding leadership to these despised Anabaptists that their movement became known by his name, the Mennonites.

Swiss and Dutch Mennonites practice adult baptism by immersion, avoid "worldliness," adopt plain costumes, refuse to serve in the army or take an oath. The movement is a catalog of schisms. Jacob Ammon, a Swiss bishop, called the Mennonites back to a stricter discipline. His followers split the church in 1693 when they condemned the new fangled buttons which were replacing the traditional hooks-and-eyes. The Old Order Amish remain the ultraconservative branch of a conservative church refusing to compromise with the world in matters of automobiles, electricity, radios, tractors, and the like.

Another serious schism in Mennonite history grew out of a dispute about the foot washing ceremony. One faction held that one person should wash and wipe the feet while another faction argued that two people were needed, one to wash and one to wipe. A lively debate also rocked Mennonite churches over the question of whether a second band of suspenders constituted a luxury.

Lancaster, Pennsylvania, became the center for Swiss Mennonites in the United States although later immigrations brought the church to the Midwest. Mennonites are universally respected as scrupulously honest and God fearing. Despite a reluctance by some to adopt mechanized farming methods they are known to be excellent farmers. All branches of Mennonites oppose war, secret societies, fashions, oaths; some groups add objections to automobiles, radio and television, shaving, higher education, electric lights, telephones, and buttons. Members who attempt marriage outside the group or who violate church laws subject themselves to shunning whereby other Mennonites, even of the same family, discontinue all social fellowship and conversation with the excommunicated offender.

With fewer than 165,000 members in this country, the Mennonite movement is split into 12 sects. The largest are the *Mennonite Church* with 74,000 members and the slightly more liberal *General Conference Mennonite Church* with 36,000. There are about 20,000 Amish.

THE REFORMED

Calvinism took early root in Holland and Dutch colonists brought their Reformed Church to New Amsterdam. Their Collegiate church in New York City, organized in 1628, is the oldest Protestant church in the nation with an uninterrupted ministry. Members of this Dutch Calvinist church also founded a college at New Brunswick which later became Rutgers.

Church affairs were closely regulated by the Classis of Amsterdam until 1771 when the American branch won the right to train and ordain its own ministers. By 1830 the exclusive use of the Dutch language had ceased and a number of German immigrants had affiliated with the church; the present name, which eliminates a national label, was adopted in 1867. This *Reformed Church in America* reports 230,000 communicants. Its best known minister is Norman Vincent Peale, pastor of Marble Collegiate Church in New York City and author of the best-selling *The Power of Positive Thinking*. He began his ministerial career as a Methodist; in some Reformed churches the great majority of parishioners come from other Protestant denominations.

THE CHRISTIAN REFORMED

A protest against laxism in the Dutch Reformed Church led to the formation of the strict *Christian Reformed Church* in 1857. Ministers of 20 congregations accused the mother church of diluting Calvinism, slighting the doctrine of predestination, and tolerating Masonry and other secret societies. Within a decade the protesters had been reduced to a handful but immigrants from Holland and anti-Masonic dissenters from the parent body added new strength.

This church supports a seminary and college in Grand Rapids, Michigan, and operates 246 parochial schools for parents of 50,000 pupils who wish to educate their children in uncompromising Calvinism. Since its founding the Christian Reformed Church has held fast to the rigid Calvinism of the Heidelberg, Dortrecht, and Belgic Confessions. This church belongs to neither the National nor World Councils of Churches. It has experienced a rapid growth in recent years and now, with 250,000 members, has finally surpassed the mother church in membership. The Christian Reformed Church gives us a glimpse of Geneva Calvinism in twentieth-century America.

THE BRETHREN

Dunkers and German Baptists are other names applied to members of the *Church of the Brethren*. They baptize by trine immersion: the adult believer kneels in the water and is immersed not once but three times in the name of the Trinity.

An outgrowth of the Pietistic movement in the state Lutheran church in Germany, the Brethren church follows the teachings of Alexander Mack. Mack baptized seven followers at Schwarzenau in 1708 and in turn was baptized by them.

Persecution by the state and the state church drove most of the Brethren to America after 1719 and most of them settled in Germantown, Pennsylvania, on invitation of William Penn. Mack himself arrived with 30 families in 1729. The Brethren have retained many Old World customs and the German language, and their churches are generally found in rural areas.

They reject the Old Testament which records wars, slavery, and divorce but reverence the New Testament in which they maintain Christ instituted four ordinances: adult baptism by trine immersion, the Lord's Supper including a foot washing ceremony and the agape or love feast, anointing of the sick with oil, and the imposition of hands on Christian workers. Strongly pacifist, they not only protest against war but undertake extensive relief and rehabilitation programs.

The Brethren Service Committee, organized in 1940, sponsored a "heifers for relief" plan in which several thousand heifers were donated by individuals and churches and sent to Europe and Asia. Brethren young people volunteered to become "seagoing cowboys" on ships which transported the cattle.

Ephrata Cloisters in Pennsylvania, a Protestant monastic community founded by Conrad Beissel, broke away from the Church of the Brethren 20 years after the church was founded. Protestant monks and nuns, vowed to celibacy, engaged in farming, printing and weaving. By 1770 the Cloisters housed 135 members but the movement declined after the turn of the century.

The 200,000 Brethren in this country are expected to observe total abstinence and to avoid luxuries such as jewelry. They operate six colleges, a seminary, and mission enterprises in India, Puerto Rico, and Africa. Four smaller Brethren sects are the *Brethren Church* (Progressive) with 25,000 members, the *Brethren Church* (Ashland, Ohio) with 18,000, the *Old German Baptist Brethren* with 4000, and the tiny *Church of God* (New Dunkards).

THE SALVATIONISTS

In its war against "slumdom, rumdom and bumdom" the *Salvation Army* adopted a military form of organization which suggests a comparison with a Catholic religious order. Popular opinion often views the Salvation Army as a relief agency with religious undertones. On the contrary, the Army is an evangelical Protestant sect which carries out its religious mission through social service.

Founded by a saintly Methodist minister in England, the "Christian Mission" carried the gospel to the vicious slums of London. But William Booth found his poor converts felt unwelcome in the "respectable" churches, Methodist or Anglican, and he found it necessary to provide separate worship services and church facilities. The name, Salvation Army, and the military organization were adopted in 1878 and Booth became General Booth.

Clergymen were officers of this army with titles from lieutenant to general. Converts became recruits and soldiers and wore a military uniform after they had signed the "Articles of War" against liquor, tobacco, and vice. Orders come from the top and are obeyed by junior officers. The Salvation Army officer wears a uniform at all times, receives "marching orders" to a new post, progresses through a system of ranks, receives a salute, takes his vacation as a "furlough," participates in "knee drills" or prayer meetings, and is lowered into his grave to the sound of taps.

Officers are recruited from the ranks of soldiers and are selected to attend an intensive 12-month course at one of the four Officers Training Colleges in the United States. On graduation he or she is commissioned a probationary lieutenant. Salvation Army officers may perform marriages, preach, christen children, and serve as armed forces chaplains. They agree to marry within the Army family and to serve at their post for life. A wife holds equal rank with her husband.

No longer does the Army confine its activities to skid row. Extensive programs for children and families have been developed. The street meeting with brass band and preaching, however, continues to be the basic Army evangelistic technique.

Converts are expected to don the military uniform as soldiers and commit themselves to saving sinners although they may keep their secular occupations. Many are reluctant to devote their lives to this work and are free to join other churches. About 5500 full-time officers supervise the volunteer local officers and soldiers in the Army's widespread activities: citadels (local churches), relief associations, summer camps, hospitals, homes for unmarried mothers, publications, nurseries and day schools, orphanages. No Protestant church approaches the scope of the Army's welfare work.

Theologically the Salvation Army follows the original Wesleyan emphasis including belief in the Baptism of the Holy Spirit or entire sanctification as preached by the Holiness sects. They uphold man's free will and deny that man's spiritual powers were utterly destroyed by the Fall, contrary to Luther and Calvin. With the Quakers they reject baptism and the Lord's Supper as unnecessary rituals. Booth debated whether to continue the Lord's Supper and his decision was based on three factors: the use of wine in the service might tempt his alcoholic converts, the public might object to women officers administering the communion, and the interpretation of the Eucharist had divided Christians in the past. The Salvation Army offers classical Methodism without sacraments.

In place of baptism the Army conducts the Dedication of Children using the following formula: "In the name of the Lord and of the —— Corps of the Salvation Army, I have taken this child, who has been fully given up by his parents for the salvation of the world. God save, bless, and keep this child. Amen." Other ceremonies in the Army are the swearing in of soldiers, the presentation of colors, covenant services, and marriage.

Two defections from the Salvation Army led to the organization of groups with similar objectives but more democratic principles. The first, the *American Rescue Workers*, was begun just two years after the Army invaded this country in 1880. In 1896 General Booth's son and his wife seceded and started the *Volunteers of America*. This sect now numbers 28,000 members and has done outstanding work among prisoners, parolees, and their families. Unlike the Salvationists, the Rescue Workers and Volunteers observe baptism and the Lord's Supper.

General Booth's devoted wife and mother of his eight children died in 1890 but the General continued his tireless efforts for the down and out. He visited America every four years. He was honored by kings and presidents, received honorary doctorates from Oxford and Brussels Universities. He died blind and penniless at the age of 84.

THE COVENANTERS

A protest against the formalism of the state Lutheranism of Sweden began in mission societies within the Lutheran church and developed into the *Evangelical Covenant Church of America*.

Transplanted to the United States by Swedish immigrants, the church was formally organized in Chicago about 75 years ago. The majority of Swedes who remained Christian, however, allied themselves with the Swedish Lutheran Church, now the Augustana Synod, or Swedish Methodist and Baptist groups. Since the local Covenant church is independent and autonomous its members are sometimes known as Swedish Congregationalists. Like the Congregationalists, they are creedless and nonliturgical.

A few non-Swedes have affiliated with this church which seems to be moving further from Lutheran orthodoxy. It supports North Park College and Seminary and reports 61,000 members. For many years it was known as the Mission Covenant Church.

Chapter XIV

THE CULTISTS

"Christian" by Courtesy

Wₕₑₙ a hapless United Nations mediator pleaded with the Arabs and Jews in Palestine to sit down and settle their dispute like "good Christians" he was voicing a current platitude. To many Americans "Christian" has become a synonym for decent, gentlemanly, and democratic.

Consequently, we find a variety of religious bodies commonly identified as Christian although they cannot make the remotest claim to the title. Some of these groups deny the most fundamental Christian beliefs such as the divinity of Christ, the existence of evil, the trinity, original sin, and the redemption, but they enjoy the prestige which accrues to a Christian church in a professedly Christian nation. Often these cults appeal to private revelations, such as those claimed by Swedenborg and Joe Smith, and to scriptures, such as *Science and Health With Key to the Scriptures,* which Christians, Catholic and Protestant, reject. Some cults make no claim to be Christian but are so identified in the popular mind. Still other cults, such as Theosophy, Baha'i, Rosicrusianism, I AM, Father Divine's Peace Mission, and Vedanta, stand wholly outside the Christian tradition and as such do not fall within the scope of our discussion any more than do Islam, Buddhism, or Confucianism.

In this and the following three chapters we will discuss a number of cults which we must classify as "Christian by courtesy." A careful examination of their tenets will disclose no warrant for

extending to them the title "Christian" even though the cultists
themselves may appropriate the name. The three largest of these
non-Christian cults are Christian Science, Mormonism and Jehovah's
Witnesses to each of which we shall devote a separate chapter.
Four of the smaller American cults constitute the subject matter
of the present chapter. These cults are no more Protestant than
they are Catholic and we must beware of labeling all non-Catholic
and non-Orthodox groups as Protestant. To establish the basic principles of Protestantism — justification by faith alone, the supreme
authority of the Bible, the priesthood of all believers — and then
classify as Protestant cults which deny any or all of these principles
would be absurd. Simply because they have arisen in Western
nations since the Reformation is no indication that they are Protestant churches and sects.

THE SWEDENBORGIANS

After a distinguished scientific career a latter day Leonardo da
Vinci by the name of Emmanuel Swedenborg turned to religion.
A Ph.D. at the age of 21, he had mastered the mathematics, anatomy,
and science of his day, traveled throughout Europe, and written
60 books and pamphlets when, at the age of 55, he announced that
he had received the power to live in two worlds, the material and
the spiritual.

This respected Swedish scientist abandoned science to produce 29
volumes in Latin which described the spirit world in detail and
presented his own peculiar version of the Gospel. He recounted his
spirit conversations with St. Paul, Luther, infidels, angels, popes, and
Moslems. He had earlier rejected the doctrine of justification by
faith alone as had his father, a Lutheran bishop. Now he discounted
the Trinity and other traditional Christian beliefs. He claimed to
have witnessed the Last Judgment which took place in 1757.

Swedenborg devised an allegorical interpretation of the Bible in
which stones always represented truth, houses meant intelligence,
snakes were carnality, cities were religious systems, and so on.

At death, Swedenborg explained, man awakens in the spirit world and continues a life quite similar to his earthly existence. Eventually each man goes to the realm in which he will feel most at home: heaven, the spirit world (similar to purgatory), or hell. Bachelor Swedenborg revealed that marriage continues in the next world as an eternal relationship although there may be some reshuffling of partners. He carefully described the flora and fauna of heaven as well as the appearance of the inhabitants of other planets such as Mercury, Jupiter, Mars, and the Moon.

Despite these bizarre revelations Swedenborg continued to enjoy the respect of his fellow Swedes. He seldom attended the state Lutheran church because he complained that spirits kept interrupting the sermons and contradicting the minister. He also won a reputation as a seer by disclosing a number of secrets and reporting events at a distance such as the details of a Stockholm fire some 300 miles from his home.

He did not found a church. An English printer and some Anglican clergymen initiated the Swedenborg movement in 1783, eleven years after the seer's death in London. Lancashire became the main center for the *Church of the New Jerusalem*. The original American branch was founded in Baltimore in 1792 and a secession produced a second, smaller body in 1890. Together the Americans make up about half of the world's 12,000 Swedenborgians.

The larger body, the General Convention, maintains a theological seminary at Cambridge, Massachusetts, and most of its members may be found on the Atlantic seaboard. Swedenborg's works are offered in inexpensive editions and a modest advertising program has been launched but no one seems particularly interested in the Swedish seer. Barron, the financial expert, and Helen Keller are probably the best known Swedenborgians. The father of William and Henry James was a Swedenborgian.

Nevertheless Swedenborg exerted an influence on modern Spiritualism by claiming immediate contact with the spirit world. His view on eternal marriage was elaborated by the Mormons. The Swedenborgian cult, however, is now intellectually stagnant and declining in membership.

THE SPIRITUALISTS

Attempts to pierce the veil of death and communicate with the spirits of the departed are recorded in man's earliest history. But modern spiritualism began with the Fox sisters in Hydesville, N. Y., and March 31, 1848, is usually given as the founding date.

The Fox family, which included two little girls, Kate and Margaret, occupied a cottage known by their neighbors to be haunted. Strange nocturnal rappings and noises had been heard in the house for some time and on March 31 little Kate addressed the noisemaker: "Here, Mr. Splitfoot, do as I do." The spirit responded and a rapping code was devised.

The two sisters, exploited by an older sister Leah, went on tour and staged public demonstrations of the mysterious rappings in many American cities. The new religion attracted hundreds of thousands of enthusiasts and gave rise to a flood of spiritualist publications. Horace Greeley of the *New York Tribune* contributed many newspaper columns of publicity to the Fox exhibitions.

Margaret eventually entered a common law marriage, gave birth to a son, turned to drink, and finally startled the Spiritualist world by announcing her conversion to Catholicism. She admitted the whole thing was a hoax and demonstrated how she and her sister Kate had produced the loud rappings by snapping their toes. "I know that every so-called manifestation produced through me in London or anywhere else was a fraud," she confessed. Her exposé failed to shake the faith of the hard-core believers and Margaret herself eventually recanted and returned to Spiritualism to eke out a living.

Meanwhile Andrew Jackson Davis, the Poughkeepsie seer, provided a systematic Spiritualist theology and terminology in 33 volumes supposedly written with spirit aid. He, rather than the discredited Fox sisters, is considered by many devotees to be the real founder of the religion but the Fox sisters are esteemed by most Spiritualists and the Hydesville cottage has become a shrine.

Spiritualism reached its membership peak within five years after its dramatic arrival on the American scene. By the first part of

the present century it had all but disappeared, only to be revived
after World War I. American Spiritualism never achieved the respectability of English Spiritualism which counted A. Conan Doyle
(and presumably Sherlock Holmes) and Sir Oliver Lodge among
its propagandists. Exposures and fraud have harried the Spiritualist
cause in the United States and few intellectuals have taken it
seriously.

Spiritualist mediums use various physical devices to prove their
powers of spirit communication. These include the time-tested rappings, the ouija board, slate writing, spirit photography, levitation,
telekinesis (moving heavy objects without visible means), clairvoyance, knowledge of foreign tongues, and automatic writing. In a
typical seance the medium sits with a circle of devotees and attempts
to establish contact by rappings or voice with the deceased. At times
a go-between or "control" relays messages from the deceased to the
medium. Healing services are also conducted by some Spiritualists.

Harry Houdini, the magician, claimed he could duplicate any
Spiritualistic phenomena by legerdemain. He exposed dozens of
mediums and published his findings after 25 years' study in A
Magician Among the Spirits. A number of Societies for Psychical Re-
search have studied alleged Spiritualistic phenomenon in the United
States and Europe.

Spiritualists ignore most Christian doctrines although they sometimes seek incorporation as a Christian church. They usually refer
to Christ as an exceptionally able medium and adduce the annunciation, transfiguration, and resurrection as spirit phenomenon. The
theology of Spiritualism pays little attention to God and ends up
as a base ancestor worship. The highest ideal apparently is to be
assured that one's loved ones are happy and contented in the spirit
world. Spiritualism is singularly free of ethical or social content.

Spiritualists describe seven levels of life after death and claim
that most of mankind begin their upward evolution in the third or
Summerland sphere. The religion is universalist and no one ends
up in hell. The first of the seven levels is thought to start about 300
miles above the earth's surface and the seventh heaven begins at
18,000 miles. Life in Summerland seems to resemble life on earth

except that sorrow and evil are missing. The dead marry their soul mates, live in houses, wear clothes, keep pets. The trite and contradictory messages received from the "other side" disappoint many who investigate Spiritualism from a religious motive.

Women dominate the movement but men usually hold the top national offices. About 500 local congregations are grouped in a dozen denominations. The oldest (1893) and largest is the *National Spiritualist Association of Churches* which prescribes rituals for worship, baptisms and funerals and ordains clergymen, licentiates, and mediums. Congregations are likely to meet in private homes or hotel rooms rather than church buildings. Other national organizations are the *National Christian Spiritual Alliance* and the *International General Assembly of Spiritualists*, a co-operative federation which claims 164,000 members. Most Spiritualist churches meet in rented halls, hotel rooms, or private homes. Perhaps 180,000 Americans are affiliated with recognized Spiritualist churches but many times this number can be considered fellow travelers to the spirit world.

All Spiritualist spokesmen admit that fraudulent mediums abound in the movement but they insist there remains a hard core of sincere devoted mediums. Some associations seek to raise the educational requirements for Spiritualist clergymen, and a seminary in Wisconsin, the Morris Pratt Institute, offers a course for would-be mediums. Summer sessions are featured at Lily Dale, N. Y., and Chesterfield, Ind.

Outside of the explanation of deliberate fraud and collusion which probably account for 95 per cent of spiritualistic phenomena, there remains the possibility of extra-sensory perception and the intervention of the devil. Catholics are forbidden on pain of serious sin to participate in a seance even out of curiosity. Some Catholic nations such as Brazil find Spiritualism a danger to the faith hardly less destructive than communism.

Spiritualism may attract some bereaved Christians by offering an assurance from the other world that the departed loved one is safe and happy. For some it supposedly offers tangible evidence of a hereafter which some Protestant churches seldom mention. Many people dabble in Spiritualism and drift in and out of the movement. Spiritualism's religious impulse is slight. Not worship of God but chats with the dead is its motivation.

THE UNITY SCHOOL OF CHRISTIANITY

Unity School of Christianity, a Christian Science heresy, propagates its religion of optimism and healthy mindedness from a 1300-acre farm and headquarters near Kansas City. Unlike Eddyism it acknowledges the reality of sin, sickness, and death but asserts that these can all be overcome by mind.

Each year millions of copies of a half dozen attractive periodicals and pamphlets are mailed from the 100-man printing plant at Lee's Summit. These include *Unity, Weekly Unity, Good Business, Daily Word, You,* and *Wee Wisdom.* Many Protestants and Catholics read Unity literature without ever bothering to investigate Unity's philosophy and religious basis.

Myrtle and Charles Fillmore were debt ridden and sickly before discovering the transforming principles of Unity. Both had studied Christian Science and the new religion which they taught after 1889 was patterned after Mrs. Eddy's creation.

Devotees were encouraged to think good thoughts, dismissing the delusion that sickness and death had any power over them. They were expected to observe a vegetarian diet and limit sex functions to procreation. From the beginning the Fillmores used the U. S. mails as their pulpit and relied wholly on voluntary contributions. Unlike Christian Science practitioners they made no charge for their healings which were published as testimonials in their magazines.

Mr. and Mrs. Fillmore established Silent Unity which offers a round-the-clock prayer service for all who phone, wire, or write for such help. A corps of Unity employees is on duty at all times to answer these appeals for prayers and to accept love offerings. An average week brings 10,000 appeals.

Myrtle and Charles Fillmore are both dead but their sons carry on the work. Unity moved to the new headquarters, eighteen miles from downtown Kansas City, in 1949. The property now includes an administration building, a 170-foot tower, a 22-acre artificial lake, training school, Unity Inn (vegetarian menu), the printing plant, swimming pool, golf course, picnic areas, and amphitheater. More than 700 Unity workers are employed at Lee's Summit.

Unity claims to be a school of practical Christianity rather than a sect, but in practice it is indistinguishable from a sect. The training school offers a four-month course for ministers which is supplemented by correspondence study. Some 500 local congregations known as Unity Centers sponsor worship services, healing services, Sunday Schools. Ministers baptize converts (sometimes with rose petals instead of water) and are authorized to marry couples.

Unity converts are not required to sever connections with their former churches as is demanded of Christian Scientists. Many find the Christianity of their own churches prosaic compared to the esoteric teachings of Unity; they are likely to rely more and more on Unity Centers and Unity ministers for their spiritual needs.

Unity students interpret the Bible allegorically and strip Christianity of its essential doctrines. A Hindu or Jew would find little to upset his religious sensibilities in Unity literature. In fact, the Hindu might feel more at home perusing Unity books than the Christian since the sect teaches that the soul passes through various reincarnations "till we all come into Unity." Unity sponsors no social welfare programs, hospitals, orphanages, or homes for the aged.

For all practical purposes Unity has become another sect and its claims to be nothing but a school of Christianity and nonsectarian are misleading. Its well-printed publications no doubt offer some comfort and inspiration to many millions who do not care about the cult's basic philosophy. Certainly, few Unity readers subscribe to Unity's belief in reincarnation. Were they to dig deeper into Unity they would find a school not of practical but of gnostic Christianity.

THE MORAL REARMAMENT MOVEMENT

What once went by the name of the Oxford Group, Buchmanism, and the First Century Christian Fellowship now calls itself *Moral*

Rearmament. Labels come and go in this movement but its destiny is still guided by the tireless Frank Buchman, an ordained but unorthodox Lutheran minister.

Buchman gained fame in the 1920's when he launched his movement among college men and women. He had spent some time as a missionary in China, pastor of a rundown parish, and Y.M.C.A. director at the University of Pennsylvania where he developed the technique of the religious house party. At these week-end parties, somewhat resembling a retreat, the participants not only engaged in prayer, meditation, and Bible study but also in open confession, including confession of sexual sins. When Buchman accused 95 per cent of Princeton undergraduates of practicing sexual perversion, the president of the university forbade him ever to step foot on that campus.

The Oxford Groupers (not to be confused with the nineteenth-century Oxford Movement in the Church of England) plan to reform the world by moral and spiritual force. They stress four absolutes: absolute honesty, absolute purity, absolute unselfishness, and absolute love. The name "Oxford" serves this American-made movement well. It was bestowed by a group of South African enthusiasts and the only connection between the movement and the university was that Buchman happened to visit Oxford in 1921.

Conversion plays an important part in the movement. The convert is asked to confess his sins openly, sever himself from all sin and surrender to the will of God, make restitution of any wrongs against God or neighbor, and cultivate the guidance of the Holy Spirit. Members are enjoined to spend at least 15 minutes each morning in Quiet Time during which they listen to the promptings of the Holy Spirit and write down the inspirations and answers they receive. Of course, Catholics who would rely on such personal messages from God would be likely to fall into the heresy of illuminism, the error of basing one's religious life on the immediate guidance of the Holy Spirit independent of the Church.

A prominent Episcopal rector lent his support and prestige to the Oxford Group for many years and the Biblical scholar B. H. Streeter endorsed Buchmanism. Today MRA employs the services of 2,000 full time workers who have turned over their possessions to the movement and receive only room, board, and a nominal allowance.

When Buchman declared, "I thank heaven for a man like Adolph Hitler who built a first line defense against the Anti-Christ of Communism," he brought the suspicion, probably undeserved, of fascism on the organization. The name "Moral Rearmament" began to be used after a meeting of the cult in the Black Forest in Germany in 1937 and is now the common name. Buchman continued to dictate all MRA policies until his death in 1961. International headquarters are maintained at Caux, Switzerland, and rallies are held at a multi-million dollar center on Mackinac Island, Michigan.

Bishop Thomas L. Noa of the Diocese of Marquette (which includes Mackinac Island) issued a pastoral directive in 1958 which bans participation in MRA to Catholics of his diocese and to all other Catholics who come within the see's jurisdiction. The bishop declared: "It is our duty to bring to the attention of Catholics that MRA, whatever its good intentions, assumes the role of spiritual direction and guidance for which it does not have divine authority."

As early as 1938 Cardinal Hinsley of England forbade Catholics under his care from taking an active part in MRA and in 1946 the bishops of England and Wales declared: "The movement is so tainted with indifferentism, i.e., with the error that one religion is as good as another, that no Catholic may take an active part therein or formally cooperate therewith. Catholics should be warned not even to attend the meetings or gatherings even as spectators." Later the Sacred Congregation of the Holy Office specifically forbade priests and religious from affiliating with MRA and discouraged participation by the Catholic laity.

Chapter XV

THE MORMONS

"What Man Is Now God Once Was; What God Is Now Man May Become"

MORE than a million and a half Americans who claim the name Christian believe:

That Christ preached to the American Indians after His ascension and founded a church among them for the Western hemisphere;

That an angel revealed the history of these people on golden plates to a young man in New York in 1827 and furnished magic spectacles to enable him to translate the record;

That this youth re-established the church of Christ which had been wiped out in the Americas and had apostasized elsewhere;

That there is not one God but many gods for many worlds;

That man lived with God in a previous existence and that after death he may become a god for his own planet;

That polygamy is the divine pattern of marriage.

These people are "Mormons" or, properly speaking, members of the *Church of Jesus Christ of Latter-day Saints*. Obviously they are neither Catholic nor Protestant and their flourishing religion is a curious mixture of paganism, Judaism, Christianity, Swedenborgianism, Spiritism, and Campbellism. Like many cults it prefers to masquerade as a Christian religion. In fact, it asserts that it is the only true Christian religion.

Preponderant in Utah and strong in Idaho, Arizona, California, and other Western states, Mormonism can boast a doubled membership in 25 years. From 215,000 adherents recorded in the 1906 census, the Utah church has grown to 1,595,000 members in 3566 congregations or wards. An unusually high birth rate, low death rate, and aggressive missionary program account for the growth of this bizarre sect into one of the leading denominations in the United States.

Anyone who knows Mormons personally or who has visited Mormondom's world headquarters in Salt Lake City will attest to the good example they present to their "Gentile" neighbors (Mormons consider all non-Mormons including Jews as Gentiles). Kindness, industry, hospitality, cleanliness, zeal, sobriety, and high moral standards characterize the believing Latter-day Saint. That the hodgepodge of heresies which is Mormonism can produce such results is a continual source of amazement.

Mormondom is split into two main branches and a handful of tiny schismatic bodies. The main branch in Utah represents the majority of early Saints who followed Brigham Young westward after the Prophet's assassination. The other significant body of Mormons, the *Reorganized Church of Jesus Christ of Latter-day Saints*, objected to Young's leadership and eventually rallied around Joseph Smith's son. Its 158,000 members look to Independence, Missouri, as their Mecca. Except where noted our comments will apply to the larger Utah or Brighamite group rather than the so-called Josephites who reject polygamy, the plurality of gods, the Adam-god doctrine, and other Utah dogmas.

Joseph Smith is popularly credited with being the founder of this religion. That he served as its Prophet for 15 years no one denies but a number of students of the movement, such as Linn, Shook, and Arbaugh, maintain that the real founder was a disaffected Campbellite preacher, Sidney Rigdon.

Smith, a Vermonter by birth, was a visionary, lazy, good natured young blood who passed his time hunting buried treasure by means of "peep stones." According to his own account and official Mormon history he was visited by a number of angels from the time he reached 14. One such angel, Moroni, informed him that all existing churches were in error, corrupt and apostate. His mission was to re-establish the true church and priesthood. Finally the angel gave him permission to dig near the top of the Hill Cumorah, near Palmyra, New York. There he unearthed a box of golden plates inscribed in "Reformed Egyptian." The obliging angel also supplied him with a pair of magic spectacles called the Urim and Thummin which enabled him to decipher the hieroglyphics.

Unable to write himself, the 22-year-old Smith employed various amanuenses, including Oliver Cowdery, an unemployed schoolteacher. Sitting behind a blanket he dictated the *Book of Mormon*, the supposed history of the original inhabitants of this continent from 600 B.C. to A.D. 421.

According to this fantastic book North and South America were peopled by Jews who came by ship from Palestine. Two nations arose, the Lamanites and the Nephites. Essentially Mormonism is based on a version of the lost tribes of Israel legend; Cotton Mather, Roger Williams, and William Penn also speculated that the American Indians were Jews. Other variations of the lost tribes legend place the Israelites in Ireland, Japan, England (Anglo-Israel cult), and the lost continent of Atlantis.

The Mormon Bible relates that Christ appeared among the Nephites, chose 12 Indian apostles and set up a church which was a counterpart of the church he had established in Jerusalem. Eventually the dissolute Lamanites destroyed the virtuous Nephites in a battle near Palmyra in A.D. 421. Moroni, son of the vanquished Nephite general Mormon, buried the golden plates which recounted the history of his race. The plates also recorded the history of the Jaredites who were supposed to have come to America after the confusion of tongues at the Tower of Babel.

After translating the Reformed Egyptian, Smith delivered the plates and goggles to the angel and they have not been seen since. Linguists know nothing about a language called Reformed Egyptian and some of Smith's early disciples urged him to submit a specimen to a scholar in order to confound the skeptics. He copied down what he called some "caractors" and presented them to Prof. Charles Anthon of Columbia College. Anthon declared that the sample consisted of "all kinds of crooked characters, disposed in columns . . .

evidently prepared by some person who had before him at the time
a book containing various alphabets." He repeatedly denied the
Mormon claim that he had declared the markings to be genuine
"Reformed Egyptian."

The original edition listed Joseph Smith, Junior, as "Author and
Proprietor" but this admission was later wisely deleted. Of the
11 witnesses who testified to having seen the plates none ever
admitted he had been duped or had perjured himself. Martin
Harris, a farmer who mortgaged his land to pay the printer, testified
in court years later that he had seen the plates "with the eyes of
faith . . . though at the time they were covered over with a cloth."
Five of the witnesses were Whitmers and three were Smiths including the Prophet's father. Harris, Cowdery, and David Whitmer
eventually apostatized; the latter pair were driven out of Missouri
by 80 Mormons who signed a complaint that they were thieves and
counterfeiters.

Lengthy passages from the New Testament were included verba-
tim in the Book of Mormon and the entire book, supposedly written
before A.D. 421, is phrased in King James idioms. It abounds in
anachronisms, contradictions, and stock Campbellite answers to the
theological questions of the early nineteenth century. At times its
hindsight prophecy becomes entangled in such statements as "the
Son of God shall be born of Mary at Jerusalem." Shakespearean students will be surprised to find the phrase "the undiscovered country
from whose bourne no traveller returns" appearing in a passage
written 2200 years before the Bard.

Some "Gentile" scholars accept the Spaulding theory of the
origin of the Book of Mormon. Solomon Spaulding, a retired Presbyterian minister, amused himself by composing a romance about
the American Indians. He offered the manuscript to a Pittsburgh
printer and left his novel with the printer when he moved from
the area. One of the frequenters of this print shop was a certain
Sidney Rigdon.

Rigdon, originally a Baptist preacher, expressed a growing dissatisfaction with the treatment accorded him by the Campbellites;
he saw an opportunity to found a church of his own as Alexander

Campbell had done. He needed a book to impress the bibliolaters of the age.

Rigdon apparently added the Campbellite theology and scriptural exerpts to the Spaulding novel and entered into a partnership with Smith whose reputation as a visionary and occultist had spread throughout the countryside. Unfortunately for the ambitious Rigdon he underestimated his stooge. He never managed to displace his accomplice or even hold his own in the church and he died as head of a minuscule splinter sect.

A few other non-Mormon critics acknowledge Smith as the real author and suggest that anyone with a smattering of the Bible and a lively imagination could have done as well in a credulous era. At least one scholar maintains that Smith was an epileptic and attributes the book to automatic writing.

Smith relates that John the Baptist appeared to Cowdery and himself in 1829 and ordained them into the Aaronic priesthood. The two baptized each other in the Susquehanna River. Later the Apostles Peter, James, and John conferred the higher priesthood of Melchizedek.

The tiny church, organized at Fayette, New York, the next year, moved to Kirtland, Ohio, where Rigdon was pastor of a church. Here they found a ready welcome, built their first temple, chose 12 apostles to assist President Smith, and attempted to establish a communist order. Another band of Mormons continued to Missouri and two Mormon settlements continued for some years 1000 miles apart.

Smith went to Missouri on a scouting expedition in 1831 and dedicated 63 acres in Jackson County which was proclaimed the exact site of the Temple of Zion where Christ would live and rule after His Second Coming. Today a tiny splinter group of Mormons owns the holy ground but has no funds to build the Temple. The schismatics say they have refused an offer of $5 million from the Utah Mormons for the property.

With the failure of a wildcat bank and impending indictment, Smith and Rigdon fled Kirtland by night and headed for the Missouri colony. Here the strange beliefs of the Mormon settlers and their suspected anti-slavery attitudes had antagonized the Missourians. Riots and incessant squabbles between Saints and Gentiles prompted the governor to call out the militia and the Mormons were expelled from the state in midwinter 1838–1839. Smith had been imprisoned for 4½ months as a hostage and when he escaped he rejoined the Saints in neighboring Illinois.

Purchasing swampland on the Mississippi River, the Saints began to build their city of Nauvoo, which Smith maintained was a Hebrew word meaning "the beautiful." Its 20,000 citizens made it the largest city in the state and it received a liberal municipal charter. Thousands of English converts followed the exhortations of the Mormon missionaries to gather in Zion. To this day both Utah and Missouri Mormons look for the establishment of Zion at the Second Coming at Independence, Missouri (also reputed to be the site of the Garden of Eden).

The industrious Saints built a handsome temple at Nauvoo, laid out broad streets, built substantial homes and factories. Smith recruited a private army, the Nauvoo Legion, and designated himself as lieutenant general.

Rumors of polygamy, envy of Mormon prosperity, fear of the Saints' political power and dominance stirred the Gentiles to provocative actions. Smith contributed to the unrest when he announced himself a candidate for the presidency of the United States on a three plank platform of abolition, nationalization of the banks, and prison reform. Rigdon ran for vice-president and Mormon missionaries were pressed into service as campaign spokesmen.

Disgruntled ex-Saints attempted to publish an anti-Smith newspaper in Nauvoo but Smith ordered his henchmen to pi the type and smash the presses. When the governor of Illinois promised Smith protection and safe conduct, he agreed to appear in Carthage to face charges of immorality, counterfeiting, sheltering criminals, and treason. But a mob of 200 men with blackened faces stormed the Carthage jail and shot the Prophet and his brother Hyrum to death. The Mormon prophet was dead at 39.

In stricken Nauvoo rivals vied for positions of leadership. The murder of Smith and his brother, the heir apparent, left the community in an unforeseen quandary. When Brigham Young returned from a mission in New England he managed to win the confidence of most of the bewildered Saints. Rigdon was banished. Many abandoned the Prophetless church and a minority which insisted that the leader should be a lineal descendant of the Prophet formed the nucleus of the Reorganized faction. Smith's widow Emma married a Nauvoo tavern keeper, raised her family in the deserted city of Nauvoo, and eventually joined the Reorganized Church.

The demoralized Saints found an outstanding leader in Young. An ex-Methodist and fellow Vermonter, Young had joined the Prophet in Kirtland and never seemed to doubt Smith's extravagant claims. Although he had the benefit of only 11 days of formal schooling, this determined carpenter would build a theocratic empire in the West.

Realizing the precarious situation of the Saints in Nauvoo Brigham Young set about organizing the epic march to the West. To all who asked why he was leading the Saints out of Illinois he had one answer: "To get away from Christians and out of the United States." The first party left the state in the middle of winter, 1846. By April the last of the Saints had bidden farewell to their homes, factories, fields and temple in Nauvoo. Thousands would never reach their destination.

"This is the place" declared Young on July 24, 1847, when his advance party reached the valley of the Great Salt Lake, then a part of Mexico. The Mormons made the desert bloom. They irrigated the land, planted trees, built homes, hauled huge blocks of granite for their new temple.

After the Mexican War the Saints found themselves subject to the same United States government from which they had fled. Congress turned down their petition for statehood for the "State of Deseret" but Young was appointed first governor of the Utah territory. Polygamy was traded for statehood in 1896 when Utah became the 45th state in the union.

After 1853 polygamy was openly practiced and defended. The Utah Mormons claim that Smith received the revelation on plural marriage at Nauvoo in 1843 but the controversial doctrine was not published until the Saints were safely entrenched in their intermountain sanctuary. Obviously polygamy was an afterthought since the Book of Mormon plainly states: "Wherefore, my brethren, hear me, and hearken to the word of the Lord: For there shall not any man among you save it be one wife; and concubines he shall have none" (Jacob 2:26). In other passages in the Mormon scriptures polygamy is called an "abomination before the Lord" and in *Doctrine and Covenants*, published in 1835, we read: "Inasmuch as this Church of Christ has been reproached with the crime of fornication and polygamy, we declare that we believe that one man should have one wife, and one woman one husband, except in case of death, when either is at liberty to marry again" (Section 101).

Nevertheless, the revelation to the Prophet no longer speaks of the "crime" of polygamy: "If any man espouse a virgin, and desire to espouse another, and the first give her consent; and if he espouse the second, and they are virgins, and have vowed to no other man, then he is justified; he cannot commit adultery, for they are given unto him; for he cannot commit adultery with that that belongeth unto him and to no one else. And if he have ten virgins given unto him by this law, he cannot commit adultery, for they belong to him, and they are given unto him, therefore he is justified" (Section 132).

Not all Saints welcomed this innovation and 4000 English converts who balked at polygamy were summarily excommunicated. In Utah the leaders of the priesthood advised the wealthier Saints to take a second or additional wife. The cult found itself with a surplus of female Saints, a theology which deprecated celibacy, and a desert which needed people. When Young died in 1877 he left his $2,000,-000 fortune to 12 widows (nine had already preceded him in death) and 47 children. Another leader of the Mormon hierarchy, Heber Kimball, supported 45 wives.

The church has never renounced its belief in polygamy which Mormons believe was revealed by God Himself. It has become a "suspended" doctrine since 1890 when President Woodruff yielded to federal law and declared: "Inasmuch as laws have been enacted by Congress, which laws have been pronounced constitutional by the court of last resort, I hereby declare my intention to submit to these laws, and to use my influence with the members of the church over which I preside to have them do likewise. And now I publicly declare that my advice to the Latter-day Saints is to refrain from contracting any marriage forbidden by the law of the land."

Opposition by the Federal Government to the practice of polygamy was registered as early as 1862 when President Lincoln signed a bill condemning polygamy in the Territories of the United States. In his inaugural address President Garfield stated: "The Mormon church not only offends the moral sense of mankind by sanctioning polygamy, but prevents the administration of justice through the ordinary instrumentalities of law." Finally, in 1890 the supreme court upheld the constitutionality of the Edmunds Law of 1882 which disfranchised any person who practiced plural marriage. When Utah finally won statehood it was on the condition that polygamy be forever prohibited in the territory.

If the Federal Government were to withdraw its opposition to plural marriages, the Saints would certainly resume the practice. They have always considered the laws against polygamy to be unjust and an infringement of religious freedom. Scores of Saints went into exile in Mexico or served prison sentences rather than submit to the Federal Government. Several Utah congressmen were denied seats because they had more than one wife. Hundreds of Mormon fundamentalists have never recognized the church's surrender on the matter of polygamy and continue its practice in secluded Western villages. Recently state officials raided a settlement of 400 Mormon fundamentalists in Arizona who were following Joseph Smith's original revelation on polygamy. Time magazine reported: "What they practice openly thousands of others throughout the West practice in secret."[1]

Mormons accept four sources of doctrine: the Bible "insofar as correctly translated," The Book of Mormon, Doctrine and Covenants, and The Pearl of Great Price.

Smith labored for months over his own translation of the Bible but the Utah Mormons continue to use the King James version. In

---

[1] Time, Jan. 23, 1956.

practice *Doctrine and Covenants* and the *Book of Mormon* receive far more attention than the Bible.

Doctrine and Covenants consists of a collection of dated revelations from God to the Prophet and a single revelation to his successor, Young. One such divine revelation set the price of the Book of Mormon at $1.25 and another presented the godhead's advice on the financing of a boarding house at Nauvoo: "And they shall not receive less than fifty dollars for a share of stock in that house, and they shall be permitted to receive fifteen thousand dollars from any one man for stock in that house." This book also includes the Word of Wisdom which forbids alcohol, tobacco, and hot drinks which the Saints have taken to mean coffee and tea.

The Pearl of Great Price is a slim volume of three sections: the so-called Book of Moses in which certain visions are described, the Book of Abraham, and a potpourri entitled the "Writings of Joseph Smith." The Book of Moses discloses that Satan originated Freemasonry in order to ensnare mankind.

The background of the Book of Abraham is instructive. At Kirtland, a traveling carnival owner invited Smith to examine the papyrus accompanying his circus mummy. The Prophet solemnly declared the hieroglyphics to be the writings of Abraham and Joseph and proceeded to produce a translation. Egyptologists realized the hieroglyphics were part of the well-known Book of the Dead and bore no similarity to Smith's efforts. Years later in Illinois the Prophet studied six brass plates with mysterious scratchings and explained that they told the history of the descendants of Ham; the wags who perpetrated the hoax could not contain their amusement. When a Protestant minister sought to test Smith's knowledge of languages he handed him a Greek copy of the Psalter. "It ain't Greek at all, except a few words. What ain't Greek is Egyptian and what ain't Egyptian is Greek. Them characters are like the letters that were engraven on the Golden Plates," explained the Prophet.

Algermissen succinctly summarizes the religion when he writes, "The doctrine of the Mormons is a primitive polytheism upon a foundation of materialism and sexual myth."[2] Their apparently

---

[2] Konrad Algermissen, *Christian Denominations*, trans. by Joseph Grunder (St. Louis: B. Herder, 1953), p. 870.

orthodox Articles of Faith were drawn up to camouflage their peculiar doctrines from their Christian neighbors. Mormon missionaries still trot out the so-called Articles of Faith in order to get a hearing in Christian homes.

Mormon theology teaches that the god of this world is a man (probably Adam), a physical being, a polygamist. God did not create matter, which existed eternally (he "organized" it), but he did create a tremendous number of spirits or souls. All humans have entered a pact with the god of this world to erase the memory of their former existence if he would send them to earth. If they faithfully follow Mormon precepts and obey the priesthood they may be given charge of a planet of their own after death. Their leading theologian states simply, "All men are potential gods," and Young himself phrased the Mormon aphorism, "What God was once, we are now; what God is now, we shall be."

They believe in a practical universalism. Of the billions of souls who have inhabited the earth only murderers and apostates, sons of perdition, will go to hell. The afterlife for all others will be spent in a graded heaven: the celestial, terrestrial, and telestial. The celestial is reserved for Mormons who are married in the mystic temple rites. Lower grade Mormons and exceptional Gentiles may attain the terrestrial heaven which is presided over by Christ. Run-of-the-mill Gentiles may expect to spend eternity in the telestial plane and fraternize neither with God nor Christ but with angels. Their conception of heaven comes closer to the Moslem paradise than the Christian beatific vision.

The distinctive Protestant doctrine of justification by faith alone receives a thoroughgoing criticism by the cult which demands ethical, ceremonial, and moral works besides faith. Of course, the sole sufficiency of the Bible, another Reformation principle, is automatically denied.

The dead may receive Mormon baptism by proxy which enables them to advance to a higher plane in the afterlife. A Saint may be baptized for his ancestors as many as 30 times in an afternoon; President Woodruff was baptized for the signers of the Declaration of Independence, John Wesley, and others. The Saints specialize in genealogical studies so that they can trace all their ancestors. Some Mormons claim to be able to identify members of their family tree to A.D. 500. These proxy baptisms for the dead are performed only in the temples. Ordinarily Mormons are baptized by immersion when they reach the age of 8.

Mormonism is Jim Crow. No Negro may enter the priesthood and colored people are not encouraged to join the church. This exclusion from the priesthood is quite significant in Mormonism since nine out of ten adult Mormon males hold some office of the priesthood. Brigham Young explained, "Why are so many inhabitants of the earth cursed with a skin of blackness? It comes in consequence of their fathers rejecting the power of the Holy Priesthood, and the Law of God." The cult considers all Negroes to be descendants of Cain, cursed by a dark skin or, as the Book of Mormon puts it, "the Lord did cause a skin of blackness to come upon them." At another time Young told Horace Greeley, "We consider slavery of divine institution and not to be abolished until the curse pronounced on Ham shall have been removed from his descendants." This Mormon position is often softpedaled in missionary work, at least in the North.

Jesus Christ is sometimes set up as a model for conduct but He receives little attention in the Mormon system. Jesus was a polygamist and Mary and Martha were two of his wives, Young informs us. Esoteric meanings are attached to the incarnation, the atonement, and the resurrection which may mislead some Christian observers.

Mormon folklore abounds in illustrations of the good deeds of the "peripatetic immortals," four men who have never suffered death and who move among men to this day doing good. They include St. John and three Nephite brothers.

The Big Fifteen who control the church consist of a "President, Prophet, Seer, Revelator, and Trustee in Trust," a First and Second Counselor, and the 12 Apostles, a self-perpetuating body which selects the President for a life term. One of these apostles, Ezra Taft Benson, has served as the controversial secretary of agriculture in

President Eisenhower's cabinet. His rank in his church corresponds to that of cardinal in the Catholic Church.

A bishop and two counselors supervise the ward, which corresponds to a parish. The wards are gathered into 366 stakes of Zion similar to dioceses. All but a few dozen of the church's personnel serve without pay and carry on daytime secular occupations.

A Mormon lad advances in the lesser Aaronic priesthood from deacon to teacher to priest. As a priest he may baptize, administer the sacrament, and ordain other priests. A priest enters the Melchizedek priesthood and may continue his advance as an elder, seventy, high priest, patriarch (hereditary in the Smith family), apostle, and president.

The cult exaggerates the importance of sex and the family. Celibacy is regarded as an inferior state and virgins have no chance of attaining the celestial plane in heaven. To remain single is considered contrary to the Word of God and those who do not marry at a fairly early age are urged to do so by the priesthood.

Large families are encouraged; birth control is condemned; family solidarity is fostered by the regular recreational "Home Evenings"; divorces in temple marriages are rare. The Young Men's and Young Women's Mutual Improvement Associations enroll thousands and the cult sponsors an extensive Boy Scout program.

Mormon temples are closed to Gentiles and to Mormons who do not tithe, observe the Word of Wisdom, and attend church regularly. Visitors may enter the 8000-seat Salt Lake City Tabernacle and attend services at ward chapels. Three main rites are performed in the eleven Mormon temples: proxy baptism of the dead, marriage for time and eternity, and the endowment.

Mormons classify marriages as those for time and those for time and eternity. The latter can be solemnized only in one of the ten temples. Christians usually marry with the formula "until death do us part" but Mormons (and Swedenborgians) consider marriage an eternal contract if performed by two Mormons in the temple rites. Saints who are unable to travel to a temple or who contract a marriage with a Gentile or who fail to meet temple entrance requirements are married "for time" in a ward chapel. Later they may undergo a second ceremony of "sealing" in the temple — if their circumstances change. Children born in a temporal marriage may also be sealed to parents in the temple.

In the day-long endowment rites young Mormons are initiated into the esoteric aspects of the cult. The endowment ceremony usually precedes the marriage rites. Twenty or thirty participants enter the temple with their temple vestments of white shirt and trousers, white robe and girdle, cloth cap, moccasins, and a Masonic-type green apron with fig leaf design.

They first bathe and are anointed with oil. After this they don their long white underwear (LDS Approved Garments as they are known in Utah haberdasheries) which they will wear throughout life as believing Mormons. Three symbols stitched in the garment signify that if the initiate should reveal temple secrets he will allow his legs to be amputated, his intestines disemboweled, and his heart cut out. Mormons are buried in their endowment garb.

The initiate then receives a new secret name and secret grips. They pass from one room to another to watch a continuing playlet which includes scenes wherein Catholic and Protestant clergymen are ridiculed for their inadequate religious beliefs. The Five Rooms of the temple are called the Creation room, Garden of Eden, World room, Terrestrial Kingdom, and Celestial Kingdom.

Masonic influence is apparent in Mormon temple rites which is not surprising since both Smith and Young were Freemasons in Illinois but were expelled from the lodge. Utah Mormons are forbidden to join the lodge.

The regular Sunday afternoon worship service includes a simple observance of the Lord's Supper. Water is used in place of wine lest the Word of Wisdom be violated. The Saints believe their church possesses all spiritual gifts such as healing, speaking in tongues, communication with spirits, and prophecy.

At one time the doctrine of blood atonement embarrassed Mormon proponents but this vicious doctrine has gradually been forgotten by Gentile critics and young Mormons alike. Early Mormon theologians argued that some sins could only be forgiven by the shedding of the sinner's blood. As Young explained: "Cutting people off from the earth . . . is to save them, not to destroy them." The Danites were a band of avenging Saints who liquidated apostates and Gentiles for their own good.

The greatest scandal in Latter-day Saint history is the famous Mountain Meadow massacre of 1857. A party of 120 people on their way to the California gold fields passed through Utah and were promised safe passage and protection from the Indians if they would surrender their weapons to Mormon Bishop John D. Lee and his men. They agreed to this arrangement but at a signal from Bishop Lee ("Do your duty, men!") the Mormons murdered the men, hacked the women to death, and kidnaped the children. Twenty years later, Lee, a Catholic in his youth, was convicted and executed; the role of Young in this affair has never been ascertained. That this was a case of blood atonement rather than simple cold-blooded murder has been suggested by some Gentile historians.

Mormonism is the largest sect in the country to insist on tithing. A member who does not contribute 10 per cent of his income to the church does not qualify as a Mormon in good standing. This source of income provides the cult with huge sums for missionary activities, relief, educational programs, building, and other enterprises. The canny Mormon businessmen undertake their major church construction projects during economic depressions, getting materials at lower prices and providing work for unemployed church members. Mormons also refrain from two meals on the first Sunday of each month and donate the proceeds to church welfare funds. The church maintains more than 100 warehouses for food and clothing for those in need.

All young men are expected to spend a year or two as unpaid missionaries and each year 4000 leave Utah in pairs to spread the message of the Prophet around the globe. All are members of the priesthood and graduates of a short course in missiology. They average 21 years of age and have memorized a sales talk, Bible proof texts, and stock answers to Gentile objections. They direct their efforts at members of other denominations rather than the unchurched and in a recent year claimed 100,000 baptized converts. Strangely the Mormon church has had little success in converting Gentiles in predominantly Mormon communities.

Rather than operate its own high schools as it once did, the church now supports 150 seminaries which supplement the secular secondary school curriculum with Mormon theology. Institutes of Religion provide a similar service for Mormon students on 25 college campuses. The church-owned Brigham Young University, largest church-related university in the nation, enrolls more than 11,000 students, 97 per cent of whom are Saints. The University of Deseret in Salt Lake City is now the state University of Utah but the faculty and student body is naturally largely Mormon.

Somewhat closer to traditional Christianity, the Reorganized church denies polygamy, blood atonement, and the Adam-god doctrine of their Utah cousins. They flatly deny Young's assertion: "When our father Adam came into the Garden of Eden, he came into it with a celestial body, and brought Eve, one of his wives with him. . . . He is our father and our God, and the only God with whom we have to do." This branch of Mormondom was organized at Beloit, Wisconsin, in 1852 and was headed by Joseph Smith III from 1860 to 1914.

Financial circles buzzed in 1960 when President David O. McKay, disclosed that the Mormon Church had sold its $10,000,000 interest in Zion's First National Bank to private interests. He squelched rumors that the immensely wealthy church planned to liquidate other assets in its huge business empire. The church owns in whole or in part a department store, station KSL and KSL-TV, the Deseret News Publishing Co. in Salt Lake City, two hotels and a motel, 70 downtown office buildings, the Utah-Idaho Sugar Co., two insurance companies, a 320,000-acre cattle ranch in Florida, a coal mine, parcels of Salt Lake City real estate, a clothing factory, and scores of farms. Its total financial holdings have never been revealed.

Although Mormonism has registered impressive gains in membership in the past half century, its advance is bound to slacken. As a world religion it has little to say to the dark races of mankind except "ye are cursed." Its early growth was fostered by the relative isolation of Utah but today Salt Lake City is 40 per cent Gentile with the Catholics second in number.

The number of "Jack Mormons," born Saints who have stopped tithing and ignore the Word of Wisdom prohibitions, is larger than the church would care to admit. Mormons who leave Utah or enter secular colleges and universities often quietly shed their Latter-day Saints beliefs.

The cult is saddled with the preposterous fable about the golden plates and magic spectacles and Mormon theologians cannot question the truth of the origin of the Book of Mormon without shaking the church's very foundations. Most Gentiles would have to agree with Ernest Sutherland Bates when he declared: "If there is one fact in American history that can definitely be established it is that the engaging Joe Smith was a deliberate charlatan."[3]

A religion built on patent fraud, a religion so vulnerable to the attacks of archaeology, anthropology, history, and philology, will attract few informed Christians. Unfortunately those Mormons who become disenchanted seldom affiliate with a Christian religion.

Conversions of Mormons to Catholicism are about as rare as the conversion of Moslems. A Utah Mormon finds his entire social, religious, and often economic life entwined in Mormonism. He no doubt holds office in the priesthood, tithes his income, attends church several times a week, supports a large family, provides religious education for his children, and finds his chief recreation in church dances and entertainments. He is kept so busy being a Mormon he has little time or inclination to investigate the claims of Christianity.

---

[3] E. S. Bates, The American Faith (New York: W. W. Norton & Co., 1940), p. 346.

Chapter XVI

THE JEHOVAH'S WITNESSES

"Millions Now Living Will Never Die."
— Judge Rutherford.

EVERY household in the United States has probably been visited by a Fuller Brush salesman, a tax assessor, and a Jehovah's Witness "minister." Once upon a time these door-to-door proselytizers toted phonographs and subjected citizens to transcribed sermons by their spokesman, "Judge" Rutherford. Nowadays most diligent Witnesses have undergone a speech training program and manage to deliver their own sales talks.

Such aggressive missionary tactics have brought impressive harvests. Jehovah's Witnesses are undoubtedly the fastest growing body of cultists in the world. From 115,000 members in 1942 their numbers have ballooned to 920,000, in 158 nations. Of these, 267,000 reside in this country. And they are still growing. Fellow travelers and subscribers to their magazines must be numbered in the millions. No other modern sect begins to match this amazing increase during the past 20 years.

A public relations face lifting, a series of successful legal battles, and shrewd leadership have pushed this fanatical eschatological sect into the forefront of modern religious movements. Most of this progress and growth has been achieved since the death of the cantankerous Rutherford in 1942 and the ascendancy of Nathan Knorr.

Compared to Jehovah's Witnesses, Calvin Coolidge's minister

who declared himself against sin was a piker. The Witnesses oppose blood transfusions, business, Catholics, Christmas trees, communism, civic enterprises, the doctrines of hell and immortality, evolution, flag saluting, higher education, liquor, lodges, Protestants, priests, the pope, public office, military service, movies, Mother's Day, religion, Sunday Schools, the Trinity, tobacco, the United Nations, voting, the Y.M.C.A., Wall street, and women's rights. This list does not pretend to be complete.

The sect tolerates no inactive or associate members. All adults save the lame and blind must devote at least 60 hours a month to canvassing, street corner pamphlet hawking, or study classes. This huge investment in time and shoe leather has paid dividends. A growing full time body of nearly 7000 Pioneers work 150 hours a month supervising congregations, handling administrative details, and distributing publications. All contributions for their books and magazines are forwarded to Brooklyn headquarters while the Pioneer lives on a small expense account and boards with sect members.

More than 500,000,000 pieces of literature have been sold or given away since 1920, most of it printed at the cult's modern printing plant. The annual output has reached 3,000,000 bound books and 27,000,000 pamphlets besides the magazines. *Let God Be True*, a 320-page doctrinal exposition, has gone through several reprints and the latest count reveals 16,000,000 copies have been printed. It is hard bound and sells for fifty cents.

The Witnesses specialize in regional national conventions. Their 1958 Divine Will International Assembly in New York City, attracted 194,000 Witnesses. Thirteen "Triumphant Kingdom" assemblies were staged in 1955 with a total attendance of 403,000 in Chicago, Vancouver, Los Angeles, Dallas, New York, London, Paris, Rome, Nuremburg, Berlin, Stockholm, The Hague, and Helsinki.

Charles Taze Russell, son of a Pennsylvania haberdasher, adopted adventist views after a Congregational boyhood and temporary loss of faith. He became distressed at the thought of hell and his Bible searching convinced him that the Hebrew word *sheol* should invariably be translated "grave" instead of "hell." He began his preaching activities in 1872 and many people found comfort in his flat denial of everlasting punishment.

"Pastor" Russell toured the nation preaching his novel Biblical interpretations on an average of six to eight hours a day. But two scandals rocked his new movement. His wife sued him for divorce charging him with infidelity and cruelty and the court declared that "his course of conduct towards his wife evidences such insistent egotism and extravagant self-praise that it would be manifest to the jury that it would necessarily render the life of any sensitive Christian woman an intolerable burden." Russell contested the divorce five times without success and eventually attempted to avoid alimony payments by transferring his property to corporations which he controlled. The cult leader's involvement in a phony $60 a bushel Miracle Wheat disillusioned other converts. He also promoted a "cancer cure" which consisted of a caustic paste of chloride of zinc, a wonderful Millennial Bean, and a fantastic cotton seed.

Russell died in 1916 on a Sante Fe Pullman after requesting an associate to fashion him a Roman toga whereupon he "drew up his feet like Jacob of old" and passed away. His successor, Joseph F. Rutherford, was a small town Missouri lawyer who preferred writing to preaching. He consolidated Russellism, quietly supplanted the founder in the memory of the devotees. His scripture-heavy polemics soon formed the bulk of the sect's printed propaganda. Later he recorded the short talks which Witnesses played for householders on their portable phonographs.

He also shrugged off Russell's pyramidism, a system by which the founder claimed to be able to foretell history by measuring the rooms of the Great Pyramid in Egypt. Several schisms erupted when old-timers objected to the mild debunking of the late "Pastor" Russell.

During World War I Rutherford and other officers of the cult were imprisoned for nine months on charges of sedition. Shortly after his release from Atlanta federal prison the "Judge" coined the slogan "Millions Now Living Will Never Die" which expressed the urgently adventist hopes of the movement and soon blossomed on road signs, handbills, and posters.

Rutherford's followers were known variously as Russellites, International Bible Students, Millennial Dawnists, Rutherfordites, Watchtower Bible and Tract People. This untidy situation was cleared up in 1931 when Rutherford disclosed that their new name would be "Jehovah's Witnesses." This proved a happy choice since any mention of "witness" in the Old or New Testament could now be adduced as evidence of the antiquity of the cult.

When not at his Brooklyn Vatican "Judge" Rutherford resided in a mansion near San Diego, California, whose deed was made out to Abel, Noah, and Abraham. This estate was kept in readiness for any Old Testament princes who returned to life before the Battle of Armageddon. Meanwhile, it served as Western headquarters. The "Judge" was not among the millions now living who will never die. He died in 1942 after dictating the affairs of the cult for more than 25 years.

The self-perpetuating hierarchy of 402 men chose the 36-year-old Knorr to succeed Rutherford. The present head left the Reformed church while in high school and was employed in various business capacities in the cult until his election to the top position. He holds office for life but is technically re-elected each year. Like all full-time workers he receives room, board, and $14 a month; insinuations that the leaders have enriched themselves on book profits seem unwarranted.

Many basic teachings of Jehovah's Witnesses resemble those of Seventh-day Adventism through whom Russell was introduced to millennial doctrines. Mankind lives in the latter days. The great battle between Satan and Christ, Armageddon, may occur any day now. Prepare. The Witnesses have learned by experience not to specify dates but all members confidently expect to see these events in their lifetimes, at least before 1984.

Satan was cast out of heaven and now rules the world; however, Jesus Christ returned to earth invisibly in 1914. We have already entered the early days of the millennium which will terminate in A.D. 2914 but only a few people recognize the theocracy. These few include Jehovah's Witnesses.

Satan is marshaling his forces for the battle of Armageddon. He finds his principal allies in an evil triumvirate: organized religion, the commercial world, and political organizations. During the course of the battle the faithful few will sit on a mountainside and watch Jesus and His angels defeat Satan and his cohorts.

After the dust has settled Satan will be bound and cast into an abyss. The righteous survivors will marry and repopulate the earth during the remainder of the 1000 year reign. The dead will remain in their graves until the resurrection but the wicked will be annihilated. Those who have died without a chance to know the Lord will be resurrected and given a second chance. If they persist in their disbelief, they too will be totally destroyed.

At the end of the 1000 years Satan will be loosed and he will try one last time to seduce mankind. A few men will succumb to his temptations and with Satan will be annihilated. The billions who have repopulated the earth and been resurrected from the dead will continue to dwell on earth forever.

Only a fraction of Jehovah's Witnesses can be members of the invisible church since they believe its number has been set at 144,-000, no more, no less. This quota has been filling up since Pentecost and few places remain. Today about one Witness out of 20 claims to belong to this select "bride's class" and only these few can entertain hopes of reaching heaven. They are the only ones who partake of the annual spring observance of the Lord's Supper in local Kingdom Halls.

The best that other Witnesses can hope for is to be counted among the Jonadabs or "other sheep" who will protect and assist the "bride's class" from their earthly habitation. To summarize the final disposition of mankind according to Russell-Rutherford-and-Knorr: 144,000 will attain heaven and reign with Christ, the wicked will be annihilated, the righteous will live on earth forever.

Witnesses reject many fundamental Christian beliefs such as original sin, the divinity of Christ, His resurrection, immortality, and the Trinity. Christ was originally Michael the Archangel, lived and died a man, and is now an exalted being. He was not God. And besides, say the Witnesses, he was born on October 1, 2 b.c. rather than December 25 which just goes to show how heathenish Christendom has become. The authoritative text *Let God Be True* explains the Jehovah's Witness views on Christ:

> Prior to coming to earth, this only-begotten Son of God did not think himself to be co-equal with Jehovah God; he did not view himself as "equal in power and glory" with Almighty God; he did not follow the course of the Devil and plot and scheme to make himself like or equal to the Most High God and to rob God or usurp God's place. On the contrary, he showed his subjection to God as his Superior by humbling himself under God's almighty hand, even to the most extreme degree, which means to a most disgraceful death on a torture stake.[1]

They agree with the Seventh-day Adventists on immortality: "Immortality is a reward for faithfulness. It does not come automatically to a human at birth."[2]

The Christian doctrine of the Trinity is ridiculed in the following passage from the same textbook:

> When the clergy are asked by their followers as to how such a combination of three in one can possibly exist, they are obliged to answer, "That is a mystery." Some will try to illustrate it by using triangle, trefoils, or images with three heads on one neck. Nevertheless, sincere persons who want to know the true God and serve him find it a bit difficult to love and worship a complicated, freakish-looking, three-headed God. The clergy who inject such ideas will contradict themselves in the very next breath by stating that God made man in his own image; for certainly no one has ever seen a three-headed human creature.[3]

The Witnesses consider all religious bodies, Catholic and Protestant, to be tools of Satan and deceivers but they reserve a special hatred for Roman Catholicism. Their literature offers kind words for Arius, Waldo, Wycliffe, Huss, and the early Anabaptists but they lament that the Reformation never really got off the ground.

Some Protestant churches ask no more of a prospective member than that he sign the register, attend church with some regularity,

---

[1] *Let God Be True,* 2nd ed. (Brooklyn: Watch Tower Bible and Tract Society, 1946), p. 34.
[2] *Ibid.,* p. 74.
[3] *Ibid.,* p. 102.

promise to read the Bible, and contribute to the support of the church. Not so with Jehovah's Witnesses. Anyone who conscientiously meets the demands of the cult finds little time for anything else. A convert completes courses in the Bible, speech, salesmanship, and missionary techniques before being assigned to ring doorbells with an experienced Witness. As long as the Witness remains in good standing he is expected to devote an average of 10 to 12 hours a month to such activities. Most members hold regular jobs and attempt to get in their required hours evenings and week ends.

A Witness may be a farmer or laborer or professional man but he cannot be a salesman or shopkeeper since these people are involved in Satan's commercial enterprises. He is encouraged to live and eat decently but invited to turn over any surplus wealth or income to the cult. Witnesses neither tithe their incomes (like Mormons and Adventists) nor pass the collection plate; members drop their contributions in a box at the rear of each local Kingdom Hall.

Mass baptisms by immersion are scheduled at the conventions and more than 4000 converts were baptized in swimming pools at the New York meeting. The baptism service, like the Lord's Supper, is more of a dedicatory than a sacramental rite.

Members must agree to abstain from liquor and tobacco, avoid motion pictures, dances, and the theater. They do not vote in local or national elections, hold public office, salute the flag, or enter military service since they consider the United States government and every other government an instrument of the devil. On this score one government is about as wicked as another be it democratic, fascist, or communist. To cast a vote or accept a public office would be supporting Satan's political ally. Oddly enough, they have never objected to paying taxes. At one time the sect discouraged marriage and the begetting of children since the theocracy was just around the corner, but this prohibition has been relaxed.

Some 700 Witnesses live a community life at Bethel House, a nine-story apartment building in Brooklyn. These members run the presses, set the type, bind the books, handle the mail and other chores at national headquarters. The Bethel residents eat in a common refectory whose food is supplied by several Witness-operated farms. Bells arouse the workers at 7 a.m. and signal lights out at 10:30 p.m. All get the same recompense from Knorr to janitor: room, board, and $14 a month.

The local congregation or "company" meets in a Kingdom Hall, usually a rented store or small building. Sixteen thousand such companies are grouped in 1000 circuits; a circuit servant visits each company once every six months. Sunday and Thursday evening meetings resemble discussion groups more than worship services. Prayer, study of scripture and Watchtower publications, reports of activities, and business comprise the meetings. Hymn singing has been considered a waste of time and music has played a minor role in Witness assemblies. A full-time Pioneer, known as the company servant, may conduct the meeting.

In recent years under the Knorr administration Witnesses have learned how to smile, to treat householders with some courtesy and tact, to inquire about the children and pet the dog. The old-fashioned belligerency and "hear me or be damned" approach antagonized most prospects. To many bibliolaters the scriptural gymnastics of a trained Witness is a sure sign of godliness. What matter if this "minister" never finished high school, knows no Biblical languages, chooses to quote out of context? As a matter of fact anyone who itches to engage an experienced Witness in a Biblical duel had better make sure he has spent as much time memorizing proof passages and persuading doubters as his opponent.

The Watchtower Bible School of Gilead at Brooklyn, N. Y., trains about 200 Pioneers a year for full-time missionary work. Almost 3000 graduates have completed the course since the school opened its doors in 1943. Only Witnesses who have spent two years in the field are admitted. Until recently this was a five-month course given at South Lansing, N. Y. The Gilead School has been moved to Brooklyn and expanded into a ten-month program.

The cult has found fertile missionary fields in West Germany, England, Canada, Northern Rhodesia, Nigeria, Latin America, and the Philippines. They enjoy high prestige in Germany since some 10,000 Witnesses were sent to Nazi concentration camps and 2000 perished. The Communists have forbidden Witness activity behind the Iron Curtain. More than 3000 missionaries are laboring in South America.

Few college graduates join the movement; only one Witness out of 100 holds a bachelor's degree. Knorr himself never studied in an accredited college. Few younger members in the cult are encouraged to extend their formal education beyond high school. The main appeal has been to the socially, economically, and intellectually disinherited. The sect promises that the rich and powerful will soon get their comeuppance. About 20 per cent are Negroes and the sect makes a special effort to win Puerto Ricans and Mexicans. Racial equality has been one of the long-time policies of the cult, but no Negro has ever held a top administrative office. Naturally the sect counts no representatives of the commercial, military, political, or academic worlds. Two well-known converts were the mother of President Eisenhower and Mickey Spillane, a sex-and-sadism mystery writer.

Evidently to many people the advantages of cult membership outweigh the burdens. Without spending years in college and seminary they can become "ministers." They can sit in other people's living rooms and command respect as they spin their peculiar doctrines and impress their listeners with heavy doses of proof texts. As "ministers" they can claim exemption from the draft, ride the railroads for half fare, preach, and baptize.

Witnesses have been stoned, imprisoned, fined, sent to concentration camps, tarred and feathered. They have become involved in dozens of law suits over their refusal to salute the flag, their peddling books without a license, their slandering of religious groups, their denial of blood transfusions to their sick children. Between 1940-45 almost 2000 were sent to federal prisons as draft dodgers although all claimed to be ministers of the gospel. They have won about two thirds of the 40 cases which have reached the Supreme Court. In most instances they were supported by the American Civil Liberties Union and in Witness gratitude they have branded the A.C.L.U. an agent of the devil.

A passage in Leviticus condemning the eating of blood is taken to refer to blood transfusions although the practice condemned was obviously a primitive tribal rite rather than a medical technique. Christmas trees are pagan-inspired since the Witnesses quote Jeremiah: "The customs of the people are vanity; for one cutteth a tree out of the forest, the work of the hands of the workman with an axe. They deck it with silver and gold."

Only unsigned articles now appear in their two magazines: *Watchtower* and *Awake*. The former is published semimonthly in 65 languages and has reached a circulation of 4,150,000 at five cents a copy. *Awake* boasts a circulation of 3,650,000 in 25 languages. A 13-story magazine publishing plant has been built to supplement the Brooklyn factory. All books are now published anonymously and neither Russell's nor Rutherford's works are being reprinted. Even correspondence from the Society is anonymous and signed with a rubber stamp.

How the Witnesses can sell a 320-page book printed in two colors and hard bound for fifty cents can be explained. They pay no author's royalties, bookseller's commissions (usually 40 per cent), profits, union printing wages. They also print these books in such tremendous quantities that the unit cost can be cut to a minimum.

Witness scholars have completed an interesting New World translation of the Hebrew scriptures. As might be expected, they substitute the "correct" word Jehovah for God in many passages. Two volumes have appeared and two more are promised. Their translation of the Lord's Prayer runs as follows:

> Our Father in the heavens, let your name be sanctified. Let your kingdom come. Let your will come to pass, as in heaven, also upon earth. Give us today our bread for this day; and forgive us our debts, as we also have forgiven our debtors. And do not bring us into temptation, but deliver us from the wicked one.[4]

Already we can observe the beginning of a transition from sect to church. The full-time Pioneers are assuming more of the duties ordinarily assigned to ministers and priests. Witnesses encourage their children to enter Pioneer work as a career. Kingdom Halls move from rented quarters to modest Witness-owned buildings.

---

[4] *Ibid.*, p. 162.

Publications have dropped their lurid illustrations and Rutherford-era vilification and a new look tempers their attitude toward the public. Anonymous leadership replaces the colorful Russell and the brooding Rutherford. The democratic congregational organization of the local company has been replaced since 1938 by the autocratic theocracy.

All but a handful of Witnesses are converts, mostly recent converts. Whether they will pass on the same enthusiasm and crusading zeal to their children seems doubtful. All expect to see Armageddon in their lifetimes. Can the movement sustain itself with a continually postponed Armageddon?

Catholics form the special target of Witness attacks but they cannot in charity reply in kind. Rather they should realize that anyone who joins a cult which demands so much of his time is serious about serving God. Angry words and slammed doors will not bring these souls to Christianity. Adult Catholics with Catholic high school or college educations should be able to demonstrate the divinity of Christ or the fact of immortality to any Witness who calls at their door. They should not buy or keep Witness literature.

Neither scandals nor persecution have stopped the growth of this American-born cult. In 1928 there were only 6040 Witnesses in the entire nation and today there are more than 267,000. We can expect their membership to continue to grow but not at the rate of the past decade. A nation with millions of fundamentalists, depressed minorities, and people in search of a cause provides a happy hunting ground for a band of dedicated fanatics such as Jehovah's Witnesses.

Chapter XVII

THE CHRISTIAN SCIENTISTS

"Man Is Incapable of Sin, Sickness and Death."
— Mary Baker Eddy.

In THIS age of antibiotics, revolutionary surgical techniques, the X-ray, and vaccinations for smallpox, diphtheria, and polio, we may forget that for religious reasons a substantial minority deprive themselves and their children of the benefits of medical science. They are following the teachings of an elderly New England matron, Mrs. Mary Baker Glover Patterson Eddy, discoverer of Christian Science.

For more than 75 years her loyal devotees have not only stubbornly denied the reality of disease but the reality of matter, of evil, and of death itself. Moreover, our Christian Science neighbors, numbering perhaps 350,000 in the United States, constitute a group of citizens of greater wealth and higher social standing and better education than most.

With Mormonism and Jehovah's Witnesses, Christian Science stands as one of the three really successful home-grown religions. Excepting Madame Blavatsky's Theosophy it remains the only religion of consequence founded by a woman. Denying every fundamental Christian dogma, it presents itself to the public as a Christian denomination and appropriates a Christian vocabulary.

How a penniless woman of 50 carried through her plans to build a church to perpetuate her strange beliefs makes a fascinating story.

185

Barely literate, she compiled a book which, doctored and edited, has been given a place next to the Bible in many cultured homes.

Born Mary Baker on a New Hampshire farm in 1821 she spent a childhood plagued by sickness and "fits." In the space of a few decades early nineteenth-century New England would witness such enthusiasms as Shakerism, Mormonism, Spiritualism, and Transcendentalism. Mary Baker had to miss most formal schooling because of her delicate health. At the age of 17 she joined the Congregational church, of which she remained a nominal member for 40 years.

At 22 she married George Washington Glover, a bricklayer and small-time contractor. The newlyweds set up housekeeping in South Carolina but in six months Glover was dead of yellow fever. His young widow returned home and gave birth to her only child, a son from whom she would be estranged for most of her life.

The tragedy aggravated her hysterical attacks and she dabbled in poetry, Mesmerism, and Spiritualism for some years. Eventually she married an itinerant dentist and philanderer by the name of Daniel Patterson. Her four-year-old son had been taken to Minnesota to be raised by foster parents and she would not see him again until he was 34. Dr. Patterson had the misfortune to visit a Civil War battlefield as an observer. He mistakenly crossed into Confederate territory and spent the duration of the war in a Southern prison.

Neither morphine nor Mesmerism seemed to help Mrs. Patterson's numerous physical complaints. But she happened to hear of a marvelous healer in Portland, Maine. To this day the healer with the Dickensian name of "Dr." Phineas P. Quimby remains the skeleton in Christian Science's closet. Quimby was simply a hypnotist, albeit a successful one, who effected certain cures to which he attached no particular religious significance.

Mrs. Patterson visited Quimby as a patient and student for three weeks in 1862 and again for three months in 1864. She received a copy of Quimby's writings on healing entitled *Questions and Answers* and expressed her appreciation for his help through letters to the press and quaint versicular testimonials. She would later explain these embarrassing tributes by commenting, "I might have written them twenty or thirty years ago, for I was under the Mesmeric treatment of Dr. Quimby from 1862 until his death" (*Boston Post*, 1883).

At any rate the hypnotist's death in 1866 evoked a eulogy by Mrs. Patterson entitled "Lines on the Death of Dr. P. P. Quimby, Who Healed With the Truth That Christ Taught in Contradistinction to All Isms." The founder and her followers have since then sought to ignore or minimize Quimby's contribution and to defend the complete originality of Mrs. Eddy's system.

Her P.O.W. husband meanwhile had returned and promptly announced that he had had enough and left home. She eventually obtained a divorce in 1873 on grounds of desertion. He left his profession, died a hermit in 1897, and was buried in a potter's field. The wife he abandoned left a fortune estimated at $3,000,000.

"The Fall at Lynn" is considered the first authentic Christian Science healing. Mrs. Glover (she had assumed her first husband's name) relates that she slipped on the ice returning from a ladies' aid meeting and suffered injuries which she (but not her doctor) pronounced incurable.

She could not appeal to the dead Quimby although she had dipped into Spiritualism. At this crisis she claims to have rediscovered the laws of healing which Christ had demonstrated in the New Testament and which had been lost through apostasy by the primitive Church. She began to read her Bible and came across the passage in St. Matthew in which Christ addressed the man sick with palsy: "Arise, take up thy bed." She now realized that death and sickness were illusions and within a few days she was walking around to the amazement of her few friends.

Her physician later signed an affidavit in which he declared, "I did not at any time declare, or believe, that there was no hope for Mrs. Patterson's recovery, or that she was in a critical condition."

Between the Fall in 1866 and 1870 she labored on her "textbook." Of *Science and Health With Key to the Scriptures* Mark Twain wrote, "Of all the strange and frantic and incomprehensible and uninterpretable books which the imagination of man has created, surely this one is the prize example." Despite the best efforts of editors and proofreaders *Science and Health* scares off most inquirers by its inconsistency, awkwardness, and abstruseness. The author shrugged off all criticisms and pointed out that "Learning was so illumined that grammar was eclipsed."

Christian Scientists consider the work inspired. "I should blush to write a *Science and Health With Key to the Scriptures* as I have, were it of human origin, and I, apart from God, its author; but as I was only a scribe echoing the harmonies of heaven in divine metaphysics, I cannot be super-modest in my estimate of the Christian Science textbook," declared Mrs. Eddy.

The first edition carried the following verse on the fly leaf *a la* Gertrude Stein:

> I, I, I, I, itself, I.
> The inside and the outside, the what and the why
> The when and the where, the low and the high.
> All I, I, I, I, I, itself, I.

This has since been deleted.

Revised and expanded many times, the book now includes chapters on Christian Science versus Spiritualism, Animal Magnetism Unmasked, Marriage, Physiology, etc. The Key to the Scriptures section was added in 1884 and consists of an allegorical interpretation of Genesis and the Apocalypse. The final edition concludes with a glossary and pages of "fruitage" or healing testimonials.

The book sold for $3 a copy when first offered in 1875 and this was mostly profit in those days. The original edition was advertised as "a book that affords an opportunity to acquire a profession by which you can accumulate a fortune." Church members and practitioners were forced to buy each new edition during the author's lifetime although the changes sometimes amounted to nothing more than a few words.

Shunted from one rooming house to another for nine years, the destitute grass widow decided to team up with a Richard Kennedy. Like the late Quimby he called himself "Dr." and advertised himself as a faith healer. She offered a series of lectures on her healing method, Christian Science. This series, originally 12 and then seven lectures, cost $300. She admits she hesitated to ask such a sum, half a year's wages for the Lynn, Massachusetts, shoe workers who comprised her early disciples, but a voice from heaven commanded it.

She taught a garbled pantheism which denies the reality of matter, evil, sickness, and death. These were not created by God and therefore constituted simply errors of mortal mind. Remove the erroneous conceptions and you remove the suffering and defeat the grave. Man's purpose in life is to free himself from these errors of mortal mind through application of the laws she had discovered. Once freed, he would find himself healthy, sinless, and immortal.

Her mechanical application of these mysterious laws forced her to conclude that if they could be employed to produce health they could be perverted to inflict sickness and death. This Yankee voodooism, a revival of New England witchcraft, she termed Malicious Animal Magnetism. In her later years she lived in terror of MAM, tormented by the malevolent forces of her enemies and critics. As protection she surrounded herself with a corps of devoted followers whose task was to ward off evil thoughts and forces. Christian Scientists who had been hexed told their troubles in a MAM column in the *Christian Science Journal*. Today this black magic aspect of the cult shares the closet with Phineas P. Quimby.

Her third venture into matrimony involved Asa Gilbert Eddy, a sewing machine agent whose name she would perpetuate. A few years later neither her healing laws nor the M.D.'s could prevent his death. She disagreed with the post mortem (post mortems were later forbidden in her *Church Manual*) and maintained that her spouse had died of "arsenic mentally administered." She added emphatically: "My husband's death was caused by malicious animal magnetism. . . . I know it was poison that killed him, not material poison but mesmeric poison." Now she had all the more reason to dread the devils of MAM she had unleashed.

Kennedy was the first of a succession of co-workers and students who left to found cults of their own or who refused to turn over royalties to Mrs. Eddy for the use of her healing techniques. All were violently denounced; all were sinisterly accused of employing MAM to destroy the frail high priestess. She became embroiled in innumerable lawsuits to collect her 10 per cent royalty on students' healing fees.

A revolt of her students at Lynn finished her career in that community and at 61 she transferred her activities to Boston. Here she founded her First Church of Christ, Scientist. She had obtained a charter for the Massachusetts Metaphysical College of which she was the sole instructor. Between 1881 and its discontinuance in 1889, 4000 students each paid $300 tuition for the course. Later three advanced options were added including Metaphysical Obstetrics. Anyone taking the full course paid Mrs. Eddy $800. She probably collected $1,200,000 in the eight years the school functioned. A few charity cases were also admitted.

In Lynn she had preached her new religion to factory workers. In Boston she managed to interest the wealthier classes for whom the cult would exert a perennial appeal. By now she had ordained herself and assumed the title "Reverend." Her organization prospered with practitioners, former students, and branch societies in the East and Middle West. She hired a retired minister to polish her textbook and by 1891 she would have sold 150,000 copies.

A 41-year-old physician, Dr. Foster, joined the college staff as instructor in obstetrics. At the age of 68 Mrs. Eddy legally adopted the doctor who changed his name to Ebenezer J. Foster Eddy. He played the role of crown prince in the cult until a falling out with his "mother" and subsequent exile.

Despite her successes, Mrs. Eddy was restless. MAM dogged her day and night; she knew her enemies were trying to poison her just as they had murdered her husband. She decided to leave Boston, close her profitable college, disband her present church structure.

A shrewd woman, Mrs. Eddy saw the need to forge stronger bonds between herself and her church. Defections and schisms were no novelty to her. A strong Boston organization with decentralized and wholly dependent branch churches seemed the answer. Now an elderly woman, she undertook a series of bold steps to insure her complete control of Christian Science not only during her lifetime but after her death.

She set up a single Christian Science church, the Mother Church in Boston. All others were and are simply branch churches of this one church — buildings where nonresident members of the Boston congregation and neophites could meet to study, sing hymns, and deliver testimonials. Only members of the Mother Church could teach Christian Science, receive the degrees C.S.B. and C.S.D., serve as Readers in branch churches. Only Mother Church members could qualify as practitioners. Those holding only branch membership had little standing in the cult.

District organizations and conferences were forbidden, which frustrated attempts at organized revolt. Next she deposed all pastors and substituted her textbook and the Bible as "pastors." First and Second Readers conducted the worship services but their terms were limited to five years. They were not allowed to preach or to elaborate on the *Science and Health* and Bible passages selected by Boston.

Mrs. Eddy encouraged each branch to sponsor an open lecture annually but all lecturers had to be approved by Boston. All lectures were submitted for censorship and no questions from the audience were tolerated. Only the Bible, the works of Mary Baker Eddy, and church periodicals could be sold in reading rooms operated by the branch societies.

A Committee on Publications set about correcting criticisms and misstatements about the cult in the press. Its boycott of the debunking Dakin book in 1930 backfired and turned the book, *Mrs. Eddy, the Biography of a Virginal Mind*, into a best seller. In recent years the Committee's methods of boycott and intimidation have managed to stifle nearly all published criticism of the cult. After her reorganization of her church all decisions and power rested in Boston and Mrs. Eddy controlled Boston. She lived at her Concord estate 70 miles away. The Mother Church, dedicated in 1895, featured The Mother's Room. Pastor Emeritus Eddy is said to have spent one night in the shrine. A light has since burned before her portrait in the room.

The faithful undertook pilgrimages to Concord to get a glimpse of their Leader (a title which replaced Mother). Many vied for a chance to serve in her household. She fussed with her textbook, collecting royalties of $50,000 to $100,000 a year. She accused her foster son of practicing MAM and disowned another devotee who claimed to have experienced a virgin birth.

The old lady's health was failing but her followers could not be disillusioned. If the discoverer and founder of Christian Science could not apply its laws and defeat sickness and death, who could? A stand-in was employed to dress like Mrs. Eddy and take her place during her daily ritual carriage rides.

After 1900 her health declined rapidly. She had worn glasses and visited dentists for years. Now a doctor was called to administer regular doses of morphine. She was too ill to attend the ceremonies for the $2,000,000 addition to the Mother Church which was completed in 1906. Some 30,000 people jammed the edifice during six identical dedication services; retouched photographs of the Leader were distributed.

Her natural son reappeared but withdrew his suit to declare his wealthy mother mentally incompetent; he received $250,000 and Dr. Foster Eddy $50,000. When she excommunicated the popular Mrs. Augusta Stetson of the New York City branch she eliminated her last rival.

Two years before her death she founded the daily *Christian Science Monitor*. The *Monitor* ranks high in any appraisal of American journalism and its sponsorship by the cult has brought Christian Science considerable prestige. It has won 60 awards for excellence in journalism since 1915 and now reports 186,000 subscribers throughout the nation. It avoids sensationalism, observes the expected taboos on news of deaths, tragedies, epidemics, etc. No advertisements are accepted for coffee, tombstones, cemeteries, undertakers, dentists, oculists, or hearing aids. It never uses the word death but prefers the euphemism "passed away." The *Monitor* news story about the World War I battlefield littered with "passed on mules" is probably apocryphal. The official publication of the church, the *Christian Science Journal*, has been published since 1883. The Christian Science Publishing Society also publishes Mrs. Eddy's works and the three other official periodicals: *Christian Science Sentinel, Herald of Christian Science*, and *Christian Science Quarterly*. Authors must be members of the Mother Church.

Mrs. Eddy could make no real provision for her impending death without compromising her religious principles. "Matter and death are mortal illusions" declares her textbook. Her associates grew alarmed but she was confident she had bequeathed a workable polity in her *Church Manual*.

Mary Baker Eddy died of pneumonia December 3, 1910, at the age of 89. Most of her fortune went to her church. Her cult had no provision for funeral rites. Probably 100,000 people called her Mother or Leader at the time of her final succumbing to error of mortal mind.

A self-perpetuating five member Board of Governors ruled the church after her death. An article of her *Church Manual* asserts that nothing can be adopted, amended, or annulled without the written consent of the Leader which has been an impossibility since 1910. A struggle between the Board and the publications officers ended in two independent corporations, one for the church and another for the publications.

Another tenet forbids the tabulation of membership so we can only guess at the present strength of the movement. The more than 3100 branches of the Mother Church in the United States enroll an average of perhaps 150 members. Only 16 are needed to found a branch society. Christian Science is a cult for city ladies; perhaps three out of four Scientists are women. The church is strongest in California, Illinois, New York, Ohio, and Massachusetts. Few cults promise devotees a boost up the social ladder but Christian Science proves to be an exception.

A true Christian Scientist will take no medicine, consult no physician. Yet she will employ the services of an obstetrician, dentist, oculist, bone setter, and mortician. She will wear glasses and dentures but will vigorously oppose public health measures, compulsory vaccination or X-ray examinations, or fluoridation of water supplies. Assured by her religion that matter is unreal, she ordinarily evinces the same interest in food, property, success, a home, and security as her Christian neighbors.

In many cases Christian Science seems to produce happy, serene, optimistic individuals. Perhaps some adjust to the make-believe world of childhood which knows no sin or death. The cult stresses self-mastery and Stoic courage.

Does Christian Science cure? Certainly. Recent research in psychosomatic medicine confirms the belief in the close interaction of mind and body. "A merry heart doeth good like a medicine" (Prov. 17:22). Any M.D. will testify that mental disturbances lie behind a large percentage of his patients' ills. Recognizing the role of mind in sickness and health is not the same thing as denying all sickness, sin, and death.

Contrast the cures effected by Christian Science with those at the shrine at Lourdes. In the first instance the illnesses are usually self-diagnosed and the cures a matter of affirmation; in the other case a thorough medical history and examinations, before and after, are demanded before any statement of cure is made. One denies the reality of disease and the value of medical science; the petitioner at Lourdes acknowledges the fact of disease and turns to God after science has failed.

Christian Scientists are encouraged to treat themselves, but a class of professional healers, practitioners, tackle stubborn cases. Like doctors and dentists these practitioners hold regular office hours, bill their clients for their services (payments are deductible for income tax purposes). They attempt to convince the sufferer, who may or may not be a Christian Scientist, that she is in error in thinking she is sick or dying. They read from the Bible and textbook in the office or at the bedside. About 7000 registered practitioners, mostly women, are listed in the *Journal* and several serve as chaplains in the armed forces. Authorized teachers of Christian Science are limited to 30 students a year.

No marriage has ever been solemnized in a Christian Science church; the ritual contains no marriage rite. Scientists are married by Justices of the Peace or obliging Protestant ministers. Thrice-married Mrs. Eddy considered marriage "legalized lust" but conceded that until mankind would fully comprehend her principles she would tolerate the marriage of her followers. A childless marriage is preferred, however, since children are "errors." Her followers were likewise urged to overcome any "depraved appetite" for alcoholic drinks, tobacco, tea, coffee, and opium.

The standardized Sunday morning service (identical in all branch churches) consists of Mrs. Eddy's version of the Lord's Prayer, alternate reading of the Bible, the Lesson-Sermon prepared by a committee in Boston, the collection, and the recital of the "scientific statement of being." Mrs. Eddy may have borrowed her term "Father-Mother God" from the Shakers, a defunct religious cult also founded by a woman, Ann Lee. The Shakers also called their main church the Mother Church.

Traditional Christian holidays such as Christmas and Easter are ignored but special services are held on Thanksgiving Day. Baptism is not administered and a spiritual communion service is held twice yearly. Wednesday evening is devoted to oral testimonials of healing by members of the congregation.

Scientists allot large sums for the erection of pretentious temples. Of course, they operate no hospitals, clinics, welfare agencies, or orphanages since this would entail coddling error. The Principia, a small Illinois college, is Christian Scientist in faculty and student body but is not owned by the church.

Practically all basic Christian beliefs, Catholic and Protestant, are flatly denied by the cult. Christian Science rejects the idea of a personal God, the Trinity, original and actual sin, the devil, the atonement, the resurrection, the divinity of Christ, judgment, heaven, and hell. Casual inquirers must be warned, however, not to assume that the use of common Christian terms in Christian Science literature supposes common meanings and interpretations.

A number of Jews have embraced Christian Science and have found little incompatible with liberal Judaism. The cult is sometimes proposed as a happy compromise in a Jewish-Gentile marriage. We might say that this fashionable cult makes its chief appeal to Jew and genteel.

The cult inculcates an attitude toward life which nonmembers find impossibly inconsistent. In this it shares the difficulties of all systems of absolute idealism. The demands of faith it imposes on its members are enormous. Christian Science claims to offer much more than health to its faithful. It is advertised as the key to success in business, marriage, financial undertakings. The writer once heard a Scientist testify at a Wednesday evening meeting that he attributed his success in obtaining travel and hotel reservations to his application of Christian Science.

Mrs. Eddy was a shrewd, tenacious, and courageous woman. She seemed an utter failure before she discovered Christian Science in 1866; she died a millionairess and the revered religious leader of 100,000 Americans.

Although Christian Science is only one of two score sects which feature faith healing, it has achieved a respectability, membership, and power which most have lacked. Its period of greatest growth may be seen between 1906 and 1926 and it seems to have reached its zenith. Its chance of becoming one of the great churches has gone.

Four main agencies are employed in its widespread proselytizing program: the open lectures, the reading rooms maintained by each branch society, the *Monitor* and other church periodicals, and radio and TV programs. In each medium the healing testimonial is the basic selling point.

Its wealthy and educated devotees, impressive temples, and dignified publications make a good impression on the public. The Committee on Publications silences adverse publicity. But a taste of *Science and Health* disenchants many inquirers. Few can dissuade themselves from the common sense view of life and the world around them. The facts of measles and murder and mortuaries appear self-evident to most of mankind.

A few people in search of the esoteric, a few who despair of medical science, a few who abandon Judaism and are looking for a substitute religion will continue to find their answers in Eddyism. As medical science banishes more of man's scourges to the halls of memory fewer people will be willing to stake their lives and those of their children on the theories of a New England lady who lived in the age of homeopathy and blood letting.

Chapter XVIII

THE RATIONALISTS

Unitarians and Universalists Challenge All Dogmas

P ERHAPS one Unitarian out of a hundred has actually affiliated with the Unitarian and Universalist churches. Certainly the membership of 147,000 for the Unitarian Universalist Association hardly represents the number of Americans who hold rationalist, deistic, and secular humanistic positions.

Denial of the divinity of Christ and of the Trinity seems to be the chief Unitarian position, but the Unitarians oppose not just one or two basic Christian dogmas but all dogmas. Not only anti-trinitarian but antisupernatural, the Unitarians-Universalists would be better classified as religious liberals who oppose all dogma and ecclesiasticism.

A union of the Unitarian and Universalist Churches was completed in 1961, with the merged denomination taking the name the Unitarian Universalist Association. For the time being the two former denominations will maintain separate headquarters until the organizational structure is completed. Recently the education, publications, and public relations departments of the two liberal denominations were co-ordinated. Although the Universalists were founded by Calvinist trinitarians who believed that God was too good to punish man eternally, they came to adopt Unitarianism through the influence of Hosea Ballou in the nineteenth century.

European Unitarianism or Socinianism sprang not from the Protestant Reformation but from the Pelagianism and rationalism of the Italian humanists. The Socinus brothers cultivated the Unitarian movement in Poland where it flourished for a time in the sixteenth century among the nobility. During the Counter Reformation the Jesuits succeeded in stamping out the remnants of Polish Unitarianism by 1638. Servetus, the Spanish Unitarian, was burned at the stake in Calvin's Geneva and his execution was applauded by Luther. Polish exiles carried the anti-trinitarian message to Transylvania and before World War II about 70,000 members were reported in this surviving Hungarian Unitarian church.

American Unitarianism grew out of New England Congregationalism and eventually split that denomination in the Boston area. The frank deism of such colonial leaders as Washington, Jefferson, and Franklin fostered Unitarianism and by the end of the eighteenth century a number of Congregational ministers and laymen, reacting against the harsh high Calvinism of the age, had accepted Unitarian views. The divinity of Christ, predestination, total depravity, the atonement, and eternal punishment were dismissed as unreasonable. The election of one of their number, Henry Ware, as divinity professor at Harvard in 1805 precipitated the revolt from Congregationalism.

By 1819 the Unitarians constituted a separate denomination, in fact if not in name, and in 1825 they organized the American Unitarian Association. By coincidence the British Unitarian counterpart, begun by Joseph Priestley, the discoverer of oxygen ,and James Martineau, was formally organized on the same day.

Actually the first Unitarian church in this country was an Episcopalian rather than a Congregational church. As early as 1785 King's Chapel in Boston eliminated all references to the Trinity and the divinity of Christ from the Book of Common Prayer, junked the Athanasian and Nicene creeds.

Boston became the main stronghold of Unitarianism and its spread beyond Boston was checked by later revivals. The typical Unitarian is said to have believed in "the fatherhood of God, the brotherhood of man, and the neighborhood of Boston." At the time of the secession most of the men of wealth and position in

Boston held anti-trinitarian views and voted to turn over the former Congregational property to the new association. The first Pilgrim church, established at Plymouth in 1620, adopted Unitarianism in 1802. The Unitarians managed to capture Harvard and retain control of that respected university through the years including the recent presidencies of Eliot and Conant.

Spokesman for the Unitarians at the time of the schism was William Ellery Channing but he was succeeded by the more radical Theodore Parker who directed the movement toward the paths of humanism and secularism which it now follows. Another prominent Unitarian was Ralph Waldo Emerson, poet-philosopher, who eventually led his Transcendentalists into the byways of pantheism.

Meantime, the Universalists were building their denominational structure on a Calvinist foundation. The pioneer Universalists or Universal Salvationists upheld the classical Calvinist doctrine that God elects some to salvation and damns others to hell. They radically modified this doctrine, however, by teaching that actually God elects all to salvation — even though He could do otherwise.

The first Universalist congregation was founded in London in 1750 and the first American group was led by John Murray, an excommunicated Wesleyan evangelist, in 1779. One of the 12 charter members of this Massachusetts church was a Negro and the Universalists went on record in 1790 as opposing human slavery.

Gradually the denomination accepted the Unitarian views of Ballou so that today no significant doctrinal differences block a fusion of the two liberal churches. Dr. Benjamin Rush, a signer of the Declaration of Independence, and Clara Barton, founder of the American Red Cross, were both Universalists. This church founded Tufts, Lombard, Buchtel, and St. Lawrence University.

Both Unitarian and Universalist churches are governed by a congregational polity, admit women to the ministry, have experienced little numerical growth in the past half century. Both pride themselves on theological liberalism but maintain a rigidly orthodox stand on what they consider liberal causes. A member of either of these churches is more or less expected to support birth control, sex education, the scientific method, civil rights, prison reform, labor unions, the United Nations, slum clearance, separation of church and state, euthanasia, public schools, cremation, etc.

Both sects are barred from the National and World Councils of Churches because they deny the divinity of Christ. Millions of Protestants, particularly the Lutherans, would protest any suggestion that they be admitted to these organized Protestant fellowships. Of course, an undetermined number of Congregationalists, Baptists, and Disciples of Christ entertain anti-trinitarian views but the official, sometimes vague, statements of their denominations satisfy other Council members.

Someone has observed that "Unitarians believe that there is at most one God." Belief in a personal God has long been abandoned as a test of fellowship by the Unitarians. Whereas the original Unitarians accepted the inspiration of the Bible and the possibility of miracles, their twentieth-century coreligionists reject original sin, the authority of the Bible, the virgin birth, hell, the devil, the resurrection, and other Christian beliefs. The Midwestern branch of the church has drifted further from its Christian moorings than the Easterners and Midwestern Unitarians were instrumental in setting up the American Humanist Association. A Unitarian Christian Fellowship attempts to preserve the Christian heritage of the church. Until 1957 the official journal of the denomination was still called the *Christian Register* now the *Unitarian Register*.

Baptism is sometimes administered to children as a dedicatory rite but like the Lord's Supper it is divested of any sacramental character. Sixteen orders of service are described in the Unitarian *Services of Religion* and the use of these liturgies is recommended to the local congregations. The Catholic would probably consider Unitarian worship cold and formal.

Little formal missionary work is undertaken but the Unitarians and Universalists sponsor campus religious foundations and the Universalists support missions in Japan. The Unitarian Beacon Press publishes Paul Blanshard's diatribes against the Catholic Church and denominational periodicals seem to bear out Peter Vierick's observation that "anti-Catholicism is the anti-semitism of the liberals."

Closest kin to the Unitarians-Universalists are the Hicksite

Friends, the Congregationalists, and the Reform Jews. They also find allies among the humanists, ethical culture enthusiasts, and modernists in other denominations.

At its 132nd annual meeting in 1957 the American Unitarian Association declared in a resolution: "It is our desire to encourage all religious liberals, whether Christian, Jewish, Buddhist, Confucianist, Hindu, Moslem or others, to unite with us."

A roster of statesmen, authors, and educators who have been Unitarians would include five presidents — Jefferson, the two Adamses, Fillmore, and Taft — Nathaniel Hawthorne, Oliver Wendell Holmes, Henry W. Longfellow, James Russell Lowell, Horace Mann, and William Cullen Bryant. Unitarians are represented out of all proportion to their numbers in *Who's Who in America* and until recently enjoyed the enormous prestige of Harvard. They have generously supported many humanitarian endeavors and often work through their own Unitarian Service Committee.

The Rationalists live in a lonely, purposeless world. If there should be a God, He does not seem to care for His creatures. Man may progress, try to serve his fellow man, shake free from his superstitions but he can hardly call this impersonal God Father or expect to live with Him forever. While the Christian prays to Our Father, the Unitarian prays, if he prays, To Whom It May Concern.

It once looked as though Unitarianism would remain a leading religious force in the United States. But its growth was halted at the city limits of Boston. It conducts no proselytizing campaigns — much less revivals; it appeals to a limited segment of the population; it can no longer capitalize on its control of one of the nation's leading universities. Despite the merger of the two churches, Unitarianism will probably continue in its role as a tiny though wealthy and influential sect of churchgoing secularists. It can claim the formal allegiance of only a fraction of those Americans who follow a secular humanist philosophy of life.

Chapter XIX

THE NON-ROMAN CATHOLICS

Who Are the Old, Polish National, and Liberal Catholics?

S CHISMATIC movements have plagued the Church since the first century of the Christian era. Most of these schismatic bodies have followed along a familiar path from schism to heresy; from refusing to recognize the supremacy of the successor of St. Peter they have advanced to positions which contradict fundamental Christian doctrines.

Nationalism has contributed fuel to the flames of schism, especially in the past century, and we find a number of schismatic groups breaking from Rome and setting altar against altar in this period. Among these may be included the Old Catholic Church in Europe, the German Catholic Church, the Czechoslovakian Church, the Mexican Church of Jesus (supported by Jaurez), and the Iglesia Filipina Indepentiente (Aglipayan). Our attention will be directed to those dissenting bodies which claim adherents in the United States, include "Catholic" in their official name, claim valid orders, and retain many Catholic forms and doctrines. These are the various Old Catholic bodies, the Polish National Catholic Church, and the strange Liberal Catholic Church.

THE OLD CATHOLICS

Opposition to the doctrine of papal infallibility which was proclaimed in 1870 led to the Old Catholic movement on the con-

202

tinent. Although 533 of the 535 conciliar fathers present for the vote on the dogma supported its definition, elements in Germany and Holland balked at its acceptance.

Led by Dr. Ignaz von Döllinger, ecclesiastical historian at the University of Munich, and by Gallican spokesman Henry Maret, these modernist and liberal sympathizers called an Old Catholic Congress in 1871. Döllinger had been excommunicated earlier in the year and had ceased to perform clerical functions.

Some 300 German, Swiss, and Austrian delegates attended the congress and adopted a preliminary platform of beliefs. A year later a second congress attracted a Jansenist and three Anglican bishops besides Anglican, Eastern Orthodox, and Protestant observers.

Döllinger cast the sole vote against the move to erect rival parishes with Old Catholic pastors and thereafter disassociated himself from the schism. In 1887 he wrote, "I have no wish to be a member of a schismatic church. I am alone." He respected the sentence of excommunication pronounced against him and received the rites of the Old Catholic sect at his death at 91, unreconciled with the Church.

Meanwhile the Prussian government saw in the new Old Catholic movement an opportunity to nationalize that Catholicism against which it was waging its *Kulturkampf*. Financial and legal support from the state enabled the dissidents to win early victories. Church property was wrested from Catholic parishioners and handed over to the favored schismatics.

Ex-priests joined the Old Catholic ranks and took charge of these appropriated parishes but no Catholic bishop could be induced to join the schism. The schismatics valued the apostolic succession and needed a bishop who would ordain new priests. They turned to the schismatic Jansenist Church of Utrecht and managed to get episcopal consecration for Prof. Joseph Hubert Reinkens of the University of Breslau by the Jansenist bishop of Rotterdam.

Perhaps we should add a few words about this Church of Utrecht from which the European Old Catholics, the Polish National Catholics, and the Liberal Catholics trace their orders.

In the seventeenth century a number of French Jansenists, who might be characterized as Catholic Calvinists, fled to Protestant Holland. Eventually they broke with Rome. In 1719, a Bishop Varlet, traveling to the Orient, stopped at Utrecht and administered the sacrament of confirmation to this group. For this unauthorized action he was suspended by the pope. Varlet returned to Holland and consecrated four bishops of Utrecht in succession, the first three of whom died before consecrating a successor. To the remnants of this group of Dutch Jansenists the Old Catholics turned for episcopal consecration in 1873.

While no official pronouncement has been made by the Vatican concerning the validity of Old Catholic orders, we have no reason to doubt that they are valid. The apostolic succession does not depend on obedience to the see of Peter but rather on the objective line of succession from apostolic sources, the proper matter and form, and the proper intention. This means that Old Catholic priests are probably true priests with the full powers of the priesthood although they would be exercising these powers unlawfully. Likewise Old Catholic bishops are bishops in the apostolic succession.

Many Old Catholics abolished compulsory confession, fasting, holydays, indulgences, veneration of relics, the *Filioque* from the creed, the Latin ritual, and the doctrine of the Immaculate Conception (defined in 1854). The Swiss Old Catholics abolished clerical celibacy in 1875, the Germans in 1877 but the Dutch not until 1922. Anglican orders were recognized as valid. Rationalism infected the movement from the beginning.

In Switzerland only three priests joined the revolt and organized the Christian National Catholic Church in 1875. One of the renegade priests, Eduard Herzog, obtained consecration from Reinkens. A married ex-priest and former Unitarian, Arnold Harris Mathew, headed the Old Catholic mission to England after 1908. We shall meet him later in discussing the hardly recognizable offspring of this mission, the Liberal Catholic Church.

Despite early state support and the intellectual stature of the instigators, the European Old Catholic movement soon disintegrated. As we have seen, Döllinger himself abandoned the rebels shortly after the break. Practically all Old Catholic clergymen were ex-Catholic priests who chafed under the obligations of celibacy or had been under suspicion of rationalism. The various state governments dumped the schismatic groups when they realized they would be weak allies in a battle with the Church. The Anglicans established intercommunion with the Old Catholics in Europe in 1931 and Old Catholic bishops have participated in Anglican consecrations and ordinations. By the end of World War II, there were an estimated 100,000 European Old Catholics, mainly in Holland and Switzerland.

An ecclesiastical adventurer by the name of Joseph Rene Vilatte introduced Old Catholicism to American shores. A Parisian by birth, Vilatte came to Canada to study for the Catholic priesthood. He apostatized while in the seminary and later became a Presbyterian minister.

Next he embraced Anglicanism and went to Switzerland where he was ordained to the Old Catholic priesthood. He returned to this country to proselytize among a group of Belgians in Wisconsin who had drifted from Catholicism. Arrangements to place his flocks under the Protestant Episcopal or Eastern Orthodox churches fell through.

Having been ordained a priest in Europe, he turned to Asia to obtain episcopal consecration. He prevailed upon the schismatic Archbishop Alvarez of Ceylon, a lapsed Latin rite Catholic and free lance bishop, to consecrate him a bishop in 1892.

Back in this country, Vilatte, now calling himself archbishop and primate, continued his missionary work among dissident groups of Belgians and later of some Poles. He consecrated a number of co-workers. In 1899, however, Vilatte made a solemn recantation of error at Rome and said he wished to be received back into the Catholic Church of his youth. He spent some time meditating in a French monastery but the following year he recanted his recantation and incurred excommunication. After 20 more years in Old Catholic activity this pathetic adventurer died in a monastery.

Today the Old Catholic movement is represented in the United States by a variety of competing sects, none of which derives its orders directly from the European Old Catholic Church and none of which is recognized by the main body of European coreligionists. The main Old Catholic sects in this country claim a membership of 100,000.

Vilatte himself set up the *American Catholic Church* in Chicago and before returning to Rome he had consecrated an ex-Episcopalian priest as bishop. Its present status is precarious and it has suffered greatly by defections and splits. It claims 4246 members and like many such sects is top heavy with an archbishop, two auxiliary bishops, and a titular bishop.

James Francis Augustine Lashley organized the *American Catholic Church, Archdiocese of New York,* in 1927. Its 20 churches, most of them in rented quarters, are all in Manhattan and Brooklyn. It reports 8435 communicants.

Bishop Mathew in England consecrated the Prince and Duke de Landas Berghes, an Austrian, in 1912 and dispatched him to this country two years later. He consecrated two men as bishops on two successive days: Henry Carfora, an ex-Catholic priest, and William Henry Francis Brothers. The quarrel between these two men led to the formation of the *North American Old Roman Catholic Church* (Carfora) and the *Old Catholic Church in America* (Brothers).

The Carfora faction managed to attract most of the Old Catholic remnants along with some disaffected Poles and Lithuanians. This North American Old Roman Catholic Church split up after the death of Carfora so that it is now difficult to distinguish the many factions. One group claims 65,000 adherents and another reports 84,000; both estimates are highly inflated.

This body "acknowledges the primacy of the successor of St. Peter" but denies his infallibility. Its statement of beliefs includes the seven sacraments, the Mass, transubstantiation, "the Veneration and Invocation of the Glorious and Immaculate Mother of God, of the Angels, and the saints, and prayers for the dead." While advocating celibacy it does not forbid its clergy to marry. English is used in the liturgy.

The Brothers organization has not been so successful, although it claims recognition by an assortment of tiny Old Catholic communities in Poland, Lithuania, France, and Yugoslavia. Both Roman and Eastern Orthodox rituals are employed in translation. A Greek and a Polish bishop assist Brothers, who holds the title of archbishop. Brothers brought himself and his church, reduced to himself and two or three priests, into union with the "Patriarchal Exarchate of the Russian Orthodox Church in America" in 1962. All were re-ordained. Brothers became a "Mitred Archpriest."

Archbishop William W. Flynn, who claims episcopal orders from Russian Orthodox, Melkite, and Old Catholic sources, heads the tiny *Reformed Catholic Church* (Utrecht Confession). This church claims congregations in Great Britain, Germany, France, Belgium, Cuba, Australia, Canada, and the United States but the number of adherents in this country is given at only 2200. The Reformed Catholic Church grants the pope a primacy of honor but not of jurisdiction, allows its clergy to marry once, and considers a general confession as valid as private confession. Archbishop Flynn recently moved his headquarters from Orange, Texas, to Los Angeles.

Old Catholicism in this country has been marked by feuds, rivalries, schisms, defections, depositions and counterdepositions, and a general state of instability. Many congregations and churches are paper institutions or fictions of the imagination of some "bishop" who may have received consecration in the Vilatte line. Peter F. Anson, the authority on these sects, estimates there are more than 20 churches claiming the Vilatte succession and about as many tracing their orders to Mathew. None of these groups is in communion with anyone but themselves.

THE POLISH NATIONAL CATHOLICS

Disgruntled and nationalistic Poles in this country organized the Polish National Catholic Church in the early part of the century. Since then this sect, the only permanent schism in the American Church in 400 years, has undergone an evolution from the rationalism of its founder to a more orthodox position following his death and the cultivation of close ties with the Episcopal Church.

Grumbling over the prevalence of Irish hierarchy and priests and

details of church administration prompted a number of local defections in Polish parishes around the turn of the century. Vilatte
attempted to interest some of the malcontents in Old Catholicism
but as usual his efforts bore little fruit. Ex-priest Anton Kozlowski
set up a Polish Catholic Church in Chicago in 1895 and obtained Old
Catholic consecration from Herzog. At the time of his death in
1907 he supervised 23 dissident parishes throughout the country.

Francis Hodur, another ex-priest and a freethinker, encouraged
a mass defection in Scranton in 1897. He established the Polish
National Church in 1904 at a synod attended by 147 clerical and
lay delegates, purporting to represent 20,000 Polish-Americans. Hodur
also became an Old Catholic bishop in Europe and succeeded in
uniting his group with the Kozlowski group after the latter's death.
The consolidated *Polish National Catholic Church* has enjoyed a
considerable growth and has been transplanted to Poland. The 1936
religious census reported 63,000 members and the present membership exceeds 282,000.

Although the P.N.C.C. eliminated the obligation of celibacy
among the clergy in 1921, their priests hesitated to contract marriages because of opposition by the laity. Their entire liturgy is in
Polish and their seminarians need not study Latin, Greek, or Hebrew.

Extensive theological tampering by Hodur has taken the P.N.C.C.
far from the mainstream of Christian doctrine. The Polish National
Catholics, once schismatic now apparently heretical, reject original
sin, the existence of hell, the necessity of faith for salvation. They
have become universalists; all men will attain the vision of God
in heaven but the degree of that union will depend on their faithfulness to God's will in this life. Their most original contribution
to doctrinal novelty consists in elevating the Word of God "heard
and preached" to the status of a seventh sacrament (they consider
baptism and confirmation as one combined sacrament).

Private confession is declared not to be essential although young
people up to the age of 20 are expected to confess to a priest. Adults
may receive absolution by a public declaration of sinfulness in the
general confession which precedes every Mass. Communion is
distributed under the species of bread only.

Future priests to staff the 162 P.N.C.C. parishes in the United States are trained at Savonarola Seminary at Scranton. All courses are taught in Polish, which is becoming less and less familiar to the younger seminarians. An average of 16 seminarians are enrolled in the three year course which includes scripture, philosophy, church history, Polish history, moral and doctrinal theology.

Since 1946 the P.N.C.C. and the Protestant Episcopal Church have practiced intercommunion. Seventy Episcopal bishops have been consecrated since then and of these exactly half were consecrated with P.N.C.C. bishops as co-consecrators. The possibility exists therefore that these 35 Episcopalian bishops may be in the apostolic succession via the Old Catholic succession of Varlet. The Episcopal priests they in turn have ordained may be true priests. However, the role of the co-consecrator has not been precisely defined and his contribution to the consecration is in question. In no instance was an Episcopal bishop directly consecrated by a P.N.C.C. bishop. Furthermore, valid orders depend on more than the apostolic succession and proper matter and form; proper intention is also demanded and the radical dogmatic variations of the P.N.C.C. must be taken into account. Despite their openly heterodox positions the Polish National Catholics remain on close terms with the Protestant Episcopal Church and the Old Catholics of Holland and Switzerland who provided them with orders in the first place.

The pastor of the largest P.N.C.C. parish in the country in South Deerfield, Massachusetts, took the logical step in 1959 and became a Unitarian. He had once been a Roman Catholic priest in Poland and was given charge of a schismatic parish by Bishop Hodur after his defection from Rome. Many of his parishioners followed him into the Unitarian Church with whose liberalism they had become acquainted under his spiritual direction.

Encouraged by Bishop Hodur a group of Lithuanians also severed connections with Rome and in 1914 set up the *Lithuanian National Catholic Church*, modeled after the Polish sect. The present four Lithuanian National Catholic parishes claim a membership of 3950 and are visited by P.N.C.C. bishops.

Prompted by nationalistic rather than religious motives, these two sects demonstrate the departure from Christian truths which such schism can effect in 50 years. Their theology and comparative strength may be attributed to the abilities of their freethinking founder, who died in 1953, and to blatant appeals to nationalism.

Perhaps continued relations with the Episcopalians, the Old Catholics in Europe, and the member churches of the National and World Councils of Churches will bring them closer to historic doctrinal positions than those proposed by Hodur.

THE LIBERAL CATHOLICS

No more bizarre religious concoction can be imagined than the wedding of sacramentalism and Theosophy in Liberal Catholicism. To the casual observer the Liberal Catholic Church may sound well suited to the needs of emancipated moderns: a theologically liberal church providing the ritual and beauty of Catholicism. A prospective convert would soon discover otherwise.

Liberal Catholicism clothes the Theosophical occultism of Madame Blavatsky and Annie Besant in Christian dress. A Roman Catholic instinctively views the sect as a fantastic religious nightmare.

Bishop Mathew of the Old Catholic Church in England seemed to exercise little judgment in choosing the men whom he would consecrate. In 1915 he had consecrated a certain F. S. Willoughby, a former Anglican. Two years later Willoughby submitted to Rome but not before he had consecrated three other men, including one James Ingall Wedgwood who was already well known in Theosophical circles.

Theosophy was the creation of a sleazy Russian noblewoman, Helena Blavatsky, who combined elements of Hinduism, Spiritualism, and a fertile imagination into an occult system. She won followers in America and in 1890 came to London where she died the following year. A devotee, Mrs. Annie Besant, accepted theosophy after abandoning Anglicanism for atheism; she succeeded Madame Blavatsky as head of the Theosophical movement. She elaborated its basic doctrines of pantheism, reincarnation, adepts and masters, astral bodies, clairvoyance, and the like.

Wedgwood scuttled the Old Catholic mission in England and transformed the apparatus into the Liberal Catholic Church in 1918. Continental Old Catholics repudiated the English branch which soon bore little resemblance to anything Christian. Charles Leadbeater, another Theosophical leader, was appointed Regionary Bishop for Australia and in 1923 succeeded Wedgwood as Presiding Bishop. He chose a man named Cooper to be bishop for the United States. All were prominent Theosophists and co-workers of Mrs. Besant.

According to the Theosophical-Liberal Catholic view, Jesus visited a Near East monastery at the age of 19 and browsed around for several years in occult lore and Buddhism. He finally acquired the status of Adept and returned to Nazareth. At 29 he delivered his body to the Great White Brotherhood in return for the Christ principle.

Liberal Catholics meticulously observe the details of the Latin rite but add their own curious interpretations. During their Mass, for example, the priest and an angel act as architects in erecting an invisible bubble over the church building. Sensitive souls may perceive this basilica-type bubble which takes on various hues. Similar bubbles are blown around Roman Catholic churches during the celebration of Mass, say the Liberal Catholics; rather lopsided and muddish-colored bubbles are erected over Anglican churches (Liberal Catholics have their reservations about the validity of Anglican orders).

Priests carry on lay occupations and officiate at liturgical functions in off hours. The pastor of a Chicago Liberal Catholic church is a practicing dentist. The church neither enjoins nor forbids marriage of the clergy. Whether such a body has preserved valid orders in the light of proper intention is questionable.

No images of the dead Christ are permitted in their churches and all references to hell and pleas for mercy are deleted from their liturgy as offensive relics of primitive religion. Liberal Catholics pride themselves on their willingness to borrow from other, particularly Eastern, religions.

An official statement of beliefs declares: "As a working basis of fellowship it asks of its members not the profession of a common belief, but their willingness to worship corporately through a common ritual, and permits to its lay members (though not, of course, to its clergy) entire freedom in the interpretation of creeds, Scriptures, tradition, and liturgy." No one is denied communion, and private confession is available but its frequent use is discouraged.

Since 1947 a division in this country has separated those stressing the original Theosophical orientation from those wishing to direct the sect toward more frankly Christian positions. The latter division numbers about 4000 members in nine churches with headquarters in the Cathedral Church of St. Albans in Los Angeles. The rival group maintains headquarters in Minneapolis. World-wide headquarters of Liberal Catholicism is in London.

We might describe Liberal Catholicism as an example of pure aestheticism whereby those who admire the liturgy, vestments, incense, symbolism, and music of the ancient church may gain some satisfaction without subscribing to any definitely Christian beliefs. In other words, Liberal Catholicism seems ideally suited to adults who like to play church.

Chapter XX

THE EASTERN ORTHODOX

129 Million Christians Comprise Orthodox World

Unlike the purely human Protestant communions, the Eastern Orthodox churches have preserved the apostolic succession and the essentials of Christian doctrine and worship. Orthodox bishops are true Christian bishops; Orthodox priests are true priests; the Orthodox Divine Liturgy (the Mass) is a true sacrifice; and the sacraments of the Oriental churches are true sacraments.

Despite participation by some Orthodox leaders in the World Council of Churches, the Eastern Orthodox are much closer to Catholicism than to Protestantism. Like Roman Catholics they venerate Mary as the Mother of God, acknowledge seven sacraments or mysteries, value celibacy and monasticism, honor the saints of God, believe in transubstantiation, recognize the authority of tradition as well as scripture. They disagree with their Catholic brethren chiefly in refusing to admit the jurisdictional primacy of the pope over the universal church although he is regarded as the patriarch of the West.

Before examining the cause of the schism between East and West we should perhaps detour to point out some problems in terminology. "Orthodox" itself means "true doctrine" and in this sense Catholics would also lay claim to the term. That branch of Christendom which we are examining in this chapter is sometimes rather inaccurately called Greek Orthodox although most Orthodox

213

are not Greek and the Greek church is only one of 17 independent
Orthodox churches. "Eastern" church is likewise misleading since
the Eastern Christian churches also include the Lesser Eastern
churches, such as the Egyptian and Ethiopian Copts and the Armenian Monophysites, which fell into heresy long before the East-
West schism. Millions of Eastern rite Catholics represent that por-
tion of Eastern Christianity which has returned to the obedience
of Rome while retaining the Byzantine liturgy and Eastern customs
and traditions.

Like a lover's quarrel whose original cause has long since been
forgotten, the reasons for the schism of the Byzantine churches more
than 900 years ago have all but been forgotten. Had no political
machinations exploited this religious disagreement we might have already witnessed a reunion of East and West. Today the rulers of
Soviet Russia employ the subservient Orthodox church as a tool in its
anti-Vatican propaganda. Reunion of Orthodox and Catholic
churches in Europe and the Western hemisphere, however, may take
place sooner than many would imagine.

When Constantine established Constantinople as the capital of
the Eastern Roman Empire in A.D. 330, he chose a relatively insignificant city whose bishop was suffragan to the Metropolitan of
Heraclea. The traditional spokesmen for Eastern Christianity were
the patriarchs of Alexandria, Antioch, and Jerusalem who occupied
sees founded by the Apostles. Eventually imperial Constantinople
surpassed Rome in wealth and splendor and the bishops of that
city, puppets of the emperor and often heretical, began to advance
the novel thesis that the ecclesiastical importance of a see depended
on the political importance of the city.

From the Council of Nicea in 325 to the consecration of Photius
in 852 the Byzantine church had spent nearly 200 years in periods
of unrest and great tension. After the barbarian invasion of Rome
the pope was obliged to devote most of his attention to seeking
solutions to the problems posed by this situation. Language barriers
arose as Rome abandoned Greek for the vernacular Latin. The
proud Byzantines began to hold troubled Rome in contempt.

Emperor Michael III deposed a critic of his regime, Ignatius, the patriarch of Constantinople, and picked Photius as his successor. This learned but ambitious layman was ordained a priest and consecrated bishop in five days. When the pope objected to the treatment accorded Ignatius, Photius countered by accusing the pope himself of heresy for adding "*Filioque*" to the creed. He insisted that the Holy Ghost proceeds from the Father alone whereas the Church taught that the Holy Ghost proceeds from the Father and the Son. Photius called a synod of Eastern bishops who excommunicated the Bishop of Rome, but soon afterward Michael was dethroned and executed and the next emperor ousted Photius. Later Photius again became patriarch and this time the pope recognized the legitimacy of the appointment. Eventually another emperor banished Photius to a monastery where he died forgotten but reconciled with Rome.

Modern scholarship assigns a much smaller role to Photius in explaining the final break. His schism was of brief duration and the instigator soon submitted to Rome, but relations between East and West were severely strained and the ground was prepared for a more serious rupture.

The election of another layman, Michael Caerularius, as patriarch in 1043 presaged an anti-Western campaign. Haughty and dictatorial, Caerularius despised all things Western and immediately launched a tirade against the pope for such supposed heresies as fasting on the Saturdays of Lent and using unleavened bread in communion. The new patriarch closed all Latin churches in Constantinople and desecrated the hosts. Unfortunately, the pope was represented by a tactless cardinal who further antagonized the Byzantines. In 1054 the legates of Pope Leo IX placed the decree of excommunication on the high altar of St. Sophia. This decree applied only to Caerularius and neither the Byzantine faithful nor any other patriarch have been formally placed under the censure of Rome.

The political misfortunes of Rome and the artificial aggrandizement of Byzantium, the ambitions of the patriarchs of Constantinople, temperamental differences between East and West, and the clashing personalities of the principals contributed to a schism which need never have taken place. No intellectual necessity led to the break. Greater Christian charity and consideration on both sides could have averted the tragedy.

Attempts to heal the breach at the Ecumenical Councils of Lyons in 1274 and Florence in 1439 did not result in permanent reunions. The Easterners agreed to a formula which recognized the pope as "the vicar of Christ, the pastor and teacher of all Christians, having the right to guide and govern the Church, without prejudice to the privileges and rights of the Eastern patriarchs." This decree was read in St. Sophia in 1452 but the political motives of the Byzantines and the resistance by the Orthodox believers frustrated the hopeful agreements of the Council.

As the years passed Byzantium fell upon evil days. The Moslems conquered Constantinople in 1453 and converted the chief shrine of Eastern Christendom into a mosque. A sultan appointed and deposed the patriarch as it suited his whims.

The humiliated patriarch of Constantinople had to be content with a primacy of honor rather than jurisdiction as the center of the Orthodox world shifted to Russia. Moscow became a patriarchate in 1589 and 100 years later Czar Peter abolished the patriarchate and organized the "Most Holy Synod" which he controlled. After the fall of the Romanovs the majority of the world's Orthodox Christians found themselves living under the only officially atheist government.

The Turks faced a series of revolts in the nineteenth century and as the Ottoman empire collapsed the Greeks, Serbs, Romanians, and Bulgarians shook off obedience to the sultan's hand-picked patriarch as well as to the sultan. The patriarch was helpless to protest the founding of a succession of national independent Orthodox churches. During the nineteenth century the patriarch of Constantinople found his spiritual domain amputated again and again.

Today we find an Orthodox world which consists of a number of equal, independent, and autonomous churches united only by a certain spiritual fellowship, the common Byzantine liturgy, and adherence to the doctrinal statements of the first seven ecumenical councils. No one church speaks for Orthodoxy and no one theologian speaks for any particular Orthodox church.

The Patriarch of Constantinople still occupies a place of honor and precedence among the five patriarchs and carries the title "ecumenical patriarch." He lives in a Moslem city with a tiny Christian flock of 120,000. Of the 239 patriarchs of Constantinople only 31 have died in office; the others have been deposed or murdered. At one time during the past century seven deposed patriarchs were living in the city.

The Patriarch of Alexandria, successor of St. Mark, lives in Cairo in the winter and Alexandria in summer and shepherds 150,000 Christians. The Patriarch of Antioch, which once embraced 220 dioceses, now resides in Damascus and leads 155,000 souls. The third apostolic patriarch, the Patriarch of Jerusalem, is the spiritual leader of 45,000 Syrians and 80 monks of the Brotherhood of the Holy Sepulcher.

Russia did not accept Christianity until late in the tenth century but when Constantinople fell to the Moslems Moscow received the mantle of Orthodox leadership. Close association of the church with the ruling dynasty provided a further excuse for persecution by the Communist masters after the 1917 revolution. Not all Russians had been satisfied with the state church but had joined the many bizarre sects — the Raskolniki, Dukhobors, Molokani, Stundists, and others. Some became Baptists. Since the Revolution and the Communist antireligious movement most Orthodox churches and monasteries have been closed or turned into museums. Only a handful of bishops and priests continue to carry on their spiritual activities and few men or young people attend church. The Soviet government refuses to estimate the number of church goers in the USSR. The estimate of 129,000,000 Orthodox Christians includes 50,000,000 in Soviet Russia. How long these Christians can keep their faith and pass it on to their children in an atheistic regime is debatable.

Other independent Orthodox churches serve populations in Cyprus, Bulgaria, Serbia, Romania, Georgia, Yugoslavia, and the United

States. Semi-independent churches are found in Finland, Poland, Czechoslovakia, and Albania and small missionary churches have been planted in Japan and China.

The first missionary Orthodox church in the United States was founded in 1794. Technically most Orthodox churches in this country are dependent on the mother churches in Europe and Asia but they are understandably reluctant to take orders from puppet churches behind the Iron Curtain which must parrot the Communist political line.

As its doctrinal standard the Orthodox churches recognize as binding any dogma defined by the first seven ecumenical councils. The last of these councils, the Second Council of Nicea, was held in A.D. 787 and an appeal to an ecumenical council today is theoretical for the Easterners since they agree that no such council could be called without including the Western Church. Orthodox theological statements lack the precision of Catholicism and since the Orthodox are 12 centuries behind the times doctrinally they have not officially adopted the dogmas defined by Rome since the schism. Many of these dogmas find expression in the Byzantine liturgy and are cherished by the Orthodox believers. While these dogmas have been defined by Rome they remain open questions in Orthodoxy and a theologian who accepted any or all of them could not be condemned as a heretic by the patriarch or synod.

The question of the jurisdictional primacy of the Bishop of Rome is certainly the most important dispute between Rome and Byzantium. Numberless texts in the Eastern liturgy indicate that the pope holds a primacy not only of honor but of spiritual authority. The most eminent theologian of the Russian church in recent centuries, Vladimir Soloviev (1853–1900), entered the Catholic Church several years before his death. In the preface to his work *Russia and the Universal Church* this Russian Newman explained why he took the road to Rome. He pointed out that as an Eastern Christian he recognized as supreme judge in religious matters the same Apostle Peter and his successors who were recognized by the great Fathers and Doctors: St. Irenaeus, St. Denis the Great, St. Athanasius the Great, St. John Chrysostom. St. Cyril, St. Flavian, Blessed Theodoret, St. Maximus the Confessor, St. Theodore the Studite, St. Ignatius, and the others.

Today Orthodox scholars are willing to concede that the addition of the *"Filioque"* to the Nicene creed did not and does not constitute heresy. That the Holy Ghost proceeds from the Father and the Son was held by large sections of the Eastern church as well as the Western before it became a shibboleth between the Catholic and the Orthodox churches. This addition to the creed was occasioned by a need in the West to defend an attacked dogma but did not change the dogma. Eastern Rite Catholic churches may omit the equivalent expression but most of them have chosen to include it in their liturgies. When Pope Pius XI celebrated an Eastern Rite Mass in St. Peter's in 1925 he omitted the controversial word. Theologians at the reunion Council of Florence were able to agree on a solution to this question and theologians on both sides today agree that the *"Filioque"* issue is no longer a major stumbling block.

Some confusion is evident in the modern Orthodox teaching about purgatory. Some Orthodox theologians flatly deny a belief in purgatory while others simply deny any material fire in purgatory. The Orthodox pray for the dead and offer the Holy Sacrifice for the faithful departed. Certain theologians teach that the souls of the dead remain in an intermediate state until the general judgment. In general we may say that Orthodox eschatological views are less developed than those of the West but that any Orthodox theologian, priest or layman, may hold views identical with Catholicism without incurring the charge of heresy by his coreligionists.

Another difference between Orthodoxy and Catholicism concerns the moment of transubstantiation in the Holy Sacrifice. The Orthodox believe that the consecration is effected not by the words of institution — "This is My body" and "This is My blood" — but by a later prayer calling upon the Holy Ghost to change the bread and wine into the body and blood of Christ. This prayer is called the *Epiklesis*. The Catholic Church teaches that the transubstantiation takes place at the word of institution.

Dogmas which have been defined since A.D. 787 are not binding on the Orthodox, such as those regarding indulgences and the infallibility of the pope. Finally, in the area of morals some Orthodox churches allow divorce with remarriage for a number of reasons such as adultery, apostasy, insanity, and desertion.

Moving from the realm of doctrine to that of discipline and practice we find a number of differences between East and West, many of which are found also in Eastern churches in union with Rome. As the Mass is known as the Divine Liturgy so the seven sacraments are called "mysteries." Infants are baptized by threefold immersion but the legitimacy of other modes of baptism has been granted. Immediately after baptism the priest anoints the baby in the sacrament of confirmation which is called "anointing with holy myron."

Parish priests may be married; they ordinarily wear a beard, cassock, and a high cylindrical headgear. Most Orthodox priests have received only a high school education and are trained mainly to function at the altar rather than to master theology. In Russia the office is hereditary with the eldest son becoming pastor when his father dies or retires. Orthodox monks follow the rule of St. Basil, remain celibate, furnish the church with its bishops, theologians, and educators. The Roman multiplicity of religious orders is not duplicated in Orthodoxy.

Orthodoxy follows the ancient liturgy of St. John Chrysostom as do the Catholic Eastern rite churches. A vernacular or archaic language is used during the services which may last several hours. The faithful kneel or stand during the services since there are no pews in traditional Orthodox churches. Women sit in the balcony. The Easterners follow the Julian rather than the Gregorian calendar, which means their fixed feasts are celebrated 13 days later than those of the Latin Church.

A picture wall or iconostasis separates the sanctuary from the nave of the church and the sacred actions take place out of sight of the worshipers. The iconostasis ordinarily includes representations of the Annunciation, St. John the Evangelist, the Mother of God, Christ, St. John the Baptist, the Archangel Gabriel, and the patron saint of the church. No statues or organs are allowed. Each church may have only one altar and only one celebration of the liturgy is allowed on a single day. During penitential seasons the liturgy is celebrated only once a week.

Leavened bread and wine are used in the communion and the faithful receive both species. Easterners make a profound bow in place of the Western genuflection and both Orthodox and Eastern rite Catholics make the sign of the cross from right to left with the thumb and first two fingers held together. Far more rigorous fasting is expected in the Eastern churches.

Cordial relations have been established between some Orthodox churches and the Anglican and Old Catholic communions. Orthodox bishops have participated in ecumenical conferences and the activities of the World Council of Churches together with evangelical and modernist Protestants. Newspapers have pictured robed and bearded Orthodox prelates walking with Salvation Army generals in World Council processions. Protestants do not seem to be disturbed by Orthodox devotions to Mary, intercession of the saints, monasticism, belief in transubstantiation and the seven sacraments, and claims to be the one true church, although these same affirmations by Roman Catholics seem distressing.

The exact number of Orthodox communicants in the United States is uncertain because many Orthodox groups count all members of their nationality as members or else offer round-number estimates. The total is probably around 2,500,000. We find independent Orthodox churches composed of Albanians, Bulgarians, Greeks, Romanians, Russians, Serbs, Ukrainians, Carpatho-Russians, and Syrians. Several tiny groups claim a connection with Orthodoxy but are not recognized by the bulk of Orthodox such as the *American Holy Orthodox Catholic Apostolic Eastern Church*. These bear somewhat the same relationship to Orthodoxy as the Old Catholic splinter groups to Roman Catholicism.

Largest Orthodox body in this country, the *Greek Archdiocese of North and South America*, under the nominal jurisdiction of the Patriarch of Constantinople, claims around 1,150,000 members in 378 parishes. This would mean nearly 3,000 members per parish compared to the average Catholic parish of 1800 and the average

Protestant parish of only 350. This Greek Orthodox church operates a seminary and a teacher's college.

Eight Russian monks entered Alaska in 1792 and built a church at Kodiak. After the United States purchased Alaska the Russian Orthodox church spread to California and thence to New York to serve the thousands of immigrants who arrived late in the nineteenth century. After the Russian Revolution attempts by the puppet Russian church to control the American branch and its property were frustrated by a declaration of independence in 1924. The *Russian Orthodox Greek Catholic Church of America* now reports 755,000 members in 352 churches. Two smaller Russian bodies agree in doctrine with the main Russian Orthodox church but differ in attitudes toward the patriarch of Moscow.

Confusion often exists in the minds of Catholics over the status of Eastern rite or so-called Uniate Catholics. These Catholics follow an Eastern liturgy, use a non-Latin liturgical language, receive communion under both species, use leavened bread in the Eucharist, and follow other Eastern customs. About half the Eastern rite priests are married and only the Malabarese rite demands celibacy. These Catholics render obedience to the pope, profess the same Catholic faith and follow the same moral code as their Latin rite brethren. Catholics may attend Mass and receive Holy Communion at either a Latin or Eastern rite Catholic church. Only in danger of death, when no other priest in available, may a Catholic confess to and receive communion from an Orthodox priest and he may not attend schismatic services.

Most Eastern rite Catholics in the United States belong to one of two jurisdictions: the Byzantine Catholic Exarchate of Pittsburg with 317,000 Catholics of Russian, Magyar, Slovak, and Croatian extraction; and the Byzantine Slavonic Exarchate of Philadelphia with 323,000 Ukrainian Catholics. Other Eastern rite Catholics such as the Maronites, Melkites, and Romanians are included in the total of 835,000 in this country. The world total approaches 9,000,000 although after World War II the Communists forced all Russian Catholics to enter the Russian Orthodox church or suffer the consequences. Eastern rite Catholic churches in the Balkans have been crippled by Soviet persecution.

In his article entitled "Will Union be Easy for the Orientals?" Fr. Martin Jugie, A.A., discusses the special role of the Eastern rite churches: "The great barrier is that of age-old prejudices created by the antipathy between Greeks and Latins, and above all by political events. In our times, what one calls the Byzantine Schism has no longer any *raison d'être*. The ancient pretexts for separation have disappeared. These pretexts were of three kinds: there were divergences in doctrinal order, differences in liturgical order, and differences in canonical or disciplinary order. Of these three categories only the doctrinal divergences merit consideration in our times. The others have practically received their solution from the day that Catholic churches of Byzantine rite maintaining their ceremonies, customs and usages proper to that rite began to function."

The schism between East and West need not have occurred. No insolvable doctrinal issues were at stake. Even today the Orthodox faithful hold the essentials of the Christian faith and participate in the sacramental life of the Church through a valid priesthood. Genuine Orthodox piety must command our respect although in some circumstances it has degenerated into superstition and mere traditionalism.

As Pope Pius XI declared: "People do not realize how much faith, goodness, and Christianity there is in these bodies now separated from the age-long Catholic truth. Pieces broken from gold-bearing rock, themselves bear gold. The ancient Christian bodies of the East keep so venerable a holiness that they deserve not merely respect but complete sympathy."

Reunion of Catholicism and Orthodoxy seems more likely than any other reunion in Christendom. We shall investigate past attempts at such a reunion and future prospects in our final chapter. Meanwhile it seems that Orthodox Christianity will suffer continued losses in the Soviet Union and its satellites since the Communists are committed to erasing religion from the lives of the people.

Chapter XXI

INTERDENOMINATIONAL ACTIVITIES

Protestants Combine Efforts for Specific Purposes

Dɪᴠɪᴅᴇᴅ Protestantism finds itself severely handicapped in carrying out large scale projects and in exerting a united influence in the community. On one level the desire for some measure of co-operation has expressed itself in local and national federations of churches and in the ecumenical movement. We shall examine these trends in the next chapter.

Churches within a specific religious tradition have formed worldwide associations. These include the Baptist World Alliance, Friends World Committee, International Congregational Council, the Lambeth Conference of Bishops of the Anglican Communion, Lutheran World Federation, Mennonite World Conference, Pentecostal World Conference, World Convention of Churches of Christ (Disciples), and World Methodist Council. These organizations exercise no real authority over member churches.

On another level Protestant denominations and individuals combine energies, prayers, and funds in interdenominational agencies established to meet some specific need. We shall survey some of these co-operative agencies in this chapter, bearing in mind that space limitations do not permit a complete listing.

THE AMERICAN BIBLE SOCIETY

Fifty-two Protestant denominations support the work of the American Bible Society which translates, publishes, and distributes complete Bibles, New Testaments, and tracts. This nonprofit society began its work in 1816 and has since disseminated nearly half a billion copies of the scriptures. The average annual circulation now exceeds 12,000,000 volumes.

Working in 40 countries, the Society furnishes Bibles at cost or gives them to those unable to contribute. Translations in more than 100 languages are available and the entire Bible is furnished to the blind in braille or on records at nominal cost.

Distributors in Latin American and other traditionally Catholic nations feel compelled to justify their activities to their financial supporters by painting a wretched picture of religious life in these areas. The Society's annual report relates the conversion of numerous Roman Catholics who left the Church and became "born again Christians" after receiving a pocket New Testament. Chief monetary support of the American Bible Society comes from the Methodists, Southern Baptists, Presbyterians, and Lutherans.

THE GIDEONS

Travelers have come to expect to see a Gideon Bible in their hotel rooms. Since 1908 the Gideons, an association of 21,000 Protestant businessmen, have placed more than 4,500,000 complete Bibles and 31,000,000 New Testaments in hotels and motels, prisons, hospitals, army and navy installations, merchant ships, railroad lounge cars, and public schools.

Three traveling salesmen formed the nucleus of the Gideons and drew up a charter in 1899. Today the organization operates in the United States and 20 foreign countries. Financial support comes from the members themselves and from the Protestant churches they visit to solicit donations; the annual budget for scripture placement amounts to $2,000,000. Most members hold a more or less conservative theological position.

MASONRY

In many American communities, especially in the South and Middle West, the local Masonic lodge serves as a sort of pan-Protestant men's fellowship, even though an occasional Jew may be initiated. In fact, for many thousands the lodge serves as a satisfactory substitute religion and in this sense Freemasonry could have justifiably been included in our examination of the cults.

Masonry regales its initiates with fanciful tales of its founding in King Solomon's temple, but modern speculative Masonry dates from 1717 when its charter members assembled in an English tavern. Masonry inherited much of its symbolism and ethical teachings from the medieval guilds of working masons who built the great Christian cathedrals. After the Reformation cathedral building slackened and the depleted guilds began to admit nonworking or associate members. Eventually Speculative Masonry composed of these associate or honorary masons, jettisoned most of its Christian orientation and diluted its ritual with doses of paganism, deism, occultism, and secularism.

A candidate entering the craft begins with the first of three degrees which comprise the Blue or Symbolic lodge. Every American Mason retains his membership in one of the 16,000 local Blue lodges even though he may enter the so-called higher degrees. The first three degrees, the basic degrees, are called initiation, passing, and raising; most Masons, joining for business or social reasons, go no further than these. Master Masons who have attained the third degree supposedly know all the important Masonic lessons.

At his initiation the Masonic candidate, Christian, Jew, Moslem, Buddhist, or Hindu, beseeches the lodge to deliver him from darkness to light. He promises to keep the secrets of the lodge in the following memorized oath: "To all this I most solemnly and sincerely promise and swear, with a firm and steadfast resolution to keep and perform the same without any equivocation, mental reservation or secret evasion of mind whatever, binding myself under a no less penalty than that of having my throat cut across, my tongue torn out by its roots and buried in the rough sands of the sea at low water mark, where the tide ebbs and flows twice in twenty-four hours, should I ever knowingly or willingly violate this my solemn oath or obligation as an Entered Apprentice Mason. So help me God and keep me steadfast in the due performance of the same." The secrets for whose protection this solemn oath is given consist of a few passwords and secret grips and signals.

The gruesome penalty for disclosing similar secrets of the second or Fellow Craft degree involves "having my left breast torn open, my heart plucked out and given as prey to the beasts of the field and the fowls of the air." The Master Mason swears "Under no less a penalty than that of having my body severed in twain, my bowels taken from thence and burned to ashes, and the ashes scattered to the four winds of heaven, that no trace or remembrance may be had of so vile and perjured a wretch as I, should I ever knowingly violate this my solemn obligation of a Master Mason." The third degree candidate also commits himself to Masonry's selective morality: "I promise and swear that I will not violate the chastity of a Mason's wife, his mother, sister, or daughter, knowing them to be such."

This third degree represents a fictitious murder in King Solomon's Temple. The blindfolded and robed candidate is conducted into the lodge room where he is struck on the shoulders by "ruffians" who try to extract the secrets of Masonry. He is beaten until presumably dead when he is laid in a coffin. After prayers and more ritual he is "raised" from the dead to the sublime degree of a Master Mason.

Those who wish to advance in Masonry may choose one or both of two progressions, the Scottish or York rite. The former involves 32 degrees topped off by the honorary 33rd degree, while the completion of the York rite series of degrees leads to membership in the Knights Templar.

Knights Templar and 32nd degree Masons may join the Masonic fun organization, the Shrine, which indulges in Islamic shenanigans but also supports 14 hospitals for crippled children. Of the dozens of allied Masonic organizations some of the better known are the Grotto, social club for Master Masons; the Order of the Eastern

Star, the women's auxiliary; the young men's Order of DeMolay
and the young women's Rainbow Girls and Job's Daughters; and
Acacia fraternity on college campuses. No women may become
Masons and Negro Masons are segregated in parallel but unauthorized lodges.

One out of every dozen adult American males is a Mason and
the 4,000,000 Masons in this country are twice as many as in the
rest of the world. The murder of William Morgan in 1826 nearly
wiped out the craft in America. Morgan was writing a book to
expose the secrets of the lodge and many thought that his disappearance and death were engineered by Masons. Membership
dropped to 5000 and anti-Masonic political parties and publications
were launched.

Each state Grand Lodge is autonomous, and efforts to establish
a national Grand Lodge as in England and most other countries have
failed. Even the ritual is subject to variation among Grand Lodges
of the 49 states. Affiliation with the Mother Lodge in England is
the test of authenticity.

Twenty-one years after the first Grand Lodge was founded in
London, Pope Clement XII officially condemned the secret society.
In 1894 this ban was extended to the Odd Fellows, the Knights
of Pythias, and Sons of Temperance, Masonic offspring. Since the
first papal condemnation no less than 17 pronouncements by eight
different popes have made the position of the Catholic Church
clear. Any Catholic who joins the Masonic lodge incurs automatic
excommunication and any Mason wishing to enter the Church
must sever all connections with the lodge.

The Catholic Church condemns Masonry in the first place as
a false religion of naturalism. What does Masonry lack to make it a
religion, a rival of Christianity? An altar occupies a place of honor
in its temples. Worship of T.G.A.O.T.U. (The Grand Architect
of the Universe) is the acknowledged chief purpose of its assemblies which are opened and closed with prayer. The lodge demands
a minimum of belief in a Supreme Being, a resurrection, and immortality. Needless to say the naturalistic god of Freemasonry is
not the Triune God of Christianity. The Bible — with all references

to Jesus Christ carefully deleted lest His name offend non-Christian Masons — is employed during these worship services. The Masonic burial service assures the survivors that the deceased is enjoying the bliss of heaven because of his faithfulness to Masonic, rather than Christian, principles. Nowhere does Masonry suggest the need for a Savior which is the core of Christianity. Masonry has its high priests, vestments, holydays, patron saints, code of morality.

Another reason why the Church opposes Masonry is that the lodge extracts a solemn oath from its initiates which the Church must declare immoral. The candidate swears to an oath concerning things of which he is ignorant. Bloodcurdling penalties for failure to keep these secrets are announced and the candidate calls upon the Supreme Architect to witness the oath. The Church cannot countenance the use of a solemn oath as a stage effect in a lodge ceremony.

Finally, the enmity between Masonry, particularly Latin Masonry, and the Roman Catholic Church is well known and the Church could hardly allow her sons to affiliate with her sworn enemy. The long and bitter history of anticlericalism which has characterized continental Masonry provides ample reason why the Church continues to warn her children against the attractions of the lodge. Even in the United States the lodge seeks to harass parochial schools, bar Catholic children from auxiliary school services, eliminate tax exemptions for religious institutions, etc. The New Age, magazine of the Supreme Council, 33rd degree of the Scottish Rite, Southern Jurisdiction, has waged a long campaign of vilification of Catholicism.

The Catholic Church does not stand alone in opposing Masonry and similar secret societies. In fact the official positions of the Catholic Church, the Eastern Orthodox churches, and a number of Protestant denominations indicate that the great majority of Christians are barred from Masonic affiliation. Several Protestant denominations such as the Christian Reformed Church support the work of the National Christian Association of Chicago which disseminates antilodge material among evangelical Protestants. Orthodox Lutheranism has always viewed Masonry with suspicion and in this country the Missouri and Wisconsin Synod Lutherans actively op-

pose Masonry and bar Masons from the communion table. Most
Mennonite bodies, the Seventh-day Adventist church, the Church
of the Brethren, the Assemblies of God and most Holiness sects,
Quakers, United Brethren in Christ, Regular Baptists, and the
Anglo-Catholic party in Anglicanism ban or discourage lodge membership. The efforts of some prominent Anglicans to expose the
naturalistic basis of Freemasonry have been frustrated lest this
disclosure compromise the position of high Anglican prelates.

John Wesley once commented, "What an amazing banter upon
all mankind is Freemasonry!" but the Methodist minister today is
likely to be a lodgeman. The English Methodists passed a resolution
in 1927 which included these words, "Freemasonry, in its ritual and
official language is of purely Theistic nature . . . the distinctive
faith of Christianity can find no expression in its formulae, and
that the Christian message of salvation, through faith in Christ,
as the basis alike for home and foreign evangelization, is wholly
incompatible with the claims which have been put forward by
Freemasons."

General Booth, founder of the Salvation Army, set the policy
for this denomination when he declared, "No language of mine
could be too strong in condemning any Officer's affiliation with
any Society which shuts Him outside its Temples; and which in
its religious ceremonies gives neither Him nor His name any place.
The place where Jesus Christ is not allowed is no place for any
Salvation Army officer."

Protestants object to the use of a mutilated Bible in which
Christ's name has been expurgated, to the Masonic oath, to lodge
secrecy, and to the dual Christian and Masonic loyalty. Not every
Protestant denomination forbids membership in the lodge, but the
fact remains that every Christian body which has seriously investi-
gated the lodge and the implications of its teachings has been forced
to issue a condemnation.

For many Protestants in this country, however, Masonry is viewed
as a godly, if not Christian, brotherhood devoted to high ideals of
morality and charity rather than the ritualistic and cultic expression
of naturalism.

NATIONAL CONFERENCE OF CHRISTIANS AND JEWS

More of a civic oriented association than an interdenominational agency the National Conference of Christians and Jews defines itself as "an educational civic organization of religiously motivated men and women." It promotes the Brotherhood of Man under the Fatherhood of God.

Founded in 1928, the NCCJ seeks ". . . to promote justice, amity, understanding and cooperation among Protestants, Catholics, and Jews, and to analyze, moderate and finally eliminate intergroup prejudices which disfigure and distort religious, business, social and political relations, with a view to establishment of a social order in which the religious ideals of brotherhood and justice shall become standards of human relationships."

A Denver priest suggested the idea of Brotherhood Week in 1934. This observance has since been sponsored by the NCCJ. Millions of Americans in some 10,000 communities participate in various phases of Brotherhood Week.

A Protestant, Catholic, and Jew hold the positions of national co-chairmen. The Board of Directors is composed of 200 men and women drawn from various religious traditions. The NCCJ maintains 62 regional offices which serve more than 330 chapters. It sponsors student conferences, workshops, publications, human relations centers, motion pictures, speakers, research, and a consulting service.

PROTESTANTS AND OTHER AMERICANS UNITED

This newcomer among interdenominational groups which is saddled with the unwieldly title "Protestants and Other Americans United for Separation of Church and State" fosters a program of sophisticated bigotry directed against the Catholic Church. A group of ministers including Bishop G. Bromley Oxnam of The Methodist Church, Charles C. Morrison, former editor of the *Christian Century*, and John A. Mackay, president of Princeton Theological Seminary, signed the original P.O.A.U. Manifesto in 1947.

Today P.O.A.U. maintains headquarters in the nation's capital, enrolls 50,000 dues-paying members, and has already circulated 9,000,000 pieces of literature. Paul Blanshard, author of *American Freedom and Catholic Power*, serves as special counsel for the group.

Ostensibly founded to protect the American principle of separation of Church and State, P.O.A.U. reveals its deeper anti-Catholic bias in its publications. For example, a single recent issue of its monthly *Church and State Review* (July, 1956) accuses the Church of intolerance in its objections to Masonry and Rotary, lambasts Catholicism in Spain and Colombia, deplores the injunctions against the use of Protestant Bibles and Protestant books by Catholics, and objects to the promises in a mixed marriage.

P.O.A.U. constantly disavows anti-Catholicism and professes to abhor the crudities of the Ku Klux Klan, the APA, and other nativist movements. However, a sampling of the literature distributed by P.O.A.U. would lead many to suggest that the new organization has simply exchanged bedsheets for caps and gowns.

One of the most popular P.O.A.U. pamphlets was written by the Rev. C. Stanley Lowell, a Methodist minister and P.O.A.U. official. Half a million copies have been distributed of his *A Summons to Americans* which was originally presented as a Reformation Sunday sermon. After branding the Catholic Church a "spiritual totalitarianism," "an ally of Hitler and Mussolini," "a divisive influence," and a "dictatorship," the author offers this sociological shocker to his readers: "Due to a liberal immigration policy the Roman Catholic proportion of our population has been rising. This increase is also due to another factor. Go into a typical Protestant home and you may find *one child or none*. Go into a Roman Catholic home and you will find anywhere from *five to fifteen*." (Italics mine.)

The original P.O.A.U. Manifesto stated: "It is no part of our purpose to propagandize the Protestant faith or any other, nor to criticize or oppose the teaching or internal practice of the Roman Catholic Church or any other." But a current appeal for funds promised that the contributed pennies and dollars "Will help counter the threat of clericalism which has cursed Europe and Latin America." These same dollars "Will help defeat the effort of the Roman Catholic hierarchy, or any church, to obtain funds for its schools, churches, orphanages or other operations."

P.O.A.U. not only publishes its monthly magazine but offers legal service for the supposed victims of Church-State violations, sponsors a lending library, and provides background materials. The organization sent speakers to 250 Protestant churches last year to describe the Romish menace to American institutions.

WORLD CHRISTIAN STUDENT FEDERATION

Uniting Protestant student associations in colleges and universities around the world, the World Christian Student Federation represents such groups in 57 nations. The movement began with a meeting of five American and European leaders in a Swedish castle in 1895.

Thirteen student movements support the American unit of the W.C.S.F., the United Student Christian Council. Related to the National Council of Churches, the U.S.C.C. sponsors student conferences, prepares study materials, and undertakes ecumenical projects. The larger "co-operative" Protestant denominations hold membership in the U.S.C.C. through their respective campus organizations: American Baptists, United Church of Christ, Disciples of Christ, Episcopalians, Evangelical United Brethren, Methodists, Presbyterians, Y.M.C.A., and Y.W.C.A.

WOMEN'S CHRISTIAN TEMPERANCE UNION

"Protection of society from the destructive end-results of the liquor drinking custom and trade" has been the chief purpose of the Women's Christian Temperance Union. The old Anti-Saloon League and the W.C.T.U. have both received strong support from Protestant denominations, and the high water mark of political Protestantism was no doubt the enactment of national prohibition.

Women join the W.C.T.U. by taking the pledge and paying their $1 annual dues; men may qualify as honorary members. Recently the ladies have extended their war to narcotics, juvenile delinquency, obscene literature, communism, and child labor.

The pledge adopted in 1876 is still administered: "I hereby
solemnly promise, God helping me, to abstain from all distilled,
fermented, and malt liquors, including wine, beer, and cider, and
to employ all proper means to discourage the use of and traffic in
the same." At noon each day the members are expected to pray
for the attainment of W.C.T.U. goals and the overthrow of the
liquor traffic. The badge is a knot of white ribbon.

Y.M.C.A.   AND   Y.W.C.A.

One out of every four members of the leading Protestant youth
organization, the Young Men's Christian Association, is a Roman
Catholic. In the Philippines and South America the proportion
of Catholics in the Y.M.C.A. approaches 95 per cent.

Catholics who join the Y.M.C.A. should know that they are
joining a youth organization completely Protestant in origin, history,
inspiration, and leadership. Time and again the Holy See has warned
Catholics against affiliating with the Y without at any time dis-
paraging the sincerity of Y personnel or the accomplishments of
the organization.

George Williams, a London clerk, founded the modern Y in 1844
and the 12 charter members included three Anglicans, three Methodists, three Congregationalists, and three Baptists. It was designed
to win back the young industrial workers in the cities to the evangelical faith and this religious orientation continues to be the Y's
chief aim although recreation has assumed a greater role.

In this country membership in the Y was long dependent on
adherence to the so-called Portland test adopted in 1869. This
test limited active membership to young men belonging to evangelical churches; others, such as Catholics, could be admitted as associate or nonvoting members. In 1925 the Y.M.C.A. decided it could
tolerate Catholics in small numbers and announced that 10 per cent
of its membership could henceforth be composed of non-Protestants.
In the early 1930's the whole question was shifted to the discretion
of the local Y.M.C.A. which may legitimately bar all Catholics,
Eastern Orthodox, etc., if it wishes.

The International Survey of the Y.M.C.A and Y.W.C.A. observes,

"The Roman Catholic Church may look with tolerance on many of the Association's activities but the underlying opposition to their religious and moral ideology remains unabated." This same book makes an admission which many Catholic young people and parents may well ponder when it reports "the participation of Catholics in such activities tends very frequently, perhaps inevitably, as Catholic leaders are well persuaded, to weaken allegiance to traditional dogmas which are essential to the Catholic faith."

Y.M.C.A. leader Sherwood Eddy, in his book A Century With Youth, freely acknowledges that "The alignment of the American Y.M.C.A.'s in North America is clearly with the Protestant forces, although its services are extended to all, without regard to creed, in America and throughout the world."[1] As a matter of fact most Y authorities are equally frank even though some local Y.M.C.A. secretaries may seek to minimize the extent of Protestant control.

In the Philippines, Italy, Poland, and South America, where the great majority of Y members are Catholics, the evangelical churches retain control by stipulating that not more than one third of the board of directors may belong to any one denomination. This assures continued control by the tiny Protestant minorities.

It is instructive to note that in the United States the percentage of local board members who are Catholics (3 per cent) and of full-time secretaries (directors) (.59 per cent) is conspicuously smaller than the Catholic membership (about 23 per cent). Of course, the co-operation of a practicing Catholic as a board member or local director of a Protestant youth movement would not be encouraged by the Church.

The Philippines hierarchy concluded its joint statement on the Y.M.C.A. and Y.W.C.A. in 1954 with these words: "Wherefore, we, the members of the Hierarchy of the Philippines, hereby declare that the Y.M.C.A. is a Protestant organization and, as such, should be avoided by Catholics, that is, no Catholic may be a member of this organization or contribute to its support or lend his name for propaganda purposes, or make use of its facilities."

---

[1] Sherwood, Eddy, A Century With Youth (New York: Association Press, 1944), p. 51.

Evangelical Christianity finds a sturdy ally in the 1300 local Y.M.C.A.'s in this country, manned by dedicated laymen, and offering a diversified program of religion, counseling, recreation, and sports. The world-wide Y.M.C.A. membership in 1956 was 4,242,800. Both the Y.M.C.A. and Y.W.C.A. hold membership in the World Council of Churches and both have advanced the ecumenical ideals of Protestantism. Neither can be recommended for Catholic young men and women.

This sampling of Protestant interdenominational agencies indicates some of the many areas in which American Protestants have learned to co-operate. Not all Protestants support all these agencies: few Lutherans or Episcopalians, for example, will subscribe to W.C.T.U. objectives; no Missouri or Wisconsin Synod Lutherans will join the Masonic lodge; few Holiness adherents will be found in student Christian associations. On the other hand, several organizations such as the Y.M.C.A. have won all but unanimous approval by Protestant Christians.

Parallel agencies operate within the framework of the Catholic Church in this country and are designed to meet similar needs. We might mention the Catholic Biblical Association of America, the Knights of Columbus, Catholic Total Abstinence Union, C.Y.O., National Federation of Catholic College Students, and the National Newman Club Federation.

We should also mention some of the other influences besides interdenominational agencies which tend to bring Protestants into a closer sense of community. Most Protestants sing the same hymns during their worship services whether held in a Methodist, Baptist, or Presbyterian church. Protestant chaplains in the armed forces minister to men of many denominations as do chaplains in hospitals, prisons, welfare homes, etc. Worldwide Communion Sunday, Reformation Day, Race Relations Day are observed by scores of denominations. Except for the recalcitrant Southern Baptists, Missouri and Wisconsin Synod Lutherans, Anglo-Catholics and fringe sects, American Protestantism can mobilize its forces today in a manner which would have seemed unbelievable one hundred years ago.

Chapter XXII

THE ECUMENICAL
MOVEMENT

Protestants Search for Church Unity

Amⓞng American Protestants a sizable minority continues to glory in the manifold divisions of Protestantism. Members of this school are likely to rhapsodize about the numberless Christian "emphases" as genuine expressions of religious democracy and freedom. They may be willing to participate in limited interdenominational enterprises but they insist on preserving distinctive sectarian patterns. No one knows what degree of rationalization enters into the formation of this attitude.

Today the more general view among Protestant churchmen is that the present fragmentation of Protestant Christianity is a sin before God. This was expressed by theologians at the Faith and Order assembly at Edinburgh in 1937 in the following words: "We humbly acknowledge that our divisions are contrary to the will of Christ, and we pray God in His mercy to shorten the days of our separation and to guide us by His spirit into fullness of unity." Faced by an aggressive and subtle secularism in the Western world and a remarkable growth of Catholicism in such traditionally Protestant nations as Holland, Germany, England, and the United States, the heirs of the Reformation press the search for some semblance of unity. Disavowing any schemes for a superchurch or a political pan-Protestantism they are nevertheless deeply interested in fostering those national and international agencies which are attempting to achieve that unity.

This twentieth-century movement has been identified by the term "ecumenical" from the Greek word meaning the "entire inhabited world." Of course, this term has long been used to designate councils of the Catholic Church and its use to describe a movement in which the majority of the world's Christians do not participate is somewhat misleading. Since 1910 this ecumenical movement has given Protestantism a new direction and hope and promises to reverse the suicidal trend toward sectarian disintegration. In this respect the ecumenical movement may provide the same service which Pietism and the Wesleyan revival furnished moribund eighteenth-century Protestantism.

On the local level ministerial associations and councils of churches often sponsor union Lenten services, a church affiliation census, co-operative radio programs, newspaper advertisements, studies of social conditions, and the like. Refusal of the Southern Baptists to participate weakens these associations in the South and the Missouri Synod Lutherans and Holiness sects either decline invitations to join or fail to receive such invitations.

In the United States a number of denominations in the Reformed tradition formed the Federal Council of Churches of Christ in America in 1908. A liberal theology and social gospel characterized this co-operative federation which eventually represented 25 denominations including the Methodists, Northern Baptists, and Presbyterians.

Later, in 1950, the National Council of Churches of Christ in the United States of America absorbed the old Federal Council and a number of specialized agencies. Through the present National Council 26 Protestant and seven Eastern Orthodox denominations co-operate in areas such as home and foreign missions, relief, religious education. At least 40,000,000 churchmen are represented by the Council although the Southern Baptist, Missouri and Wisconsin Synod Lutheran, Seventh-day Adventist, Christian Reformed, Holiness and other conservative bodies have boycotted the Council. Those denominations which do work through the Council are sometimes referred to as "co-operative Protestantism." The Unitarians have been denied membership because of their unorthodox views of the Trinity and the divinity of Christ; the cultists such as Mormons, Christian Scientists, Jehovah's Witnesses, Spiritualists have not been invited to join.

Two splinter groups enroll dissatisfied fundamentalists. The deposed Presbyterian minister, Carl McIntire, organized his American Council of Christian Churches in 1941. It considers the National Council to be infected by modernism and communism. A few tiny fundamentalist sects still support the McIntire movement. Another federation of fundamentalists who share the A.C.C.C.'s suspicion of the National Council's liberalism but do not approve of the obstreperous criticism of the Council by McIntire is the National Association of Evangelicals. Both factions win newspaper publicity out of all proportion to their membership and succeed in embarrassing the National Council in many situations.

In general the National Council speaks for the predominant activist evangelicals but not for the militant fundamentalists, the liberal Unitarians and Universalists, or the "Christian" cults. No creedal uniformity is expected of member denominations and co-operation of the 30 denominations is confined to practical, external affairs rather than extended to theology. The Council has undoubtedly succeeded in presenting a more united front of Protestant opinion and has eased tension among rival churches and sects.

When delegates from 179 churches in 54 nations assembled in Evanston, Ill., in August, 1954, under the auspices of the World Council of Churches, the ecumenical movement marked another milestone. The theme of this largest interdenominational conference in history was "Christ, the Hope of the World." Six years before at Amsterdam some 147 churches had pledged themselves to stay together in a "World Council of Churches." Even though no Roman Catholics and few Eastern Orthodox attended the subsequent Evanston meeting, this assembly did succeed in attracting almost all Protestant bodies which taken together comprise about a third of Christendom. As might be expected the same groups which ignore the National Council declined to participate at Evanston.

No Russian Orthodox were present but Orthodox delegates were sent by the churches of Greece, Bulgaria, Romania, and Serbia. As a matter of fact Orthodox interest and financial support was negligible. Those Orthodox who did attend felt obliged to remind their Protestant brethren of a common Catholic-Orthodox tradition at several points during the proceedings.

At the third assembly of the World Council of Churches in New Delhi, India, in 1961 the Russian Orthodox Church was admitted to membership, making it the largest single church in the Council. Five official Roman Catholic observers attended the New Delhi sessions.

The Protestant doubts that the Church was ever united, begins his search on the assumption that it is not united now, and hopes that mutual understanding and good will will bring the various churches to that unity which Christ willed. The Catholic sees that unity in the one, holy, Catholic, and apostolic church from the date of her founding to the end of time.

The Holy See has made the Church's position clear regarding the modern ecumenical movement: she cannot enter into an assembly of equal and independent churches and communions; she cannot allow men to judge the Church; she cannot subject divine doctrine to parliamentary debate; she cannot deny her own unity and divine authority. This position has been stated and restated in a number of encyclicals and replies to invitations to attend ecumenical sessions. On the other hand, Catholics can see the working of the Holy Spirit at Amsterdam, Evanston, and New Delhi. A united Protestantism would be closer to Christian unity than a fragmented Protestantism; a united Protestant witness in the face of secularism, materialism, hedonism, and communism would advance the cause of Christ in the world.

Since formal participation in the World Council of Churches by the Catholic Church would be tantamount to a denial of the Church's unity and divine authority, we may not also conclude that informal approaches such as the German *Una Sancta* movement are forbidden or discouraged. On the contrary, such dialogues between qualified Protestant and Catholic theologians are expressly recommended in the 1948 *Instruction on the Ecumenical Movement* issued by the Sacred Congregation of the Holy Office. Catholics can and should sympathize with their separated brethren as they search for ways to reach Christian unity.

The ecumenical movement is a phenomenon of this century. The initial impulse came from problems encountered by Protestant missionaries in foreign lands. The scandal of competing Christian missions occupied the attention of delegates to the first World Missionary Conference at Edinburgh in 1910. Bishop Charles Brent, Episcopal bishop in the Philippine Islands, proposed that a later conference consider the doctrinal disagreements which formed the basis of this disunity. World War I interrupted these plans and it was not until 1927 that the First World Conference on Faith and Order was called at Lausanne, Switzerland. Here the doctrinal foundations of the present World Council were laid. The minimal doctrinal standards included acceptance of the Old and New Testaments, the Nicene Creed, the sacraments of baptism and holy communion, and the episcopal form of church government. Naturally this last point bothered those standing in the presbyterian tradition.

Meanwhile the Lutheran Archbishop of Uppsala, Nathan Söderblom, had promoted a similar conference which was sponsored by the King of Sweden two years before the Lausanne meeting. The First Conference on Life and Work met at Stockholm to consider the implications of Christianity for industry, race relations, politics, and other social areas. Stockholm was sociological where Lausanne was doctrinal.

The two conferences, Faith and Order and Life and Work, decided to hold simultaneous conventions in 1937 at Edinburgh and Oxford, to investigate an amalgamation of the two. The following year a committee met at Utrecht to draw up a plan for the proposed World Council of Churches and to set a date for the first world assembly in 1941. Again war disrupted these plans and the assembly was postponed until 1948.

At Amsterdam the delegates adopted a report which confessed: "We are one in acknowledging Christ as our God and Savior. We are divided from one another not only in matters of faith, order and tradition, but also by pride of nation, class and race. But Christ has made us His own and He is not divided. In seeking Him we find one another." During the course of the conference the Catholic bishops of Holland issued a pastoral letter which urged priests and people to pray for the delegates and for non-Catholic Christians "who lovingly seek for unity, who truly follow Christ and live in His love and who, although they are separated from Christ's flock, yet look to the Church, be it often unconsciously, as the only haven of salvation."

The World Council theoretically limits membership to those who recognize the divinity of Christ since the Constitution states: "The World Council of Churches is a fellowship of churches which accept our Lord Jesus Christ as God and Savior." Protestant, Catholic, and Orthodox churches are all eligible to join the Council.

Plans for the Evanston meeting were outlined at Amsterdam. We might point out that for most European Protestants the ecumenical movement falls under the heading of foreign relations. Continental Protestants stand in either the Lutheran or Reformed traditions and find no counterpart in their countries of the fantastic conglomeration of churches and sects which complicates the U. S. religious scene.

Again the fundamentalists balked at the position of the World Council and formed a rival organization, the International Council of Christian Churches. Not only do they brand the World Council as modernist but they protest the invitation to membership extended to Roman Catholics and Eastern Orthodox.

Several large-scale mergers of Protestant denominations have been undertaken since the turn of the century. The United Church of Canada, for example, consolidated the Presbyterian, Congregational, and Methodist churches in that country and now enrolls about 20 per cent of the Canadian population. The Anglicans, Lutherans, and Baptists remain outside the union. A later unionistic attempt is the Church of South India formed in 1947 through a combination of Anglican, Methodist, Reformed, Congregational, and Presbyterian bodies. A curious adaptation of episcopacy distinguishes the Indian experiment.

At least 14 major unions have been carried through in American

Protestantism and the temper of the times indicates more such mergers may be expected. Sometimes, of course, the merger of two denominations results in three denominations: diehards refuse to compromise on some principle and set up protesting sects.

The first significant merger in this century brought together the Presbyterian Church, U. S. A., and the Cumberland Presbyterians in 1906; however, a remnant of the Cumberlands held out against the move and now report 85,000 communicants. The United Lutheran Church in America was organized in 1918 and the American Lutheran Church arose from a fusion of several synods which came together in 1931. The Congregationalists united with the unitarian Christian Churches in 1931. When the Evangelical and Reformed Church was organized in 1934 it represented a merger of the product of two earlier mergers. And for the first time two churches of diverse backgrounds, the Congregational Christian Churches and the Evangelical and Reformed Church, joined forces in 1957 under the name the United Church of Christ. The three Methodist churches which had divided over slavery and issues of church government reunited in 1939 to form the largest single Protestant church in the nation. The Evangelical United Brethren trace their united history to a 1946 agreement and the northern Presbyterians and the United Presbyterians will join hands in 1958.

Numerous other unions are in the exploratory stage. Once there were 150 Lutheran synods; today there are 17; eventually there may be five or fewer major Lutheran groupings. The Unitarians and Universalists have already taken steps toward a union of liberal churches. The Methodists and EUB's find little to prevent a union and the Baptists and Disciples hold nearly identical positions.

These unions of Protestant denominations have been effected only where churches shared common theological heritages or where religious indifferentism had smoothed the path. Most unions have in fact been reunions of churches which once divided over slavery, language, or other dead issues.

So far the national and international accomplishments of the ecumenical movement have been confined to areas of improved efficiency. Ecumenical proponents urge patience; before tackling doctrinal questions the scores of Protestant churches must learn to work together in external matters such as missions and religious education. Bishop Brent's desire to get to the doctrinal heart of disunity remains unfulfilled.

While Catholics prefer a united to a disunited Protestant witness in a pagan world and while they discern the work of the Holy Spirit in the ecumenical movement and its leadership, they know that the unity which their separated brethren seek can be found only in the Church which Christ founded. Pope Pius XI expressed this truth in his encyclical *Mortalium animos:* "The unity of Christians cannot be otherwise obtained than by securing the return of the separated to the one true Church of Christ from which they once unhappily withdrew."

Chapter XXIII

PROSPECTS FOR THE REUNION OF CHRISTENDOM

"There Shall Be One Fold and One Shepherd."

Humanly speaking, the reunion of Christendom appears extremely remote. The schism between East and West has hardened over a millennium; the revolt of Protestantism now encompasses four centuries of divergent traditions and doctrinal developments. And yet no Christian, certainly no Catholic, can allow himself to view the present tragic disunity of the followers of Jesus Christ as a permanent state of affairs.

We must hope and pray that somehow before the end of time Christians will again unite under one Lord, one faith, and one baptism. The ideal of the oneness of those baptized in Christ pervades the New Testament. All Christians — Catholic, Orthodox, and Protestant — must strive for the fulfillment of Christ's petitions "that all may be one" and "that they may be perfected in unity" (Jn. 17:21 and 23).

Pope Leo XIII declared: "Let not this hope (of reunion) be considered Utopian, for that were unworthy of Christians. The promise of Our Lord must be fulfilled, 'There shall be one fold and one Shepherd. . . .' Difficulties there are, but they shall in nowise discourage our apostolic zeal and charity. It is true that rebellion and estrangement have fostered a deep-rooted dissent in men's hearts, but shall this make us give up hope? Please God, never!"

True to her divine mission the Catholic Church insists on one path to that desired unity: acceptance by our separated brethren of the unity of the One, Holy, Catholic, and Apostolic Church. Pope Pius XI expressed this necessity in these words: "Unity can result only from one single rule of faith and one same belief among all Christians." The fervent hope of eventual reunion was revealed in the encyclical *Sempiternus rex* by Pope Pius XII in 1951: "All those specially marked by baptism . . . cannot continue to remain divided and separated."

Catholics especially must beware of complacently accepting the many Protestant churches and sects as permanent institutions. On the other hand, we cannot realistically expect that the wounds of centuries will be healed overnight or that reunion will take place in our short lifetime or our century. We may and must further the cause of reunion but that reunion will be the work of God not the work of man.

Reunion can be accomplished in one of two ways: corporate reunion and individual conversion. By corporate reunion we mean the reconciliation of an entire dissident church or a large section of such a church. In these cases the diocesan organization, liturgical language, and traditions are preserved. The churches so reunited with the Holy See must, however, possess valid orders which means that this path is closed to Protestant communions. A number of corporate reunions by Easter Orthodox bodies and Lesser Eastern Churches have taken place in recent centuries. Where no priesthood and episcopacy has been preserved, no corporate reunion is possible.

On a practical level the prospects for reunion are brighter for the Eastern Orthodox than for any other dissident group. Of course, as we have seen, Orthodoxy itself consists of a score of more or less autonomous national churches.

The Holy See considers the Orthodox world technically in schism rather than in heresy since no heretical doctrines have been or can be defined by Orthodoxy without an ecumenical council. Orthodox theologians agree that such a council would necessarily have to include the Western Church. We have reviewed the temporary rapprochements of Lyons and Florence in the fifteenth century;

technically the breach between Byzantium and Rome is hardly more than a few years older than the Protestant revolt. Millions of former Orthodox Christians have entered the Catholic Church, especially since the seventeenth century, and they maintain their Eastern rites and traditions.

With few exceptions the Orthodox believer holds dear the same Christian truths as his Catholic brother. Once he accepts the supremacy of the Sovereign Pontiff he can join his Catholic brothers in the Mystical Body of Christ. Today we observe that the political ambitions of Soviet Russia are served by a subservient Orthodoxy which the Communists hope will rally the Russians and Slavs against the Vatican. In the United States and in free Europe where Communist machinations are less obvious we may entertain moderate hopes of reunion of Orthodoxy and Rome within the next few decades.

As early as 1577 the Holy See established the Pontifical Greek College in Rome. The more immediate Protestant threat occupied the attention of the Western Church for several centuries but the latter part of the nineteenth century saw a renewal of interest in Eastern Christianity. Pope Leo XIII set up the Armenian College in 1886, the Melkite College in Jerusalem in 1896, and the Coptic College in Cairo in 1897. Pope Benedict XV founded the Oriental Institute in Rome in 1917 which was later reorganized as part of the Gregorian University. The Russicum in the Eternal City dates from 1929. A somewhat comparable institute at Fordham University prepares Eastern Rite Jesuit priests for the day when missionary activity may be resumed in Russia and also undertakes translations, publishes books and articles on Eastern Christianity, and fosters an understanding of non-Latin rites among American Catholics. All these educational agencies are carrying out the wishes of Leo XIII who urged that Catholics "know well" the separated Eastern churches.

St. Procopius Abbey, a Benedictine foundation in Lisle, Illinois, has been designated by the Holy See as the center of unionistic work in this country. A Church Unity Congress in 1956 attracted 100 Catholic bishops, priests, and scholars of both Latin and Oriental

Rites deeply interested in reunion. All separated churches were invited to send delegates, and representatives of the Antiochene Syrians and the Old Catholics were present at the conference.

An Institute for Reunion aiming at the conversion of Orthodox priests and laity has been formed in the Byzantine Rite Diocese of Pittsburgh. Headquarters of the new Institute adjoin the SS. Cyril and Methodius seminary which trains priests for the diocese. Eleven priests in this Eastern Rite diocese are former Eastern Orthodox Christians and 2703 Orthodox have been received into the Catholic Church in this diocese in the past ten years.

A modern movement of corporate reunion was initiated in India in 1930 with the conversion of the Jacobite Metropolitan Ivan and his suffragan bishop. Since then about 35,000 Jacobites have followed their bishop into the Catholic Church. These, together with Uniate Syrians and Maronites, form the Syro-Malankar Rite.

Sections of the Old Catholic Church in Europe and the United States which have withstood modernist infiltration may also find their way back to the Mother Church. The Old Catholics, like the Orthodox, possess a valid priesthood; therefore, corporate reunion is a possibility.

Turning to the Anglican communion we see a schism which developed into a heresy after the time of Henry VIII. Interest in reunion was fanned by the Oxford Movement but Pope Leo XIII was forced to declare Anglican orders invalid in 1896. An effort in this century to investigate the possibilities of corporate reunion was sponsored by the Anglican Lord Halifax and Cardinal Mercier of Belgium. These so-called Malines Conversations were held with the approval of the Holy See from 1921 to 1926 but they remained unofficial and private. After the deaths of Cardinal Mercier and the Abbe Portal the conversations were discontinued.

Meanwhile recent decisions on the Church of South India, the approval of contraception by the Lambeth Conference, the reluctance to examine the religious basis of Freemasonry have forced thousands of Anglican Papalists and Anglo-Catholics to re-examine their positions. During a single recent year, 1956, twenty-seven clergymen in England joined the Catholic Church. Most of these converts were former Anglicans and a number are now studying for the priesthood.

The lack of valid orders, the infection of modernism and liberalism, a persistent anti-papal bias, and the widespread disunity within Protestantism render the task of reunion with the Lutheran, Reformed, and Free churches far more difficult. Nevertheless, through the centuries individuals in several traditions have labored for greater understanding and eventual reunion: Hugo Grotius, Comenius, Leibnitz, Bishop Bossuet, Cardinal Mercier, the Abbe Portal, Lord Halifax.

Recent developments in Protestantism have encouraged further explorations in the delicate area of reunion. Many Christians believe that the time is propitious and optimism is higher than in many centuries.

Large sections of Protestantism have now come around to a view of the Church which closely approximates the traditional Catholic definition. They see the present division of Christendom as a sin and not a badge of honor or triumphant individualism. Calvinistic predestination and the concomitant denial of free will have been assigned to theological limbo and Luther's external justification is refuted in practice by most denominations. The role of tradition in fixing the scripture canon of the New Testament, in observing the Christian rather than the Jewish Sabbath, and in interpreting scriptural passages is no longer denied. Nor do Protestant scholars hesitate to admit the authenticity of the widely quoted passage from Matthew "Thou art Peter . . ." and the fact that St. Peter did travel to Rome.

Ancient Catholic practices and symbols have been taken over by a Protestantism which once considered them popish and pagan. A cross or even a crucifix replaces the weather vane on the church spire; an altar occupies the central position once pre-empted by the pulpit or pipe organ; the Prince Albert coat gives way to cassock, surplice, and stole or even beyond this, to the chasuble and cope. Protestants no longer argue about the propriety of stained glass, the observance of Christmas, the kneeling posture for prayer, the use of candles on the altar, or the desirability of more beauty in ritual and architecture. Some German Lutherans as well as Anglicans have revived the institution of private confession. Anglo-Catholicism reintroduced monasticism in the Anglican Church and the Reformed pastor, the Rev. Max Thurian, founded a successful "Protestant monastery" in France. In Germany, the cradle of the Reformation, 70 Protestant women, most of them Lutherans, devote their lives to God as "Sisters of Mary."

Recent trends within Catholicism also narrow the gap between the external practices of the two traditions: increased lay activity and initiative, wider use of the vernacular in the liturgy, encouragement of congregational singing, interest in the publication of new Catholic hymnals, simplification of the rubrics, deeper appreciation of the Bible, and others.

Indicative of the vastly improved relations between Catholics and Protestants in Europe and especially in Germany where Christians have shared a common battle against godless Nazism and Communism is the Una Sancta movement. Founded by Fr. Max Joseph Metzger about 30 years ago, this movement has now spread throughout Germany. Father Metzger was martyred by the Nazis in 1944.

Backed by the German Catholic Bishops' Conference and by individual Lutheran bishops Una Sancta brings together priests, ministers, theologians, scholars, and laymen for discussion of mutual problems and of a foundation for Christian reunion. No compromise of doctrinal positions is suggested nor does Una Sancta bear any relation to the World Council of Churches. Archbishop Lorenz Jaeger of Paderborn and a commission of 12 theologians guide the movement from the Catholic side. Fr. Karl Adam, the distinguished author of *The Spirit of Catholicism* and *One and Holy*, has given his full support to the objectives of Una Sancta.

Another significant European contribution to reunion is the quarterly *Unitas* edited by Fr. Charles Boyer, S.J., dean of the theological faculty of the Pontifical Gregorian University. This university recently added lectures on modern Protestant theology and missionary techniques to its annual series on Anglicanism. A highly specialized library on Protestantism has been dedicated.

Pope Pius XI asked the Benedictines in 1924 to assign monks to study ways and means of bringing separated Christians, especially the Orthodox, back to the Catholic Church. Today 37 monks at the Benedictine priory in Chevetogne, Belgium, devote their lives to the cause of Christian unity. They publish *Istina* which is probably the most respected Catholic journal in this field. Mass is celebrated in the monastery in both Latin and Eastern rites but most of the monks belong to the Byzantine rite.

In the United States the promotion of reunion has been the special interest of the Graymoor Franciscans of the Society of the Atonement. The history of this religious community is an example of reunion itself. Founded by an Anglican priest, the entire society was received into the Church in 1909. The spiritual sons of the Very Rev. Paul James Francis Wattson, S.A., have since led the way in bringing the problems and possibilities of reunion to the attention of American Catholics. The Graymoor friars sponsor the Chair of Unity Octave, January 18 to 25. This octave, inaugurated under Episcopalian auspices, has since been blessed by four popes and is now observed by the universal Church and by Orthodox, Anglicans, and a few Lutherans. On separate days prayers are offered for the return of all the "other sheep" — Oriental separatists, Anglicans, Lutherans and other Protestants, American Christians, lapsed Catholics, Jews, and those living in mission territories.

An outgrowth of the Octave, the League of Prayer for Unity, continues the intentions of the Chair of Unity Octave through the year. Members recite the official prayer for unity daily and may receive plenary and partial indulgences. The Graymoor Friars, Garrison, New York, will gladly furnish further information.

Besides the Society of the Atonement, other religious communities which have entered the Catholic Church in a body since the turn of the century include the Benedictine monks of Caldey, the nuns of Milford Haven, the Servants of Christ the King and the Sisters of the Love of Jesus in Canada. All were former Anglican congregations.

For some modernist Protestants even the divinity of our Lord and the redemption have ceased to be normative beliefs. Reunion dialogues with such groups are futile; they can claim only squatter's rights in Christendom. Orthodox Protestants, however, may yet disentangle the negative from the positive insights of the Reformation and thereby see the true fulfillment of these principles in the Church. Stripped of their nominalist shackles we would find a justification by faith which disowns extrinsic justification and no longer denies the worth of good works; a reaffirmation of the sovereignty of God without the monstrous legalism of Calvinistic predestination; a personal religion which no longer arbitrarily denies the magisterium of the Church; an honoring of the Word of God in the scriptures without a disparagement of tradition; a priesthood of all believers which finds its true expression in the Mystical Body.

At this point the individual American Catholic may ask, "What can I do to promote the cause of reunion?" The answer is that there are many avenues of activity open to priest, religious, and layman.

Prayer takes precedence over all other means of furthering the reunion of separated Christian brothers. The 1948 *Instruction on the Ecumenical Movement* began and ended with a plea that the entire Catholic world pray that non-Catholic Christians be given the "light and strength" to embrace the fullness of Christianity. Observance of the Chair of Unity Octave is one of the best ways to join with Catholics and other Christians the world over in praying for reunion.

Good example is indispensable. The *Instruction* states: "Nothing will contribute more toward preparing the way for those who are in error to embrace the truth and the Church than the faith of Catholics being testified to by their edifying lives." Likewise the bad example of Catholics can set back reunion for many more decades. Many Protestants have been nurtured on the belief that Catholics are a superstitious and idolatrous lot. Catholics must endeavor to eradicate all taint of superstition in any area of religious life even though they know that a great deal of Protestant criticism in this regard is unfounded and biased. Such practices as prayer chains, spurious private devotions, misuse of the St. Christopher medal, recourse to magical claims for novenas and special prayers cannot be countenanced.

Encouraging a wider use of the vernacular in the liturgy can bring the truth and beauty of the public worship of the Church to millions of non-Catholics to whom it remains a closed book. One of the popular appeals of the sixteenth-century Reformers was the promise of a liturgy in a language the people could understand. Latin replaced Greek as the language of the Mass in the fourth century. Had it not been for the violence of the Reformers and the need to erect barriers against novelty in religion, we would probably have seen a natural evolution from Latin to the vernaculars. There is no longer the same urgent need to bolster the ancient faith by preserving the exclusive use of Latin in the liturgy.

Recent decrees have authorized the use of vernaculars for the administration of the sacraments of baptism, matrimony, and extreme unction besides a score of blessings. The next step seems to be the adoption of the vernacular for the Mass of the Catechumens. Priests and lay Catholics can prepare the way for any change in the exclusive use of Latin in the Mass by reminding their fellow Catholics that God understands all languages, that Latin is one of a dozen liturgical languages in the Church, that the use of Latin is in no way fundamental, that Latin was not the language of the first Mass or the early Church, and that the foremost goal of the liturgical movement is not aesthetic or even cultural but the participation of the faithful in the public worship of the Church.

If English were adopted for most of the Mass, millions of Protestants would get some understanding of what the Mass is about for the first time. The similarities of the Mass to their own worship services, especially Lutheran and Episcopalian liturgies, would become apparent.

"Our fathers divided over the Bible and under the Bible we shall unite again," declared Bishop Beeson. A neglect of the Bible by Catholics is indefensible. In recent decades we have witnessed a renewed interest in the scriptures by Catholic lay people, new translations, greater publishing activity, more attention to scripture study in Catholic colleges and universities. Positive encouragement of scripture study and reading was given in the encyclical *Divino afflante* in 1943; Catholics may receive indulgences by prayerfully reading the Bible for at least 15 minutes a day. The Catholic Biblical revival may be furthered by organizing discussion groups with priest-moderators, distributing Bibles and New Testaments, promoting family Bible reading, and incorporating more scripture courses in the schools. Catholic and Protestant scripture scholars have begun to talk about a common translation of the Bible acceptable to all Christians.

Protestants usually find a rich social life centered in their church. In many communities church suppers and socials attract more people than any other affairs. The Protestant church member greets his minister at the church door on Sunday morning, visits with his fellow worshipers after the service, entertains the minister on pastoral visits, joins ladies circles, men's clubs, and missionary aid societies, extends a hearty welcome to the stranger and traveler who attends his church. Converts often testify that the friendly spirit in their former church homes is one of the things they sacrificed when they entered the Catholic Church. The simple comparison of the average Protestant congregation of fewer than 350 souls and the average Catholic parish of more than 1800 explains in part the difference in hospitality, neighborliness, and fellowship. The minister can know all his parishioners with little effort; the Catholic pastor may be a stranger to hundreds of his own people. Smaller parishes would seem to be a partial answer even though the economics of operating a Catholic church, grade school, rectory, and convent are quite different from a Protestant church and parsonage. Lay initiative as expressed by the Legion of Mary and the Christian Family Movement is creating a deeper awareness of the community of Christians.

A study of the Eastern Rites of the Church will enable Latin Rite Catholics to get an insight and understanding of Eastern Christianity. The temptation to equate Catholicism with the particular liturgy and customs of one's own rite is always with us. If a married parish clergy, a vernacular language in the liturgy, and communion under both species are found in our Eastern Rites we know that these cannot be contrary to Christian doctrine. We can better discriminate between the essentials and the nonessentials of our faith, between doctrine and discipline. Indeed, the Holy See insists that Eastern Rite Catholics preserve their distinctive liturgies and practices, discourages Catholics of these rites from changing to the predominate Latin Rite. Latin Rite Catholics may take advantage of the opportunity of attending an Eastern Rite divine liturgy and receiving the body and blood of Christ under both species. Of course, they must not confuse the schismatic Orthodox Church with the Eastern Rites of the Catholic Church.

An open door policy would enable many non-Catholics of good will to gain a new appreciation of the Church and her work. We should make it clear that non-Catholics are welcome to attend Mass at any time, not just Midnight Mass on Christmas Eve. Too often our parochial schools remain under suspicion because they have isolated themselves from the life of the community. A surprising number of sincere people believe that a Catholic grade school teaches nine parts religion and one part 3 R's. Perhaps the threats of convent inspection laws during the nativist crusades produced a cultural claustrophobia among some Catholics. Annual open houses in our schools and colleges, hospitals, children's homes, churches, and welfare institutions would enable many Americans to see for themselves the scope of the Church's activities and to meet our devoted priests, sisters, brothers, and lay people who staff these institutions.

Just as Catholics should make an effort to understand the beliefs and practices of their separated brethren, so they should facilitate the dissemination of information about the Church. This may take the form of information centers on Main Street, inquiry classes, newspaper publicity, public lectures, books and periodicals for public libraries and secular colleges, radio and TV programs, gift subscriptions to Catholic magazines, correspondence courses, street preaching, distribution of pamphlets, and the like. Above all the individual Catholic layman must cultivate his own knowledge about his faith.

A number of areas lend themselves to interdenominational cooperation in national and community life. One example is the National Conference of Christians and Jews. The Catholic-inspired but nonsectarian Christopher Movement is another. Committees for the observance of Good Friday, for the elimination of Sunday shopping, for a cleanup of comic books and pornography can be organized on a wide basis. Provided the limits of such co-operation are understood and observed these group experiences can at least get Catholics and Protestants on speaking terms and lay the groundwork for further co-operation.

Creation of a special secretariat to deal with the question of Christian unity at the Second Vatican Council confirmed the view of many that unity would be a dominant theme at the Council. Pope John XXIII is known to cherish the hope that the groundwork may be laid for a reunion of Orthodox and Catholic Christians. For many years he served in papal diplomatic posts in nations with large Orthodox populations.

The recent statements of the Holy Father establish the ecumenical approach which Catholics should employ with their separated brethren: "We do not intend to conduct a trial of the past; we do not wish to prove who was right and who was wrong. The blame is on both sides. All we want is to say 'Let us come together. Let us make an end of our divisions.'"

We have examined the tenets of scores of non-Catholic churches and sects to which millions of our fellow Americans pay allegiance. No Catholic can survey this bewildering array of denominations, all professing loyalty to our Lord, without thanking God for the gift of faith, a faith which is firm because it is built on a Rock. "And I say to thee: Thou are Peter; and upon this rock I will build my Church, and the gates of hell shall not prevail against it" (Mt. 16:18).

Of this we may be sure: that the long desired reunion for which we pray and labor will come about not through compromise in essentials or intransigence in nonessentials, not through indifference or contentiousness, but through the power of Christian love.

CHURCH MEMBERSHIP
STATISTICS

Compiled for the *Yearbook of American Churches* for 1963, Benson Y. Landis, editor, and published by the National Council of Churches of Christ. Only denominations with a membership of 1000 or more are listed; the figures are mainly for the calendar year 1961 or a fiscal year ending in 1961.

Name of Religious Body	No. of Churches Reported	Inclusive Church Membership
Adventist Bodies:		
Advent Christian Church	420	30,676
Church of God (Abrahamic Faith)	116	5,700
Seventh-day Adventists	3,054	329,152
African Orthodox Church	24	6,000
American Rescue Workers	34	2,350
Apostolic Faith	40	4,884
Apostolic Overcoming Holy Church of God	300	75,000
Armenian Church of North America	54	127,000
Assemblies of God	8,273	514,317
Baptist Bodies:		
American Baptist Convention	6,272	1,521,052
American Baptist Association	3,117	650,800
Baptist General Conference	545	75,613
Bethel Baptist Assembly, Inc.	27	6,925
Conservative Baptist Association of America	1,351	300,000
Duck River (and Kindred) Associations of Baptists	28	3,141
Evangelical Baptist Church, Inc., Gen. Conf.	31	2,200
Free Will Baptists	2,150	193,664
General Association of Regular Baptist Churches	992	143,782
General Baptists	779	58,443
National Baptist Convention, U.S.A., Inc.	26,000	5,000,000
National Baptist Convention of America	11,398	2,668,799

Name of Religious Body	No. of Churches Reported	Inclusive Church Membership
National Baptist Evangelical Life and Soul Saving Assembly of U.S.A.	264	57,674
National Primitive Baptist Convention of the U.S.A.	1,125	85,983
North American Baptist Association	1,980	330,265
North American Baptist General Conference . .	312	51,611
Primitive Baptists	1,000	72,000
Regular Baptists	266	17,186
Separate Baptists in Christ	85	7,358
Seventh Day Baptist General Conference . . .	61	5,803
Southern Baptist Convention	32,598	9,978,488
United Baptists	568	63,641
United Free Will Baptist Church	836	100,000
Bible Protestant Church	47	2,423
Bible Way Churches of Our Lord Jesus Christ World Wide, Inc.	140	35,000
Brethren (German Baptists):		
Brethren Church (Ashland, Ohio)	114	18,207
Brethren Church (Progressive)	175	25,355
Church of the Brethren	1,070	200,788
Old German Baptist Brethren	54	4,110
Brethren in Christ (River Brethren)	150	7,358
Buddhist Churches of America	55	60,000
Catholic Apostolic Church	7	2,577
Christadelphians	500	15,000
Christian and Missionary Alliance	1,028	60,252
Christian Churches (Disciples of Christ), International Convention	7,968	1,797,466
Christian Catholic Church	4	7,000
Christian Union	122	7,300
Church of Christ (Holiness), U.S.A.	146	7,621
Church of Christ, Scientist	No statistics furnished	
Churches of God:		
Church of God (Cleveland, Tenn.)	3,338	179,651
Church of God (Anderson, Ind.)	2,292	142,823
Church of God (Seventh Day)	7	2,000
The (Original) Church of God, Inc.	35	6,000
The Church of God	1,852	71,606
The Church of God (Seventh Day), Denver, Colo.	123	3,900
Church of God by Faith	101	2,380
The Church of God of Prophecy	1,301	35,349
Churches of God in N.A. (General Eldership)	376	37,390
Church of God and Saints of Christ	217	38,127

Name of Religious Body	No. of Churches Reported	Inclusive Church Membership
Church of God in Christ	4,000	411,466
Church of Illumination	7	5,000
Church of Our Lord Jesus Christ of the Apostolic Faith, Inc.	155	45,000
Church of the Nazarene	4,486	315,697
Churches of Christ	18,501	2,250,000
Churches of Christ in Christian Union	207	6,270
Churches of God, Holiness	42	25,600
Churches of the Living God:		
Church of the Living God	268	37,425
House of God, Which is the Church of the Living God, the Pillar and the Ground of the Truth, Inc.	107	2,350
Churches of the New Jerusalem:		
General Convention of the New Jerusalem in the U.S.A.	52	4,053
General Church of the New Jerusalem	12	1,805
Congregational Holiness Church	147	4,664
Conservative Congregational Christian Conference	34	6,090
Eastern Churches:		
Albanian Orthodox Archdiocese in America . .	14	16,000
American Carpatho-Russian Orthodox Greek Catholic Church	65	100,000
American Catholic Church (Syro-Antiochean) .	40	4,563
The American Holy Orthodox Catholic Apostolic Eastern Church	27	3,000
Apostolic Episcopal Church	46	7,086
Assyrian Orthodox Church	4	3,300
Bulgarian Eastern Orthodox Church	22	86,000
Church of the East and of the Assyrians . . .	10	3,200
Greek Archdiocese of North and South America	382	1,200,000
Holy Ukrainian Autocephalic Orthodox Church in Exile	16	5,000
Romanian Orthodox Episcopate of America . .	53	50,000
The Russian Orthodox Church Outside Russia .	81	55,000
The Russian Orthodox Greek Catholic Church of America	321	850,000
Serbian Eastern Orthodox Church	73	130,000
Syrian Antiochian Orthodox Church	81	110,000
Syrian Orthodox Church of Antioch	5	50,000
Ukrainian Orthodox Church of America . . .	37	40,250
Ukrainian Orthodox Church of U.S.A.	98	86,700
Ethical Culture Movement	30	7,000
Evangelical Congregational Church	164	29,968

Name of Religious Body	No. of Churches Reported	Inclusive Church Membership
Evangelical Covenant Church of America	513	61,108
Evangelical Free Church of America	468	31,543
Evangelical United Brethren Church	4,299	747,932
Evangelistic Associations:		
Apostolic Christian Church (Nazarean) . . .	38	2,030
Apostolic Christian Church of America	64	8,535
The Christian Congregation	187	35,376
Church of God as Organized by Christ	14	2,192
Missionary Church Association	117	8,015
Pillar of Fire	61	5,100
Federated Churches	508	88,411
Fire-Baptized Holiness Church (Wesleyan) . . .	53	1,007
Free Christian Zion Church of Christ	740	19,826
Friends:		
Five Years Meeting of Friends	501	71,552
Ohio Yearly Meeting of Friends Church (Independent)	92	6,721
Oregon Yearly Meeting of Friends Church . . .	63	5,665
Pacific Yearly Meeting of Friends	30	1,805
Religious Society of Friends (Conservative) . .	21	1,696
Religious Society of Friends (General Conference)	270	31,550
Religious Society of Friends (Kansas Yearly Meeting)	88	8,302
Independent Churches	384	40,276
International Church of the Foursquare Gospel . .	726	84,741
Italian Christian Church of North America . . .	148	17,500
Jehovah's Witnesses	4,333	273,131
Jewish Congregations	4,079	5,500,000
Latter-day Saints:		
Church of Christ	12	3,000
Church of Jesus Christ (Bickertonites)	44	2,233
Church of Jesus Christ of Latter-day Saints . .	3,566	1,595,390
Reorganized Church of Jesus Christ of Latter Day Saints	957	157,873
Liberal Catholic Church	8	4,000
Lithuanian National Catholic Church	4	3,940
Lutheran:		
Evangelical Lutheran Synodical Conference of North America		
Lutheran Church — Missouri Synod	5,276	2,464,436
Wisconsin Evangelical Lutheran Synod . . .	840	348,184
Evangelical Lutheran Synod	77	14,302
Synod of Evangelical Lutheran Churches . .	50	19,802

Name of Religious Body	No. of Churches Reported	Inclusive Church Membership
Negro Missions of the Synodical Conference .	54	8,600
National Lutheran Council:		
American Evangelical Lutheran Church . . .	76	23,808
American Lutheran Church	4,622	2,295,188
Augustana Evangelical Lutheran Church . .	1,219	619,040
Finnish Evangelical Lutheran Church (Suomi Synod)	153	36,274
Lutheran Free Church	334	90,253
United Lutheran Church in America	4,363	2,390,075
Church of the Lutheran Brethren of America .	51	5,889
Evangelical Lutheran Church in America (Eielsen Synod)	44	4,220
Finnish Apostolic Lutheran Church of America	60	6,567
National Evangelical Lutheran Church	56	10,545
Protestant Conference (Lutheran)	10	3,000
Mennonite Bodies:		
Beachy Amish Mennonite Churches	29	2,562
Church of God in Christ (Mennonite) . . .	38	5,000
Conference of the Evangelical Mennonite Church	22	2,457
Evangelical Mennonite Brethren	26	2,536
General Conference, Mennonite Church . . .	209	35,491
Hutterian Brethren	20	2,215
Mennonite Brethren Church of N.A.	87	13,000
Mennonite Church	878	74,321
Old Order Amish Mennonite Church	260	17,857
Old Order (Wisler) Mennonite Church . . .	31	4,742
Unaffiliated Conservative and Amish Mennonite Churches	27	1,378
Methodist Bodies:		
African Methodist Episcopal Church	5,878	1,166,301
African Methodist Episcopal Zion Church . . .	4,083	770,000
African Union First Colored Methodist Protestant Church, Inc.	33	5,000
Christian Methodist Episcopal Church	2,523	444,493
Congregational Methodist Church	223	14,274
Congregational Methodist Church of U.S.A. . .	100	7,500
Evangelical Methodist Church	116	6,044
Free Methodist Church of N.A.	1,156	55,520
Holiness Methodist Church	27	1,060
The Methodist Church	39,850	10,046,293
Primitive Methodist Church, U.S.A.	90	12,805
Reformed Methodist Union Episcopal Church .	33	11,000
Reformed Zion Union Apostolic Church . . .	52	12,000
Southern Methodist Church	48	4,608
Union American Methodist Episcopal Church .	256	27,560

Name of Religious Body	No. of Churches Reported	Inclusive Church Membership
Wesleyan Methodist Church of America . . .	1,073	45,336
Moravian Bodies:		
Moravian Church in America (Unitas Fratrum)	168	56,195
Unity of the Brethren	32	6,151
National David Spiritual Temple of Christ Church Union (Inc.), U.S.A.	66	40,815
New Apostolic Church of N.A., Inc.	162	14,762
Old Catholic Churches:		
American Catholic Church, Archdiocese of N. Y.	18	4,369
North American Catholic Church	50	65,235
North American Old Roman Catholic Church .	64	84,565
Old Catholic Archdiocese of Americas & Europe	24	7,100
The Reformed Catholic Church (Utrecht Confession), Province of North America	20	2,217
Open Bible Standard Churches, Inc.	275	26,000
Pentecostal Assemblies:		
Calvary Pentecostal Church, Inc.	22	8,000
Elim Missionary Assemblies	75	4,000
Emmanuel Holiness Church	56	1,200
International Pentecostal Assemblies	92	15,000
Pentecostal Assemblies of the World, Inc. . .	550	45,000
Pentecostal Church of Christ	44	1,198
Pentecostal Church of God of America, Inc. . .	1,099	109,900
Pentecostal Free Will Baptist Church, Inc. . .	127	7,000
The Pentecostal Holiness Church, Inc.	1,248	55,502
United Pentecostal Church, Inc.	1,900	175,000
Pilgrim Holiness Church	1,027	33,505
Plymouth Brethren	665	33,250
Polish National Catholic Church of America . .	162	282,411
Presbyterian Bodies:		
Associate Reformed Presbyterian Church (General Synod)	144	27,690
Cumberland Presbyterian Church	971	83,642
Cumberland Presbyterian Church in U.S. & Africa	121	30,000
Evangelical Presbyterian Church	69	5,956
Orthodox Presbyterian Church	92	11,175
Presbyterian Church in the U.S.	3,998	917,449
Reformed Presbyterian Church in N.A. (General Synod)	18	2,110
Reformed Presbyterian Church of N.A. (Old School)	76	6,060
United Presbyterian Church in the U.S.A. . .	9,162	3,242,479
Protestant Episcopal Church	7,155	3,269,325

Name of Religious Body	No. of Churches Reported	Inclusive Church Membership
Reformed Bodies:		
Christian Reformed Church	572	250,934
Hungarian Reformed Church in America . . .	40	11,110
Netherlands Reformed Congregations	14	2,500
Protestant Reformed Churches of America . . .	21	2,924
Reformed Church in America	907	230,200
Reformed Church in the United States	21	3,467
Reformed Episcopal Church	70	8,928
Roman Catholic Church	23,374	42,876,665
Salvation Army	1,243	257,832
The Schwenkfelder Church	5	2,500
Social Brethren	28	1,629
Spiritualists:		
International General Assembly of Spiritualists .	209	164,072
National Spiritual Alliance of the U.S.A. . . .	34	3,205
National Spiritualist Association of Churches . .	198	5,438
Triumph the Church and Kingdom of God in Christ	600	65,763
Unitarian Universalist Association	992	147,031
United Brethren in Christ	313	20,405
United Church of Christ	8,120	2,254,835
United Holy Church of America, Inc.	470	28,980
United Missionary Church	204	10,566
Vedanta Society	11	1,000
Volunteers of America	203	28,330

BIBLIOGRAPHY

Adam, Karl, *One and Holy* (New York: Sheed & Ward, 1951).
———— *The Spirit of Catholicism* (New York: Macmillan, 1944).
Addison, James Thayer, *The Episcopal Church in the United States* (New York: Charles Scribner's Sons, 1951).
Algermissen, Konrad, *Christian Denominations* (St. Louis: B. Herder, 1953).
———— *Christian Sects* (New York: Hawthorn, 1962).
Andrews, Theodore, *The Polish National Catholic Church in America and Poland* (London: S. P. C. K., 1953).
Arbaugh, George, *Revelation in Mormonism* (Chicago: University of Chicago Press, 1932).
———— *Gods, Sex and Saints* (Minneapolis: Augustana Press, 1957).
Attwater, Donald, *The Christian Churches of the East* (Milwaukee: Bruce, 1946, 1947); 2 vols.
———— *The Dissident Eastern Churches* (Milwaukee: Bruce, 1937).

Bach, Marcus, *Report to Protestants* (Indianapolis: Bobbs-Merrill, 1953).
———— *They Have Found a Faith* (Indianapolis: Bobbs-Merrill, 1946).
Bainton, Roland H., *Here I Stand: A Life of Martin Luther* (New York and Nashville: Abingdon-Cokesbury, 1950).
———— *The Reformation of the Sixteenth Century* (Boston: Beacon Press, 1952).
Barnes, William Wright, *The Southern Baptist Convention* (Nashville, Tenn.: Broadman Press, 1954).
Bates, Ernest Sutherland, *American Faith* (New York: W. W. Norton & Co., 1940).
Bates, Ernest Sutherland, and Dittemore, John V., *Mary Baker Eddy, the Truth and the Tradition* (London: George Routledge and Sons, 1933).
Baum, Gregory, *That They May Be One: A Study of Papal Documents* (London: Bloomsbury, 1958).
———— *Progress and Perspectives* (New York: Sheed and Ward, 1962).
Beasley, Norman, *The Cross and the Crown* (New York: Duell, Sloan and Pearce, 1952).
Bellwald, A. M., *Christian Science and the Catholic Faith* (New York: Macmillan, 1922).
Billington, Ray Allen, *The Protestant Crusade, 1800–1860* (New York: Macmillan, 1938).
Bossuet, James, *Variations of the Protestant Churches* (New York: Kenedy, 1902).

Bouyer, Louis, *The Spirit and Forms of Protestantism* (Westminster, Md.: Newman Press, 1956).

Boyer, Charles, *One Shepherd* (New York: Kenedy, 1952).

Braden, Charles S., *These Also Believe* (New York: Macmillan, 1953).

———— *Christian Science Today* (Dallas: Southern Methodist University Press, 1958).

Brauer, J. C., *Protestantism in America* (Philadelphia: Westminster Press, 1953).

Brinton, Howard, *Friends for 300 Years* (New York: Harper & Brothers, 1952).

Brodie, F. M., *No Man Knows My History: The Life of Joseph Smith* (New York: Knopf, 1945).

Brooks, Melvin R., *LDS Reference Encyclopedia* (Salt Lake City: Bookcraft, 1960).

Brown, Robert McAfee and Weigel, Gustave, *An American Dialogue* (New York: Doubleday, 1960).

Brunner, Emil, *Our Faith* (New York: Charles Scribner's Sons, 1954).

Cady, H. Emilie, *Lessons in Truth* (Lee's Summit, Mo.: Unity School of Christianity, 1961).

Callahan, Daniel J., ed., *Christianity Divided* (New York: Sheed and Ward, 1961).

Calvin, John, *Institutes of the Christian Religion*, 7th American ed. (Philadelphia: Presbyterian Board of Christian Education, 1936).

Catholic Encyclopedia, Charles G. Herbermann and others, ed. (New York: Encyclopedia Press, 1928).

Chorley, E. Clowes, *Men and Movements in the American Episcopal Church* (New York: Charles Scribner's Sons, 1948).

Church, Brooke Peters, *A Faith for You* (New York: Rinehart, 1948).

Clark, Elmer T., *The Small Sects in America* (New York and Nashville: Abingdon-Cokesbury, 1949).

Clark, Walter Houston, *The Oxford Group* (New York: Bookman Associates, 1951).

Clayton, Joseph, *The Protestant Reformation in Great Britain* (Milwaukee: Bruce, 1934).

Clitheroe, Eric L., *The Mormon Religion*, unpublished manuscript.

Cole, Marley, *Jehovah's Witnesses: The New World Society* (New York: Vantage, 1955).

———— *Triumphant Kingdom* (New York: Criterion, 1957).

Congar, M. J., *Divided Christendom* (London: Bles, 1939).

Cox, Norman W., *We Southern Baptists* (Nashville, Tenn.: Convention Press, 1961).

Creedon, Lawrence P., and Falcon, William D., *United for Separation* (Milwaukee: Bruce, 1959).

Cristiani, Leon, *Heresies and Heretics* (New York: Hawthorn, 1959).

Curran, Francis X., *Major Trends in American Church History* (New York: America Press, 1946).

Dakin, Edward F., Mrs. Eddy: The Biography of a Virginal Mind (New York: Charles Scribner's Sons, 1930).

Daniel-Rops, Henri, The Second Vatican Council (New York: Hawthorn, 1962).

Davies, Horton, The Challenge of the Sects (Philadelphia: Westminster, 1961).

DeMille, George E., The Episcopal Church Since 1900 (New York: Morehouse-Gorham, 1955).

Dillenberger, John, and Welch, Claude, Protestant Christianity (New York: Charles Scribner's Sons, 1954).

Doctrines and Discipline of the Methodist Church (Nashville and New York: Methodist Publishing House, 1952).

Drummond, Andrew L., The Story of American Protestantism (Boston: Beacon Press, 1951).

Duff, Edward, Social Thought of the World Council of Churches (New York: Association Press, 1956).

Dvornik, Francis, The Photian Schism (Cambridge: Cambridge University Press, 1938).

Eddy, Mary Baker, Science and Health with Key to the Scriptures (Boston: Christian Science Publishing Society), various editions.

Eddy, Sherwood, A Century with Youth: A History of the YMCA from 1844 to 1944 (New York: Association Press, 1944).

Episcopal Church Annual 1959 (New York: Morehouse-Gorham, 1959).

Ferm, Vergilius, The American Church of the Protestant Heritage (New York: Philosophical Library, 1953).

——— Religion in the Twentieth Century, ed. (New York: Philosophical Library, 1948).

——— What is Lutheranism? (New York: Macmillan, 1930).

Fox, Paul, The Polish National Catholic Church (Scranton, Pa.: School of Christian Living).

Freeman, James Dillet, The Story of Unity (Lee's Summit, Mo.: Unity School of Christianity, 1954).

Furniss, Norman F., The Fundamentalist Controversy, 1918–1931 (New Haven, Conn.: Yale University Press, 1954).

Garrison, Winfred Ernest, The March of Faith (New York: Harper & Bros., 1933).

Gee, Donald, The Pentecostal Movement (London: Elim Publishing Co., 1949).

Gerstner, John, The Theology of the Major Sects (Grand Rapids, Mich.: Baker Book House, 1960).

Goodall Norman, The Ecumenical Movement (New York: Oxford University Press, 1961).

Grisar, Hartmann, Martin Luther: His Life and Work (Westminster, Md.: Newman Press, 1954).

Gulovich, Stephen C., *Windows Westward* (New York: Declan X. McMullen, 1947).

Hall, Clarence W., and Holisher, Desider, *Protestant Panorama* (New York: Farrar, Straus and Young, 1951).

Hanahoe, Edward F., *Catholic Ecumenism* (Washington, D. C.: Catholic University of America Press, 1953).

Hannah, Walton, *Darkness Visible* (London: Augustine Press, 1952).

Hardon, John A., *The Protestant Churches of America* (Westminster, Md.: Newman Press, 1956).

——— *Christianity in Conflict* (Westminster, Md.: Newman, 1959).

Hedley, George, *The Christian Heritage in America* (New York: Macmillan, 1948).

Henson, Herbert Hensley, *The Church of England* (Cambridge: Cambridge University Press, 1939).

Herberg, Will, *Protestant — Catholic — Jew* (New York: Doubleday & Co., 1956).

Herndon, Booton, *The 7th Day: The Story of the Seventh-day Adventists* (New York: McGraw-Hill, 1960).

Hinckley, Gordon B., *What of the Mormons?* (Salt Lake City: Church of Jesus Christ of Latter-day Saints, 1947).

Horton, Douglas, *The United Church of Christ* (New York: Thomas Nelson, 1962).

Houdini, Harry, *A Magician Among the Spirits* (New York: 1924).

Howard, Peter, *Frank Buchman's Secret* (Garden City, N. Y.: Doubleday, 1961).

Hughes, Philip, *A History of the Church*, Vol. III (New York: Sheed & Ward, 1947).

——— *A Popular History of the Catholic Church* (New York: Macmillan, 1947).

——— *A Popular History of the Reformation* (Garden City, N. Y.: Hanover House, 1957).

Janelle, Pierre, *The Catholic Reformation* (Milwaukee: Bruce, 1948).

Janin, Raymond, *The Separated Eastern Churches* (St. Louis: B. Herder, 1933).

Jehovah's Witnesses in the Divine Purpose (New York: Watch Tower Bible and Tract Society, 1959).

Jenkins, Daniel, *Congregationalism: A Restatement* (New York: Harper & Bros., 1954).

Johnson, Humphrey, *Anglicanism in Transition* (London: Longmans, 1938).

Kane, John J., *Catholic-Protestant Conflicts in America* (Chicago: Regnery, 1955).

Knox, Ronald A., *Enthusiasm* (New York: Oxford University Press, 1950).

Krull, V. H., *Christian Denominations* (Chicago: 1936).

Küng, Hans, *The Council, Reform and Reunion* (New York: Sheed and Ward, 1961).

Latourette, Kenneth Scott, *A History of Christianity* (New York: Harper & Bros., 1953).
———— *History of the Expansion of Christianity*, Vol. IV (New York: Harper & Bros., 1937–45).
Leeming, Bernard, *The Churches and the Church* (Westminster, Md.: Newman, 1960).
Let God Be True (Brooklyn: Watch Tower Bible & Tract Society, 1946).
Lickey, Arthur E., *Highways to Truth* (Washington, D. C.: Review and Herald Publishing Co., 1952).
Linn, William A., *The Story of the Mormons* (New York: Macmillan, 1902).
Littell, Franklin Hamlin, *From State Church to Pluralism* (Garden City, N. Y.: Doubleday, 1962).
Loescher, Frank, *The Protestant Church and the Negro* (New York: Association Press, 1948).
Lunn, Arnold, *Enigma: A Study of Moral Re-Armament* (London, 1957).

Macmillan, A. H., *Faith on the March* (Englewood Cliffs, N. J.: Prentice-Hall, 1957).
Manross, W. M., *History of the American Episcopal Church* (New York: Morehouse-Gorham, 1950).
Martin, Walter R., *The Rise of the Cults* (Grand Rapids, Mich.: Zondervan, 1955).
Mayer, F. E., *The Religious Bodies of America* (St. Louis: Concordia, 1954).
McKinney, George D., *The Theology of Jehovah's Witnesses* (Grand Rapids, Mich.: Zondervan, 1962).
McNeill, John T., *The History and Character of Calvinism* (New York: Oxford University Press, 1954).
Mead, Frank S., *Handbook of Denominations in the United States* (New York and Nashville: Abingdon-Cokesbury, 1951).
Milmine, Georgine, *Life of Mary Baker G. Eddy and History of Christian Science* (New York: 1909).
Moehlman, Conrad, *Protestantism's Challenge* (New York: Harper & Bros., 1939).
Moorman, J. R. H., *A History of the Church in England* (New York: Morehouse-Gorham, 1954).
Morrison, Charles Clayton, *Can Protestantism Win America?* (New York: Harper & Bros., 1948).
———— *The Unfinished Reformation* (New York: Harper & Bros., 1953).
Moss, C. B., *The Old Catholic Movement* (London: S.P.C.K., 1948).

Myers, Gustavus, *History of Bigotry in the United States* (New York: Random House, 1943).

Neal, Harry Edward, *The Hallelujah Army* (Philadelphia: Chilton, 1961).

Neve, J. L., *Churches and Sects of Christendom* (Blair, Neb.: Lutheran Publishing House, 1952).

Nibley, Hugh, *An Approach to the Book of Mormon* (Salt Lake City: Deseret News Press, 1957).

Nichol, Francis D., *Reasons for Our Faith* (Washington, D. C.: Review and Herald Publishing Co., 1947).

Nichols, James Hastings, *Primer for Protestants* (New York: Association Press, 1949).

Niebuhr, H. Richard, *The Social Sources of Denominationalism* (New York: Holt, 1929).

Nygaard, Norman E., *Trumpet of Salvation: The Story of William and Catherine Booth* (Grand Rapids, Mich.: Zondervan, 1961).

O'Dea, Thomas, F., *The Mormons* (Chicago: University of Chicago Press, 1957).

Pauck, Wilhelm, *The Heritage of the Reformation* (Glencoe, Ill.: Free Press, 1950).

Peel, Robert, *Christian Science: Its Encounter With American Culture* (New York: Holt, 1958).

Piette, Maximin, *John Wesley in the Evolution of Protestantism* (New York: Sheed & Ward, 1937).

Pike, Royston, *Jehovah's Witnesses* (New York: Philosophical Library, 1954).

Powell, Lyman P., *Mary Baker Eddy* (New York: Lyman P. Powell, 1930).

Redford, M. E., *The Rise of the Church of the Nazarene* (Kansas City, Mo., Nazarene Publishing House, 1951).

Religious Bodies, 2 vols. (Washington, D. C.: U. S. Department of Commerce, Bureau of Census, 1936).

Religious History of New England (Cambridge, Mass.: Harvard University Press, 1917).

Richards, Le Grand, *A Marvelous Work and a Wonder* (Salt Lake City: Deseret Book Co., 1950).

Rosten, Leo, *A Guide to the Religions of America*, ed. (New York: Simon & Schuster, 1955).

Rouse, R., and Neill, S. C., *A History of the Ecumenical Movement*, eds. (Philadelphia: The Westminster Press, 1954).

Roy, Ralph Lord, *Apostles of Discord* (Boston: Beacon Press, 1953).

Russell, Charles Taze, *Studies in the Scriptures*, 6 vols. (East Rutherford, N. J.: Dawn Bible Students).

Russell, Elbert, *The History of Quakerism* (New York: Macmillan, 1942).

St. John, Henry, *Essays in Christian Unity* (Westminster, Md.: Newman Press, 1955).

Schattschneider, Allen W., *Through Five Hundred Years: A Popular History of the Moravian Church* (Bethlehem, Pa.: Comenius Press, 1956).

Smith, James Ward and Jamison, A. Leland, *The Shaping of American Religion* (Princeton, N. J.: Princeton University Press, 1961).

Smith, C. Henry, *Story of the Mennonites* (Newton, Kans.: Mennonite Publications Office, 1950).

Smith, Hyrum M., *Doctrine and Covenants Commentary* (Salt Lake City: Deseret Book Co., 1950).

Smith, Joseph, *The Book of Mormon* (Salt Lake City: Church of Jesus Christ of Latter-day Saints, 1952).

———— *Pearl of Great Price* (Salt Lake City: Church of Jesus Christ of Latter-day Saints, 1949).

Snowden, J. H., *The Truth About Mormonism* (New York: George H. Doran Co., 1926).

Soloviev, Valdimir, *Russia and the Universal Church* (London: Bles, 1948).

Sperry, Willard L., *Religion in America* (New York: Macmillan, 1947).

Spiritualist Manual (Washington, D. C.: National Spiritualist Association, 1944).

Stephenson, Anthony A., *Anglican Orders* (Westminster, Md.: Newman Press, 1956).

Stephenson, George M., *The Puritan Heritage* (New York: Macmillan, 1952).

Stroup, H. H., *Jehovah's Witnesses* (New York: Columbia University Press, 1945).

Stuber, Stanley I., *How We Got Our Denominations* (New York: Association Press, 1948).

Swedenborg, Emmanuel, *The True Christian Religion* (New York: E. P. Dutton, 1936).

Sweet, William Warren, *The Story of Religion in America*, 2nd rev. ed. (New York: Harper, 1950).

———— *American Culture and Religion* (Dallas: Southern Methodist University Press, 1951).

Talmage, James E., *Articles of Faith* (Salt Lake City: Deseret Book Co., 1925).

Tavard, George H., *The Catholic Approach to Protestantism* (New York: Harper, 1955).

———— *Protestantism* (New York: Hawthorn, 1959).

———— *Holy Writ or Holy Church* (New York, Harper & Brothers, 1960).

———— *Two Centuries of Ecumenism* (Notre Dame, Ind.: Fides, 1960).

Thurston, Herbert, *The Church and Spiritualism* (Milwaukee: Bruce, 1933).

Todd, John A., *Catholicism and the Ecumenical Movement* (London and New York: Longmans, 1956).

Troelsch, Ernest, *The Social Teachings of the Christian Churches*, 2 vols. (New York: Macmillan, 1931).

Trowbridge, George, *Swedenborg: Life and Teaching* (New York: Swedenborg Foundation, 1944).

Underwood, Kenneth W., *Protestant and Catholic* (Boston: Beacon, 1957).

Van Baalen, Jan Karel, *The Chaos of Cults* (Grand Rapids, Mich.: Wm. B. Eerdmans, 1955).

Van de Pol, W. H., *The Christian Dilemma* (New York: Philosophical Library, 1952).

Wach, Joachim, *Sociology of Religion* (Chicago: University of Chicago Press, 1944).

——— *Types of Religious Experience* (Chicago: University of Chicago Press, 1951).

Ward, J. W. C., ed., *The Anglican Communion* (New York: Oxford University Press, 1948).

Weigel, Gustave, *A Survey of Protestant Theology in Our Day* (Westminster, Md.: Newman Press, 1954).

——— *A Catholic Primer on the Ecumenical Movement* (Westminster, Md.: Newman Press, 1957).

——— *Churches in North America* (Baltimore: Helicon, 1961).

——— *Faith and Understanding in America* (New York: Macmillan, 1959).

——— *Catholic Theology in Dialogue* (New York: Harper & Brothers, 1961).

Wentz, Abdel Ross, *A Basic History of Lutheranism in America* (Philadelphia: Muhlenberg Press, 1955).

West, Ray B., *Kingdom of the Saints* (New York: Viking, 1957).

West, Robert F., *Alexander Campbell and Natural Religion* (New Haven, Conn.: Yale University Press, 1948).

Whale, J. S., *The Protestant Tradition* (Cambridge: Cambridge University Press, 1955).

Whalen, William J., *Christianity and American Freemasonry* (Milwaukee: Bruce, 1958).

——— *Armageddon Around the Corner: A Report on Jehovah's Witnesses* (New York: John Day, 1962).

——— *Faiths for the Few* (Milwaukee: Bruce, 1963).

White, W. R., *Baptist Distinctives* (Nashville, Tenn.: Convention Press, 1946).

Wilbur, Earle Morse, *History of Unitarianism* (Cambridge, Mass.: Harvard University Press, 1946).

Wilbur, Sibyl, *The Life of Mary Baker Eddy* (Boston: Christian Science Publishing Co., 1938).

Williams, J. Paul, *What Americans Believe and How They Worship* (New York: Harper, 1952).

Wilson, Bryan, R., *Sects and Society* (Berkeley and Los Angeles: University of California Press, 1961).

Winehouse, Irwin, *The Assemblies of God: A Popular Survey* (New York: Vantage, 1959).

Woodman, Charles M., *Quakers Find a Way* (Indianapolis: Bobbs-Merrill, 1950).

Yearbook of American Churches, 1963 Edition, Benson Y. Landis, ed. (New York: National Council of the Churches of Christ in the U. S. A., 1962).

Yearbook of Jehovah's Witnesses, 1963 (Brooklyn: Watch Tower Bible and Tract Society, 1962).

Zeeden, Ernest Walter, *The Legacy of Luther* (London: Hollis and Carter, 1954).

INDEX

Acacia fraternity, 228

A Century With Youth, 235

A.C.L.U., and Jehovah's Witnesses, 182

Activism, Methodist, 73 f

Act of Supremacy, English, 63

Act of Toleration, English, and Quakers, 115

Adam, Karl, on Luther, 30; and Una Sancta, 250

Adam-god, Mormon doctrine of, 158, 167

Address to the German Nobility, 36

Advent Christian Church, 137

Adventism, Alexander Campbell on, 98

Adventists, 3, 15; anti-Catholicism of, 130; in armed forces, 136; Seventh-day, 128 ff

African Methodist Episcopal Church, 9, 80 f

African Methodist Episcopal Church Zion, 9, 80 f

Against the Murderous and Thieving Hordes of Peasants, 37

Albright, Jacob, 86

Alexander VI, pope, 31

Alexandria, patriarch of, 217

Algermissen, Konrad, 22; on Mormonism, 166

Allegorical interpretation of Bible, Unity School, 154

American Baptist Convention, 88, 90; decrease in, 6; and Disciples, 99

American Bible Society, 225

American Catholic Church, 206; Archdiocese of New York, 206

American Church Union, 67

American Council of Christian Churches, 56, 239

American Freedom and Catholic Power, 232

American Friends Service Committee, 117

American Humanist Association, 200

American Lutheran Church, 41 f, 43, 243

American Rescue Workers, 146

American Revolution, Anglicans in, 65 f; Methodists in, 78; Presbyterians in, 54

American Unitarian Association, 198

Amish, 141

Ammon, Jacob, and Mennonites, 141

Anabaptists, 88; and German peasants, 38; Luther and, 30, 37; Mennonites, 140; revolt against Lutheranism, 23

Angelus Temple, 126

Anglicanism, 60 ff; and Apostolic succession, 61; "biretta belt," 67; branch theory in, 61; established in colonies, 65 f; extent of, 70; nature of, 3; reunion with, 248; schism of, 2; in U. S., 65 ff; *see also* Protestant Episcopal Church

Anglican orders, declared invalid, 61

Anglicans, communion service, 26; number in England, 65

Anglo-Catholics, 61, 65; and Eucharist, 67 ff; and Masonry, 230; possible reunion of, 248; and Presbyterians, 56

Anselm, St., of Canterbury, and papal power, 62

Anti-Catholicism, Adventist, 130; of Churches of Christ, 100

Anti-Christ, Lutherans and, 46

Antimission Baptists, *see* Primitive Baptists

Antioch, patriarch of, 217

Anti-Saloon League, and Methodism, 82

Apology for the True Christian Divinity, 114

Apostolic succession, Anglican view of, 61; and Old Catholics, 204; in Orthodoxy, 213; Charles Wesley and, 77

273